THE REVELATION
of JUDE

TREVOR VELTKAMP

Copyright © 2025 by Trevor Veltkamp

All rights reserved.
No part of this publication may be reproduced, stored in a retrieval system, or transmitted in any form or by any means—electronic, mechanical, photocopying, recording, or otherwise—without the prior written permission of the publisher, except in the case of brief quotations embodied in critical articles or reviews.

Published by Pietà Press

For permission requests, contact Trevor Veltkamp (drveltkamp@gmail.com).

ISBN (Paperback): 979-8-9939069-0-4
ISBN (Hardcover): 979-8-9939069-1-1
ISBN (eBook): 979-8-9939069-2-8

Cover and interior formatting by
KUHN Design Group | kuhndesigngroup.com

Scripture quotations, if any, are from the Holy Bible and are used by permission. All rights remain with their respective copyright holders.

This is a work of creative nonfiction. Some names and identifying details may have been changed to protect privacy. Any resemblance to actual persons, living or deceased, is coincidental.

Printed in the United States of America.

For Jody

*Whose heart reveals there
is no love like a mother's love*

CONTENTS

Foreword (by Jerry Sittser) 7

Prologue 11

Jude's Journey 13

REFLECTIONS

Prayer 319

Bitter Cruelty 329

A Hole Without Measure 343

Epilogue: *The End of the Journey* 353

Acknowledgments 355

FOREWORD

In our home we like to say that "hard" and "good" are not mutually exclusive, even if applied to the same experience. A rigorous backpacking trip can be both hard and good. The first months on a new and demanding job can be both hard and good. An intense conversation or conflict can be both hard and good.

But there would seem to be limits to this paradox. Can an experience be so hard that it simply can't be good? Such would appear to be so in the case of catastrophic and irreversible experiences of loss.

The apostle Paul claims that suffering, which he calls a "slight momentary affliction," actually prepares us for "an eternal weight of glory beyond all measure." It that true in every case? Every time?

As Simone Weil describes it, affliction is rarely "slight." It is more like the physical and psychological equivalent of a multisystem organ failure. Far from preparing for us an eternal weight of glory, it imposes on us an internal weight of pain, misery, and gloom.

Trevor Veltkamp, the author of this unusual, evocative, and profound book, is my nephew. He tells the story of the long, slow, tortuous death of his son, Jude, who suffered from cancer for sixteen months before finally yielding to it at the age of nineteen. As Trevor recounts, it was an incomprehensibly hard experience, hard beyond measure, so hard that any thought of a good outcome would appear impossible. If anything, such a hope and expectation would seem immoral and unjust.

The Revelation of Jude is an odd title. It is also the right title. Jude was Trevor's firstborn child. His early childhood sweetness gave way to a long and trying period of difficulty during his teenage years, which resulted in a great deal of frustration and conflict at home. I remember those years. They were hard.

Something happened, however, almost immediately after Jude commenced his years of university education, something that changed the entire narrative and the people who played major roles in it: Trevor; his wife Jody; their two other children, Simone and Johann; family; and a few friends. And Jude, especially Jude. It was the transformation of Jude that became a revelation to the entire family, including Jude himself. It transformed me, too. I am confident it will do the same to you, the reader, as well.

As I'm sure you have, I have witnessed suffering of one kind or another my whole life, not only among my own circle of family and friends but also among a much wider circle of people I somehow knew or came to know. I have witnessed spouses lose husband or wife, parents bury children, friends suffer the ravages of cancer and mental illness, good people face the trauma of some heinous act of injustice, and leaders violate minimal standards of morality, wounding followers and fracturing institutions. These experiences of suffering crush the human spirit, erode trust, do violence to the human community. The "hard" turns into granite, making any thought of a good outcome unimaginable.

Yet Jude's story, as his father writes it, begs to differ. Somehow, mysteriously and miraculously, good was still there, awaiting discovery. Rainer Maria Rilke's poem, "Go to the Limits of Your Longing," gives voice to this mystery and miracle. As if God were speaking, it reads in part, "Let everything happen to you: beauty and terror. Just keep going. No feeling is final. Don't let yourself lose me." Terror and beauty, sorrow and joy, brokenness and healing, despair and hope. Good and hard. God's grace moves through all of it like water flowing through a canyon, which eventually wears down even the hardest granite.

The Revelation of Jude was a terror to read. It was also full of beauty: transformation, love, sacrifice, goodness, reflection, and redemption. And yes, faith—a faith that limps, falters, and endures.

Read this book. And then live because life itself—no, God himself—demands nothing less from us and gives nothing less to us.

Gerald L. Sittser,
Professor Emeritus of Theology, Whitworth University,
and author of *A Grace Disguised*

PROLOGUE

Recently, my wife, Jody, and I were packing for a trip. Like most good husbands, I'm in full possession of the gene that prevents me from finding things. As a single man, this gene remained mostly dormant. After multiple decades of marriage, however, it was fully activated.

While I struggled to decide what to bring, I realized I did not have the correct carry-on bag. Our luggage is stashed artfully throughout the house. This meant a trip downstairs and a painstaking, likely fruitless, hunt for discovery. Before I even threatened to leave the bedroom, Jody rescued the better part of my evening by quickly retrieving the bag.

"Thanks for grabbing that, sweetie." My words were ritualistic, like a well-worn melody woven into the tune of our marriage. "I really appreciate—"

As I glanced up, the notes abruptly died in my throat.

Jody stood in the doorway, tears streaming down her cheeks. In one hand, she held my bag. In the other, cradled gently against her chest, was a neatly folded, drab gray hoodie. I slowly rose, mystified by her reaction.

"It still smells like him," she sobbed. She unfolded the sweatshirt with care, then pressed her cheek against the fabric, breathing in deeply. Everything became clear. That hoodie was our son's armor, a piece of clothing he donned for many of the battles he fought. I wrapped my arms around Jody and that sacred piece of cloth, allowing the aroma of our beautiful boy to mercilessly grip our tender hearts. The memories came rushing in, carried on a tide of tears…

I DON'T KNOW WHERE I'M GOING... BUT I'M ON MY WAY

"The wisdom of the prudent is to understand their way, but the folly of fools is deceit."

PROVERBS 14:8

There is an amusing irony in today's culture. Our most influential decisions—who we marry, whether to have children, how we are educated, where we settle—are, at the time we make them, decisions we are the least qualified to make. These are all decisions best made with a heavy dose of experience and hindsight. But we are not afforded that opportunity. It is a cart-and-horse problem. We paint our futures as colorblind artists.

I find this irony both terrifying and frustrating. I wish I could propose a solution. Unfortunately, it's a paradox without a cure.

This is not to say we are incapable of making good choices. Proof is evident in the existence of wonderful marriages, upstanding children, fulfilled parents, and thriving communities. Thankfully, through reason, leaning on the wisdom and experience of others, a study of history, prayer, and blind luck, successful choices do happen. But this does not prove you were qualified to make them.

When I chose to marry Jody, I'd love to say I had carefully considered all our personality quirks and flaws, thoughtfully projected how we'd complement each other in the years ahead, and accurately anticipated the pitfalls and peccadillos that might challenge our marriage. I'd also love to say I was fully aware of the selflessness and grace it would take to help our union thrive for a lifetime.

Of course, I did not. I still don't fully grasp all that's required. But hindsight, growth, and a bit of hard-won wisdom have given me a working understanding of what it takes. Before I was married, I truly had no idea how to build a fruitful, fulfilling, and lasting relationship. And yet, I still chose to move forward with that momentous, life-altering decision despite my limited understanding.

The same irony is magnified when choosing to raise a child. At least with marriage, there is the opportunity to meet prospective spouses, enter a courting routine, and project, however feebly, how your personalities may intertwine. There are no mechanisms present by which one can practice being a parent. It is the ultimate Rubicon.

Now, there are plenty of ways one can practice taking care of children, but those exercises are not synonymous with parenting. Being an older sibling, participating in daycare, babysitting, or working as a nanny is enlightening and eye-opening. Serving as a coach or teacher also possesses some obvious cognates. Our current society provides numerous opportunities for the uninitiated to encounter, or participate in, a child's upbringing. There is, however, a vast gulf between acting within a child's sphere of influence and being solely responsible for their evolution.

Most reasonable future parents can anticipate the classic struggles—dirty diapers, sleepless nights, bloody noses, car sickness—and factor those challenges into the equation of whether to become a parent. But many parenting experiences are so outlandish, so wildly unexpected, they stretch far beyond the limits of imagination. I knew there would be laughter when I had children. I just never imagined the pinnacle of that joy would involve Jude and

Simone sneaking into the guest bathroom to gleefully splash toilet water on each other's faces, competing to see who could dunk their head deeper into the bowl, while I cluelessly fixed lunch on the other side of the house. I also knew my children would ask innumerable questions. I eagerly awaited the opportunity to answer, and never once considered a three-year-old might submit an inquiry I could not resolve with clarity. And yet one day Jude ran into the home, stark naked (we had sent him outdoors fully clothed, so his new presentation was a bit alarming), and sprinted down the hallway, his face alight with confusion, terror, and curiosity. "Hey!" he yelled, while simultaneously tugging his groin. "Why do I have a beehive attached to my penis?" My burst of uncontrolled laughter masked my failure to tackle his remarkable question. He was not impressed with my response.

As a parent, you are, at least for a time, the primary gatekeeper of the influences that shape your child. You are responsible for their behavior and actions. You create their growth environment, including their recognition and understanding of moral responsibilities, the values they embrace, and the interactions to which they are exposed. Your input holds the greatest weight in shaping how they perceive themselves and the tools they develop to evaluate their own path as they mature. In short, their personal development and sense of identity may deeply reflect your own. This is both humbling and frightening.

When you chose to have a child, did you reflect on that level of responsibility? I know I didn't. Dwelling too intensely on those responsibilities would be incapacitating. Maybe this is a psychological defense mechanism subconsciously employed to guard ourselves against the gravity of the decision? If we were fully aware of the depth of our responsibility, would any of us choose to be parents? Truth be told, I did very little thinking at all.

Before we were married, Jody informed me she felt a strong calling to become a mother and was looking forward to having children. She did not say how many, or when, other than that it would be in her future. I was too blinded by my blossoming infatuation to allow her comments to resonate.

Before marriage, my thoughts regarding children could be summarized as a great big pile of ambivalence.

Approximately ten minutes after our marriage ceremony she reminded me of that long-forgotten conversation and, much to my chagrin, elaborated on the tenuous nature of our age. She believed we were already quite "old" and needed to move along with the process. I found this assertion incredible. Even though we were married, we still weren't living together. I was finishing a residency in Dallas, and she had both a private practice and was teaching at a college in Connecticut. It made the most financial sense for her to maintain her employment while I finished my practicum and dissertation. We were separated by half a continent. The idea of children seemed a logistical absurdity.

One week a month Jody would fly to Dallas and visit. We would have a mini honeymoon, and then she would be gone. While I don't necessarily recommend this as the best way to start a marriage, it made for an interesting break-in period. We were exposed to each other's rhythms and eccentricities without having the trauma of being inextricably immersed without amnesty. On the other hand, we didn't begin deciphering how to live with each other for nearly a year into our union. One of our most revealing (and worrying) moments as a couple occurred two days after the completion of my residency.

Jody had been methodically shipping boxes from her Connecticut abode to my Dallas apartment, recognizing we would eventually be living together. We slowly collated our possessions, understanding Dallas was merely a temporary home base from which to launch. As it happened, I took a position thousands of miles away in the middle of the state of Washington. This necessitated transporting everything across the country. We rented a U-Haul truck and set to work, packing and loading.

Thankfully my parents came to Dallas for the graduation ceremony and were able to help. As fortune would have it, even though it was August, the weekend was cloudy and cool—by Dallas standards. This meant it was in the mid to high nineties and rather humid. We lived upstairs. The city had just survived sixty consecutive days exceeding one hundred degrees. The diminished heat wave felt like a blessed reprieve. My father lived in the cool Pacific Northwest, where eighty degrees is considered unusual and oppressive. Each time I watched him trudge up those cursed stairs, wet as a bedraggled muskrat, I thought we were going to lose him. Jody's overweight book boxes weren't helping.

After staggering to the finish line, Jody and I said farewell to my parents, Texas, and the rigors of residency and hopped in the truck, nervous and excited, yet silently aware of our unique situation. While approaching the state line, my typically composed wife suddenly appeared a bit frazzled, and in a mostly serious and inquisitive tone exclaimed, "Boy, I hope we like each other." We'd been married nearly a year, and yet the longest consecutive stretch of time we had spent together was eight days. And that was on our honeymoon! Needless to say, a honeymoon is hardly an adequate representation of what actual married life is like. Her statement rattled me. It was a touch too late for cold feet.

We settled in the small town of Ellensburg, Washington. The change was jarring. We had spent most of our adult lives living in large cities. Jody had lived in Los Angeles and the greater New York metropolitan area. I'd had the childhood experience of a small town—but that was a decade past. For Jody especially, Ellensburg seemed like the dark side of the moon.

Our house shopping consisted of a real estate agent driving us through the county pointing out, rather infrequently, potential homes for sale. Resources were scarce. As we toured one of the few available sales, we noticed the adjacent home ("adjacent" being relative, all the homes were on three- or five-acre plots) appeared rather fetching. We queried our agent and immediately received a firsthand demonstration of small-town sociability. She told us to relax in her vehicle while she calmly ambled over to the house in question. I still am not sure what sort of exchange occurred, but ten minutes later she came back and casually declared, indeed, the owner would be happy to sell us her home. She was an older lady, recently widowed, and was planning on putting the house on the market. So, with no concept of rural life, an appreciation for the location, the specter of student loans mocking us, and blindly ignorant of the serviceability of the home's layout, we whimsically put down money and purchased our first home. It was another life-altering, momentous decision we obliviously transacted.

I am quite certain I had not even finished sweeping out the U-Haul before Jody brought up the idea of starting a family. I was primarily focused on starting a marriage, which, relatively speaking, was a rather large family. I had been a family of just me—now I was doubled. That was plenty of change. Not to mention, the two of us were new to private practice, and we knew nothing about country home ownership or our community. Additionally, we were piled under a mountain of debt and had never spent any time together. Any one of those variables should have been a viable deflection point. Somehow logic manages to flee the premises, however, when discussions of this nature ensue.

"Are you sure you can even have kids? I mean, shouldn't you get a checkup or something?" To this day, I have no idea what I was asking or why blurting those questions had any place in the discussion. Not only did I offend my wife by questioning her health, but I also misplaced the key point in the discussion.

I followed those initial gaffes by asking, "Don't we need permission or something?"

Jody was incredulous. "Permission from who?" Her bafflement was appropriately humiliating. Granted, we did not know each other well, but even I could tell she was wondering who this person was in front of her.

I really did not want to have this conversation but was backed into a corner. Escape and evade were no longer options. So, I chose to seriously engage her inquiry. "Are you confident this is a wise idea?" As embarrassingly poor as my initial salvo had been, this question was the one I should have led with, and likely the only necessary question to ask before adopting any endeavor. It was really a succinct version of what my sister dubs "The Newspaper Rule": If you pick up the newspaper (or online article in today's world) and read about the choice you were about to make from the perspective of an uninformed bystander, how would the apparent outcome be perceived? If the answer contains words like foolish, idiotic, crazy, or stupid, then altering your intended choice is appropriate. "What is the wise thing to do?" sounds more holistic and philosophically mature but is built on the same principle.

Unfortunately, Jody had lost patience with me long before I asked that last, all-too-important question. She rightfully ignored my careless blathering and simply looked at me as if I was a foolish child and couldn't be bothered by my silliness. That critical question hung in the air, waiting to be dissected, but she did not take it seriously. A whimsical hug and a kiss thwarted any more possible remonstrations, and with an air of absurd confidence she replied, "Of course."

It was settled. I can be rather pedantic at times. I invariably suffer from buyer's remorse if I rush into a decision without applying thorough, labored research. Until marriage I'm not sure if I had ever made an impulsive decision. I have been known to agonize for weeks over the simple act of purchasing a single golf club. In this instance, there was no long discussion. No research. There were no goals, dates, or milestones fabricated to serve as gatekeepers before starting a family. The topic was broached, my mind became a sophomoric quagmire of illogic, and we moved ahead with the mundanities of the day. I think about that occurrence now, and it was so out of character I hardly recognize the person I'm remembering. But I also wonder if it would have made any sort of difference. In that moment, if I had two decades of parenting squarely behind me, would all that experience have altered our trajectory? Would hindsight have changed our plan? Are we ever truly ready to be parents?

BIRTH

"It takes courage... to endure the sharp pains of self-discovery rather than choose to take the dull pain of unconsciousness that would last the rest of our lives."

MARIANNE WILLIAMSON

"Jude was born." That is usually the finishing sentence of any male's retelling of a birth story. It is almost always the opening sentence as well. If you assembled a small group of ten couples, split them into their respective genders, and asked them to recount their experience with pregnancy and birth, all ten males will have finished their tales long before the first female had even completed her preamble. Most likely, by about the fourth or fifth male, the conversation would consist of grunts and nods of agreement. "Yeah, just like he said. You know, we went to the hospital, and my kid was born." (An elaborate tale may recall details of a harrowing drive, or a missed dinner, but most of those incidentals are left out.) With ten males it is doubtful ten stories would even be told. Why keep repeating the same thing?

According to modern statistics, nearly 100 billion humans have walked this earth. That is a lot of births. One would think that at least a handful of those births would be so similar the events would be indistinguishable. And yet I have never met a mother who did not possess an exquisitely unique birthing story.

Because Jude has a mother, he also is in possession of a unique birthing story. This story started long before he was actually born. When Jody informed me it was her intent that we start a family, we decided it was also up to her to reconnoiter prospective OB-GYN doctors. Turns out in Ellensburg that effort, which can be agonizing and anxiety laden in other cities, only took seconds. She had one option. Fortunately, he was well-trained and fantastic.

As a young, newlywed male, I had very little interest in learning about my wife's search for a gynecologist or the details of her visit. In fact, I had anti-interest. If the topic was broached, no matter how discreetly, I would quickly find myself occupied with something desperately important requiring complete attention. Details of her endeavors were an assault on my sensibilities. The last thing I wanted to do was talk about, or heaven forbid, *meet* the man who was intimately inspecting my wife.

One pressing task, upon arrival, was finding a church home. Our first month, we attended five different congregations and were not close to making a choice. Every congregation was welcoming and lovely. This presented a strange problem, even if the trend was positive. We did not know how to choose. And unlike many of our other impulsive choices, we were deliberate with this one. Our faith was the core of our marriage. We believed our church family should be an extension of that.

While attending yet another wonderful congregation, the couple sitting just ahead introduced themselves, as well as their children (one of whom was a special-needs child), and spontaneously invited us for a home-cooked meal directly after the service. We thankfully obliged, excited to get to know others in the community.

The dinner was relaxed and simple. The father, John, proved energetic and affable. He appreciated adventure and served as a knowledgeable repository of the local customs and unique history of Ellensburg. While his wife worked at dinner we chatted about mountaineering adventures, logging, rebuilding old cars, photography, and the bubonic plague. I enjoyed his eclectic approach to conversation, and to life. A couple of times during the conversation he took his leave for a quick minute but would return and pick up right where we left off. I assumed he was attending to his special-needs child while his wife managed the preparations.

Just as we settled into dinner, John was again called away from the table. His special-needs child was contentedly sitting across from me and required no attention. I became curious. And then his wife also excused herself to the kitchen to attend to part of the meal, leaving Jody and I alone together for the first time.

"Where do you think he keeps going off to?" I asked her. "What could possibly keep pulling him away on a Sunday afternoon?"

"I'm sure he's on call," Jody replied. "He's probably checking in with the hospital."

"The hospital?" I responded, a little incredulously. "You think he's a doctor?" I had never asked John what he did. I know some people consider that rude, but I hate to make judgments about people based on what they do. Besides, our conversation had been much too lively to focus on the banalities of life.

"Well, of course," Jody stated, as if it was obvious. "He's my gynecologist."

Thankfully we hadn't started eating or I would have spit my food all over the floor. I still managed to choke. "Why didn't you tell me sooner?!"

"I didn't think it was important, and I wasn't sure who he was at first," she replied. In my wife's defense, she's never been great at recognizing faces or remembering names. Still, one would assume that something as intimate as a gynecological exam might earn a more prominent place in one's immediate memory. Suddenly I was conflicted. My first impression of John had been nothing but positive. So should I be upset? Intimidated? Or just accept the fact that my wife found my discomfort hilarious? For the next hour, I sat squirming at the table, trying to banter casually with the man who had recently evaluated my wife's physical suitability for bearing a child. No one else at the table—including the adult women—seemed remotely disturbed. On the contrary, they were entirely angst-free and clearly enjoying themselves.

Very few of us are gifted with perspicacious self-assessment. What we think of ourselves and what others consider us to be is never coincident. But even my obtuse faculties allowed a disheartening epiphany: I was not the most mature newlywed. Simultaneously, an even deeper, more significant thought occurred to me, and I desperately wish it would have taken root. Unfortunately, it took years to sprout. I recognized, during my bout of unsophisticated shame, that many of the relational difficulties, social frustrations, and familial embarrassments we encounter are a *me* problem, not a *you* problem.

When I sat at that welcoming table, the only one put out was me. Everyone else possessed the wisdom and grace to appreciate the event within its proper context. My wife certainly was not ashamed. She did not even initially remember who the man was. And his wife obviously could not have cared less that her husband had recently seen my wife naked. The only person in conflict was me.

The parable of the speck of dust is particularly meaningful here. It is tempting to consider the parable only for its initial offering: Don't be a hypocrite. Upon further examination, one realizes the deeper intent is to foster humility, self-examination, and compassion. Only then will this self-actualization provide enough clarity for you to remove a possible speck from the eye of others. Or more likely, let you recognize that what you initially mistook as a splinter in someone else's eye was a branch from the log lodged in your own.

We see this all the time in marriages. There are marriage encounters, couples' retreats, marriage counseling, couples therapy, marriage Bible studies—and they all have significant merit. More often than not, however, when someone says they are going to "work on their marriage," what they really mean is, "I am going to describe to my spouse where they fail." Some days, when they are feeling rather charitable, they will be receptive to their spouse describing their own shortcomings. If we take the parable seriously, however, we would be much better off beginning with the difficult process of "working on ourselves" instead of "working on our marriages." I think you will be pleasantly surprised when you discover how much easier and fulfilling your marriage becomes when the only variable that changes is you.

Hindsight now makes it obvious how necessary it was for me to engage in some serious self-work. It is remarkable how blinding pride, contempt, self-righteousness, and insecurity can be. They produce no positive fruit in a marriage, and they are devastating for parenting. Jude's journey would have been markedly different had I cultivated this nascent thought with the care and respect it deserved.

・・・

A few weeks after her initial appointment, Jody returned to the obstetrics clinic with the intent of procuring an ovulation test kit. Difficulty conceiving was a strong family trait. She, herself, was a product of a first-generation fertility trial in the 1960s. At the time I was not concerned, as this additional variable only appeased my growing apprehension about becoming a father. Statistically, in America, the average time from attempting to start a family until conception is approximately nine months. I was already clinging to that knowledge and selfishly hoped it would take us longer. Her family history was playing in my favor.

She returned empty-handed. This was not alarming, as I had no idea what a test kit contained or how it would be packaged. It could have been in her pocket or something she swallowed, for all I knew. I secretly imagined they were out of stock. What had me more concerned was her serious demeanor.

"How do you feel about being a dad?" she inquired. I could tell from her body language this was not a rhetorical question. She had asked me this several times in the last year, but even though the words were the same, the essential delivery evoked an altogether different quality. I've been married for a long time now and have discovered, sometimes in rather irrepressible fashion, an immense amount about spousal interaction. I have not learned as much as I should or could, nor does my learning always translate into the wisest interplay. However, I could immediately ascertain, even as embryonic as our marriage was, that this question fell into that all-so-sensitive arena of "questions that require an expected and definitive response for which no male is capable of answering appropriately." Examples include:

"Do you think these jeans are flattering?"

"How do you feel about this pot roast? It was my mom's special recipe and we loved it as kids."

"On a scale of 1–10, what number would you rate our marriage at right now?"

"Do you ever think about other women?"

These are subjective questions for which "truth" is relative. Their delivery is instigated by the exigencies of the moment but are asked for reasons much more nuanced.

"Well..." I eloquently stammered. I was not sure what she was searching for. Had she just been informed she was barren? Were we going to have to go through a laborious fertility process? Was she simply looking for reaffirmation about our previous decision? Was it as mundane as trying to make simple conversation? Just like when she had pressed me to consider starting a family, my alacrity of thought screeched to a halt. I anxiously stalled, granting my sluggish brain a chance to grasp an apt reply.

"I thought we talked about this?" I finally responded with a reassuring smile. Her eyes got a little moist and my heart sank. But then she smiled, squeezed me into a rapturous embrace, and exclaimed, "You're going to be a daddy!"

I've never done well with surprises. My default reaction is to withdraw and become emotionally flaccid. This was a shocking surprise—a surprise which required an exuberant display of excitement, disbelief, and joy. I failed miserably. For a moment, I was catatonic. Fortunately, my wife, who has a much richer grasp of my personality flaws than I do, immediately forgave my lifeless response.

"What... what are you talking about?" I stuttered. "Are you sure about this?"

"Yes," she beamed. "I went there with the intention of talking about fertility. They suggested I take a pregnancy test first. I thought it was silly to even bother, but it came back positive!"

We were shocked, flummoxed, and not a little excited. We were crossing the marital Rubicon. It was exhilarating. As we sat together and digested the significance of our stunning revelation, we looked at a calendar. September. The realization that by next summer we would be solely responsible for the care and nurturing of a human being dominated our faculties. This was no light duty. Had we known then how life-altering parental responsibility is, humility and apprehension would have won the day. At the time we relished the notion of embarking on a marital adventure, fully confident in our parenting capabilities. Blissful naivete is a powerful antidote for the concerns of the future.

...

As a male it is tempting to claim Jude's gestation was uneventful. I am sure Jody has a different tale to tell. We did have one anxiety-inducing period which unnecessarily led to premature grieving and many sleepless nights. As a matter of routine most pregnant women are administered the "triple screen" blood test. This screen measures certain hormone levels in the blood and, depending on the results, may be an indicator of something amiss with fetal development. Jody's results were positive for Down syndrome.

We were not ready for this. So much of our lives are tempered and characterized by expectations. As new parents we prayed daily for the health and well-being of our unborn child. Down syndrome was not on our radar. We were devastated. All the hopes and fantasies we built with each other crumbled into rubble. How would we handle this? Why would God let this happen? The injustice of this radical development overwhelmed our thoughts. We reinterpreted Jody's miraculous pregnancy as a curse. Our exuberance, once so energizing, transformed into enervating melancholy. We interacted with our broader community as if we'd recently experienced a long illness and untimely death in the family.

Jody and I are both healthcare providers. We possess intimate working knowledge of medical jargon, and thanks to hospital and university affiliations have access to nearly unlimited amounts of obstetric information.

After a rather deep dive into the triple screen, it became abundantly clear the predictive validity of the test was heavily dependent upon precise dating of the time of conception. Although there are numerous avenues to attain this date, most algorithms usually employ a simple "walk forward" from the first day of the woman's last menstrual cycle. In Jody's case, they used the number fourteen—which is standard practice. However, in biological systems it is rare when one size fits all. Jody's body does not fit this mold. The fourteen-day "walk forward" was, for her, completely erroneous. Much to our relief, this rendered the test virtually meaningless and significantly eased our anxiety. With Jody's next pregnancy, the same prediction occurred, but almost one hundred times higher. The results were so many standard deviations from the norm they were laughable. According to the triple screen, Simone, our second child, was guaranteed to have a disability—likely several. Although unnerving, we were able to dismiss the prediction due to our unique understanding of Jody's physiology. For our third child, Johann, we elected to forgo the test entirely.

It is both embarrassing and pathetic how unprepared first-time parents are. I had completed graduate and postgraduate courses in embryology and child growth and development. I could recite, on the cellular level, exactly how a fetus knits itself together. I could talk for hours about physical maturation from infancy to adolescence. For some reason I correlated this working knowledge with parenting. In my naïve intellectual hubris, I considered myself overqualified.

Jody is a relentless self-educator. She purchased a myriad of child-rearing instructional manuals. For a time, in our house, it was impossible to find a place to set down a drink without overturning a stack of books dedicated to parenting. She effortlessly worked out a child-rearing plan. Much to my dismay, this plan was generously shared with me. She also possessed a doctorate degree in psychology, which provided an overabundance of insight into the nuances of child maturation. Most importantly, as an older sister, she had taken responsibility for her younger brothers at an impressionable age, managing their childhood while her mother taught piano lessons during the after-school hours. Confidence was high. Expectations were higher.

Jude never had a chance.

DELIVERY

"Making the decision to have a child is momentous. It is to decide forever to have your heart go walking around outside your body."

ELIZABETH STONE

For modern, developed, First World countries, the birthing process is rigorously sanitized. Unless you live on a farm or work in a dedicated healthcare field, most people—especially males—are ignorant of the details. I am not sure this is a bad thing. I am certain that those who grandiloquently express "the life-affirming beauty of the birthing process" likely were not present at the time of the actual event. "Beauty" is a gross misapplication of the adjective.

Jody was ten days overdue. She was enormous. The June desert heat arrived with force, adding to her misery. She evinced no signs of going into labor. We tried every natural way to induce her, including forced, manual work. During her ninth month she vigorously helped me tear out and replace our entire lawn and commenced restoring and refinishing our oversized, careworn cedar deck. This did nothing for the labor induction process and only served to ensure she was tired and grumpy.

Our obstetrician planned his yearly vacations around the due dates of his patients. He had a wall-sized calendar in his office with his expectant mothers' due dates artfully checkered like a piece of second-rate modern art. Wherever he could locate a respectable gap between due dates, he would arrange to leave town. Jody's predicament was fouling his system. She was on a weekly check-in system with his office, and they both agreed, when it was apparent that Jude was already well north of nine pounds and rapidly accelerating to ten, that it was time to chemically induce. Jody is a planner. The fact that she could pick the time and date to go into labor was very attractive to her. Excitement began to build. Monday, June 17, 2002, would be the date Jude would arrive.

We knew nothing about forced induction. When your body is unprepared for active labor, it is usually also unwilling. Jody started the process on Monday at noon and was instructed to check into the maternity ward at dinner time. We were too excited to eat. Hunger was not a concern, however, as I assumed I would grab some food after the birth—a nice kickstart to the celebration. We giddily called our parents when Jody checked in, assuring them we would apprise them of the arrival of our firstborn child, likely later in the evening. They instructed us not to worry about waking them if it was late. They wanted to know right away.

Ellensburg Hospital had just remodeled their obstetrics ward. We were led into a beautiful, spacious, and comfortable room. At least it was comfortable for me. Jody, in a rather ungainly fashion, crawled onto the bed and began her work in earnest. The chemicals were starting to express their magic. Undoubtedly Jude would come shooting out in short order.

As it happened, Jude entered this world the same way he left it—with extreme reluctance. Monday proved a washout. Jody suffered through heavy contractions, but nothing of significance occurred. All through the night I sat there and watched her labor. Our anticipation and excitement metamorphosed into concern and frustration. The chemically induced contractions were rather fierce, but they produced no positive effects. Early Tuesday morning the doctor cheerily arrived to check her progress.

"Where is she at?" he asked the evening nurse who had just finished examining Jody.

"Nothing," the nurse unhappily replied.

"What do you mean nothing?" the doctor responded. "I can see she isn't ready to deliver yet. But how far along is she?"

"Nothing," the nurse repeated. Her expression was grim. I was not sure what they were talking about.

"Well, where's she dilated? We might as well start tracking her progress."

"Like I said," the nurse unhappily responded, "it is zero. She is not dilated at all. There is no softening. There is nothing." The doctor was incredulous. He put the gloves on and immediately examined Jody.

"Hmm," he muttered. "We need to get the show on the road." In one sense I completely agreed and silently urged him on. I was starving and exhausted—and I was not even the one in labor. The only suffering I experienced was boredom. Neither of us had any idea what "getting the show on the road" meant.

Some hushed conversation, a few approving nods, all followed by more intense whispers in the corner apparently were the necessary precursors to moving the process along. They did not consult with Jody or me about anything. It appeared rather ominous. I do not know why the clandestine approach. Were they attempting to protect us from something? We felt like we were plague ridden and no one was quite sure how to deal with our infestation.

Nothing happens quickly in a hospital. I expected the secretive, intense conversations would elicit a crash cart and all sorts of fanfare. What we got was three more hours of monotonous drudgery, punctuated with painful contractions. By midday, however, they had adjusted Jody's induction cocktail several times. All it served to do was increase the intensity of her contractions. Agony hardly suffices to characterize her situation. I felt terrible for her, but other than offering some lame, unenergetic platitudes, there was not a lot I could do. At one point I wandered off with the excuse of "informing our parents" just to garner some relief from that miserable torture chamber. I stayed away as long as I dared and even had the temerity to utilize the services of a vending machine upon my return. I resumed my stalwart position at Jody's bedside while eagerly diving into a delicious bag of Cheetos. I took exactly one bite of those life-affirming morsels before noticing Jody's look of pure venom. The rest of the bag went uneaten.

Tuesday afternoon turned into evening. Jody was a sweaty mess. I was starving. We were both frustrated. Neither one of us wanted to have a kid. We just wanted to go home. Thankfully, after twenty-eight hours, she began to dilate. This change brought with it an anesthesiologist who pleasingly provided an epidural.

The temperature in the room dropped precipitously. Normal, adult conversation resumed. With an effusive smile, Jody began introducing herself to nurses and orderlies—and even allowed herself a bite of food. Her sudden shift in demeanor gave me a chance to sit down and breathe. It was incredible how tense her discomfort had made all of us. I was so relieved to see Jody coherent and functional, it was like tossing off a weighted blanket. The downside was that if giving birth is like climbing a skyscraper, then we were still in the lobby. After thirty hours into this campaign, no one was feeling tip-top. The remaining staircase was daunting. Jude was also exhibiting signs of birthing distress, which began to alarm everyone.

By midnight she began "real" labor. I have no idea what she was in before if it wasn't real, because it had certainly appeared real to me. Nonetheless, despite his best intentions, Jude was going to make a reluctant entrance—or so we thought. He reserved one last trick to thwart us. Just when he was starting to move along, Jody's uterus stopped contracting. The artificially induced contractions had pressed it beyond maximal fatigue. It was the equivalent of a uterine heart attack. The doctor implored me to help her push.

"Do your breathing," he commanded. "It's time to put to use everything they taught you in your birthing class."

Everyone in the room seemed upset with me. It wasn't my uterus that pooped out. How does one jumpstart a uterus? Fortunately, despite my dim-witted fatigue, I possessed enough savvy to recognize this was not the time or place to confess my lack of attendance at Lamaze classes.

At four in the morning, with frayed nerves and the threshold of exhaustion a distant memory, the fetal distress monitor began squawking violently. Dr. Sands brandished the birthing forceps and began clacking them together. My wife is a neuropsychologist. She assesses mental function for a living and knows an immense amount about human intellect. She had read every study on forceps births and the potential deleterious effects they may have on cognition. There was no possible way Jude's delivery would be mechanically aided. So, despite a nonfunctioning uterus, and drawing on an inner strength which could have only been tapped from the deepest well of love for our unborn child, she forced Jude to emerge.

I would love to say there were cheers, handshakes, and general merriment, but then this book would be fiction. Everyone was so exhausted that after the nurses whisked Jude away to clean him up, we all slumped into our respective corners and absorbed the silence. The nurse quickly returned, however, and placed Jude gently upon Jody's chest. She broke into a huge grin, which slowly turned into an odd stare, as if something about Jude's countenance was disturbing. I had no idea what the appropriate response should be, but this seemed strangely out of place. Once again, I was frozen with confusion.

She finally glanced up and gave me an exhausted smile. A faint tear ran down her cheek. The switch flipped. After thirty-six hours of miserable, torturous labor, one would think there would be nothing left to give. But in those wee hours of the morning, amidst the exhaustion, frustration, and chaos, I bore witness to the ineluctable bond forged between a mother and child. The ancient adage states, "There is no love like a mother's love." I testify to its veracity. Anything her son required, whatever the circumstances, and whatever her condition, Jody would provide. To observe this melding of a mother's love was, from my vantage, nothing short of a miracle. In that moment time stood still. Peace reigned.

Jody interrupted our idyllic tableau with an embarrassed giggle. "Well, this is weird." She let her head fall back onto the pillow while Jude lay comfortably on her chest. Her comment confused me.

"Ummm... what's weird?" I asked cautiously.

"He looks just like me. He's a boy. Isn't he supposed to look just like you? That's what I've been imagining all this time!"

Expectations are dangerous for a parent. This would not be the last time Jude surprised us.

DADDY DAYS

"If there is anything that we wish to change in the child, we should first examine it and see whether it is not something that could better be changed in ourselves."

CARL JUNG

There is an interesting fact about parenting. Once you've joined the fraternity, there is no exit. Regardless of your level of investiture, the title remains. An absent parent is still a parent. So is a doting parent, a helicopter parent, a smothering parent, or an estranged parent. They are all parents. The mantle can never be discarded.

After the initial bonding with Jude, the nurses carefully carried him away. I did not know if this was standard operating procedure, but for an exhausted Jody and me, it was much appreciated. We crashed for a few hours.

I was woken from my slumber by the pediatrician explaining to Jody that they were going to have to keep Jude for a few days for observation. We both immediately grew apprehensive, as there had been no indication at the time of delivery that anything was amiss.

"Just a touch of transient tachypnea," the doctor stated, as if expressing a technical term would ease the concern. My groggy wits evaporated quickly, replaced by a strangely primal parental concern. It was the first time I had experienced this, and it was revelatory.

"Why is he breathing quickly?" I asked, trying not to sound concerned but feeling the sweat start to drip down my back. My classes in pediatric pathology were not too distant. All manner of infant horrors flashed through my mind.

"It's just wet lung," she reassured. "We have him in an oxygen tent, just as a precaution."

Well, that did not sound the least bit good to me. My mind started racing. A few hours ago, we had a healthy, happy boy, and suddenly, I was catastrophizing him into an iron lung. The pediatrician, well experienced with this sort of parental behavior, smiled benignly.

"No need to worry. You can go see him if you wish. We'll just keep him there for a day or two in order to ensure everything is perfect."

That was two days of quiet bliss. Jody mostly slept and recovered. I did much of the same. We did not have a baby in our room, and the only time he inserted himself into our lives was to be fed. Parenting is a piece of cake when you have someone else doing all the work. I could come and go as I pleased. Jody got to experience Jude at his best and handed him over when he became agitated. We were in parenting utopia.

This ended abruptly at discharge. Suddenly, we had to deal with the reality of managing and caring for a creature that was utterly helpless. For much of my life, and certainly the entirety of my adult life, when I wanted to engage in an activity, all I had to do was grab my personal necessities and go. Now I had to figure out how to pack and carry a diaper bag, remember to stock it, manage an infant seat and stroller, anticipate the needs of someone whose only form of communication was wailing, and ensure my destination was also infant-friendly. A nurse accompanied us on our way to the car. It was her job to make sure we strapped our son properly into the car seat. I thought this attention was ridiculous and patronizing. Jody and I were practical, thoughtful adults with advanced degrees. We would not need instruction and oversight when it came to placing Jude in a vehicle.

Five-point infant restraining harnesses are nearly impenetrable. I fumbled and fussed with that silly device for several minutes while the nurse, who was certainly a few years my junior, just gave me a knowing smile. I was not the first incompetent father she'd monitored. Fortunately, I was able to get everything clicked into place and locked down without her assistance, and for that, my ego is still grateful. Upon completion, Jude appeared ready to handle escape velocity. The mischievous part of me wanted to wreck the car just to test the restraints. They appeared impregnable.

. . .

Arrival home proved surreal. Everything was just as we had left it. The house was tidy and bathed in sunlight. The yard was meticulous, the deck still unfinished. Everything was the same, except it was radically different. We walked into the kitchen, plopped down the car seat with Jude locked inside, cautiously surveyed the surroundings, and took a few deep breaths. "Now what?" we both asked.

Both Jody and I can be ambitious and motivated. If there is a job to do, we like to dive in and complete it. Tasks left unfinished are anathema. We attacked parenting like it was another task, a hoop to jump through in the obstacle course of life—one of many such hoops we had already managed to navigate. This was a wonderful, beautiful, accepted challenge we could attack with all the vigor granted to a young couple. The prospect invigorated us.

Parenting is nothing like that. I quickly learned it is a marathon, not a sprint. Except that "marathon" implies there is a finish line. The work of a parent is never complete. Yes, it changes over time, even day to day, but it is never finished. Parenting is not a discrete part of your life, akin to coaching, serving on the school board, or church council. Nor is it a vocation-consuming part of each day that you can hold at arm's length when it suits you. It is not a social club or a friendship. It is not even a way of life—like a behavior pattern, or ideology, or habit—that one can adopt or discard depending on the exigencies of the moment. Parenting *is* life. And once instituted, it is your irrepressible responsibility, forever.

We discovered very quickly—within hours, really—that our idealistic parenting plans would transmogrify into a flexible "work in progress." This was difficult for two planners to apprehend. We can both be rather intransigent and possess a keen appreciation for, and faith in, our personal intellects. That is a nice way of saying we were pridefully stubborn. Now, this may come as a shock, but *stubbornness* and *pride* are not helpful parenting traits. Unbeknownst to us, we were about to experience the difficult and necessary work of being refined by our child. Jude had embarked on his journey. His work began in earnest.

...

Around the time Jude was born, SIDS—or sudden infant crib death—was hot on every parent's radar. There was a great deal of anecdotal evidence regarding its manifestation. Current wisdom, expounded by most pediatricians and parenting manuals, was to never let your child sleep on his stomach. We were instructed to be vigilant about this.

Obviously, Jude's well-being was of paramount importance. We were willing to capitulate to nearly any living arrangement to ensure his safety. In a fit of rookie parenting insanity, we deduced it was in Jude's best interest to sleep at the foot of our bed. We erected an antique crib next to our footboard. This assured us that while Jude slept, if anything happened, we could leap into action.

In theory, this plan was, at best, mediocre—and that may be a generous assessment. If all three of us were going to be sleeping, and Jude happened to stop breathing, would we notice? I'm not sure, in a fatigued state, either of us would really be capable of detecting the absence of something. What we could both readily detect was the presence of something. And that was the obnoxious, stentorian breathing of our infant child. He sounded like an asthmatic bulldog. I lay in bed, staring at the ceiling, silently praying for him to stop breathing. It was maddening. Jody can usually sleep through anything, but even this was overwhelming her talent. Finally, after three hours of his grunting, gasping, and snorting, I completely lost patience and found myself dragging his crib down the hall and into his newly remodeled nursery. We weren't planning on introducing Jude to his private bedroom for at least a couple of months. Plans changed.

This was the first time our plans changed. It would not be the last.

His breathing difficulties plagued us for months. Although he was in a different room, the baby monitor transmitted the sound directly to us. Granted, it was comforting knowing he was alive and well, just down the hall. Unfortunately, for a light sleeper such as myself, it was exacting a chronic toll. In desperation, I began turning off the baby monitor once Jody fell asleep. She did not appreciate this. I considered it a survival tactic.

Out of desperation, I began researching SIDS. Most scientists thought it was a brain stem defect, which no amount of vigilance could defend against. There was also a strong contingent who believed that when an infant slept on their stomach, the brain stem defect could be exacerbated. It was also proposed that even if an infant did not have a defect, sleeping on their stomach could cause a child to suffocate if they lacked the capacity to free their head from a soft mattress or the strength to pull away from stuffed animals or wadded blankets.

Being the firstborn child is hard work. You are afflicted daily by parents who do not know what they are doing. Every new day for you is also a novel parenting day. There is a line in the movie *The Natural* when Robert Redford's love interest says, "I believe we have two lives: The life we learn with, and the life we live after that." Firstborn children are afforded the double insult of sowing the life their parents learn with and reaping the life they must live with after that.

Jude became my SIDS test subject. One day, when Jody was working, I put Jude down for a nap on his stomach. He fell asleep instantly. It was like covering the head of a chicken. There was no snorting, gasping, or retching. As he calmly drifted in his peaceful abyss, I took the opportunity to strategically place all manner of stuffed animals around his head, nose, and mouth. I started small and watched carefully. Whenever he moved, causing an animal to roll close to his face, he would jostle as much as his feeble muscles would allow, creating an air gap. I began stuffing multiple animals around his head. He still managed to push them away—steadfastly sleeping through each assault. I eventually took his head and turned it facedown into the mattress, attempting to ascertain if he had the strength to lift away and avoid asphyxiation. His infant survival skills thwarted my most nefarious intentions.

I could not have been more delighted. Not only had we solved the noisy sleeping problem, but we also had some assurance that Jude was likely not susceptible to SIDS. When I divulged my studious experimentation to Jody, she was less than pleased. Granted, my methodology likely would have garnered an investigation from child protective services had they been publicized, so her objections were vindicated. Sometimes it is easier to ask for forgiveness than apply for permission. However, even I was wise enough to recognize that a Machiavellian approach was not the best strategy for cultivating a healthy marriage. Using our son to satisfy my own curiosity, however beneficial the outcome, would be best served as a historical fact, not a future enterprise.

Interestingly, after Jude officially became a stomach sleeper, we called both our parents and asked what our preferred position had been. "The stomach," was their unanimous reply. Apparently when we were infants the conventional wisdom was that sleeping on your back could cause breathing problems. Sometimes the best way to parent is to ask others who have done it.

* * *

Jody is many things, including determined. She was determined to take six weeks of parenting leave and then resume work. Why she decided on six weeks is something of a mystery, as she was self-employed and not beholden to an employee contract, but once that number was decided then that was the timeline to which she would adhere. I was proud of both her determination and desire to be a working mother. I was also working, and the imposition of Jude in our lives introduced some logistical hurdles. Our autonomy was suddenly hampered. There is no such thing as only parenting when it is convenient. With no relatives in immediate proximity, and as recent transfers to town with a growing yet limited social base, Jude would need to be placed in childcare.

Childcare centers are wonderful developments. They have enabled many women, and men, the opportunity to maintain careers while parenting. Not all childcare facilities are created equally, however. We were very reticent to place the care and nurturing of our son into the hands of a stranger. To mitigate this, we modified our own work schedules so that while one of us was seeing patients, the other could be at home. Hence the advent of "daddy days."

I've heard countless parents describe the moment of their child's birth as "the happiest day of my life." If subjected to a lie detector test, I am curious how many of those people would revise their statement. Although I am not proud to admit it, at 4 a.m. on day three of labor, I was only feeling frustrated, bewildered, and impatient. That would not be the last time Jude would make me feel that way. When he arrived, "happy" is not a descriptor I would employ.

Many fathers grow into love for their child instead of having love thrust upon them. The moment Jude rested against Jody's bosom, love materialized. I am sure I loved Jude as well, but it was a fledgling emotion, nascent and feeble. We were strangers. How much can you love a stranger?

I have no professional training in elucidating the psychology of relationships. I certainly have no scientific background dedicated to dissecting the nuances of father-son bonding strategies. My observations and impressions are purely anecdotal. Having the privilege of surveilling countless interactions between parents and their children—as a coach, friend, and healthcare provider—has provided unlimited data from which to draw a general conclusion. It has also allowed me to recognize that the style and shaping of parental relationships can be quite different for fathers than for mothers. For mothers, relationships mature, intertwine, and flourish through clear, honest, and intentional communication. For fathers, relationships seem to thrive amid shared experiences. I recognize those statements are not without controversy.

They are broad observations, for which there is ample evidence to the contrary. In my experience, especially with Jude, that observation seemed to hold true.

Our shared experience created an operating dynamic which forged our future. And we had a great number of shared experiences, much to Jude's chagrin. I was determined to not let having children "slow me down." In retrospect, I do not know what that pithy statement even means. At the time I believe I thought it meant I would not let Jude's arrival derail my personal time. Obviously, I was not the brightest parent. How could the care and nurture of a tiny human, fully dependent upon someone else for their survival, not impact the caregiver's activities?

* * *

We had just purchased a home which we decided needed some remodeling. As a true Dutchman, newlywed saddled with immense debt, and someone who is relatively handy, the idea of hiring outside help for any project was unfathomable. Jude became my handyman. Essentially this meant he got to observe what his father was doing, without getting in the way or having any needs. When he was an infant, it was simple. I would place him in his baby seat while I got to work. If I remembered I would provide him with some occasional nourishment and usually place him in his crib. For the most part, he did not interfere with my progress. After he learned to crawl, and then walk, his radius of interference became infinite. It turns out that kids are curious. I could not do anything without Jude surreptitiously appearing underfoot. His curiosity and my grim determination proved to be a trying combination.

Rough carpentry was manageable. Anytime I turned on a fixed power tool, like a chop saw, he would scream and run out of the room. I had little fear of him interfering while I was cutting lumber. Small power tools were more of a problem. He was fascinated with my electric drill and pad sander. One day, I was prepping a room for painting—calking some imperfections, removing outlet covers, taping corners, etc.—when I heard the drill fire up. There was Jude, all of eighteen months, toddling around the room with the trigger fully depressed, ready to "work." Before I could intervene, he had punched multiple holes in the drywall with ecstatic delight. I had never seen him more pleased.

Painting was impossible. One day I decided to paint the bathroom. Fortunately, the doors had locks so I could keep him out. Why I thought it was advisable to lock myself in a small room with no windows and give my toddler the run of the house is beyond my capacity to reason. Of course, as is the case with any small child, they simply want to be with their parents. Never mind that he could have gone anywhere or done anything, he just wanted to be where I was. He pounded on the door, wailing for ingress while I desperately attempted to apply a first coat. The cacophony was unrelenting. I finally conceded.

"Can you stay nice and quiet and not touch anything?" I asked.

"Yes, Daddy," he responded through his sniffles.

"It's important that when you're in the room, you stand exactly where I tell you and don't move." I was very serious and stern. His eyes grew wide, and he nodded vigorously. He was trembling with excitement. His dream of witnessing the profound mystery unfolding in the forbidden room was about to be realized.

I let him enter and closed the door, allowing full access to the walls. He stood in the center of the room in mute fascination, exhilarated to bear witness to the project that, until that point, had been strictly off-limits. As I cautiously began applying more paint, he moved in closer to inspect the proceedings.

"Don't get too close," I warned. "I don't want to accidentally get paint on you." He took a cautious step back, and then another. "Careful!" I exclaimed. "Don't touch that wall." I pointed to the wall directly behind him, glistening with newly applied paint.

"Why?" he asked.

"Because there's wet paint on it," I explained. He leapt away from the paint like it was a striking cobra and shot across the narrow bathroom entryway directly into the adjacent wall, also freshly painted.

"NO!" I cried. "Step away from that wall." In my mind, "step" meant to move a single pace away from the wet paint and hold still. For an excited toddler, "step" meant spinning around while maintaining full contact with the wall, then careening across the floor and inadvertently slamming his chest, cheek, and open palms squarely against all the adjacent surfaces.

"Stop!" I yelled. "What are you doing?" My disbelief was overwhelming. Jude started hopping around like the floor was on fire. My booming admonition unhinged him. Not a single part of his person was free of paint. "We need to get you out of here. Stop moving," I demanded. He was beyond reason with fear and alarm, crying, shaking, and stumbling about. He managed to splash one foot into my roller pan, splattering paint everywhere and igniting absolute panic. We were both beside ourselves. I desperately clutched him by his stained shirt and hauled him away at arm's length, plopping him in the utility sink. Paint was on his foot, in his hair, all over his hands and every article of clothing. The only thing that didn't have paint on it was his disposable diaper. We spent the next hour trying to get him clean and hiding the evidence from Mom. We were unsuccessful on both counts.

An uncommon supply of stubbornness and a deficiency of foresight can be a stout combination for inducing trauma. Jude and I engaged in many home projects. He managed to keep his fingers and toes. I managed to work through numerous tasks, albeit with limited efficiency and quality. For fear of being investigated by CPS, even two decades later, I will avoid speaking of his interactions with the nail gun, impact hammer, and jigsaw. Despite those altercations, after his sister, Simone, was born, I redoubled my efforts to not let my children "slow me down." This all came to a regrettable head the day, with a sixteen-month-old and a not-quite-three-year-old, I attempted to lay slate on the guest bathroom floor. It was a complicated room and the slate we picked out was rather irregular, both in shape and surface texture. The room was far from square, and there were several awkward angles requiring precision and attention. It was a difficult undertaking even in ideal conditions.

Those of you with toddlers can attest they require constant supervision.

That supervision entails interaction, guidance, instruction, and vigilance. You are their caretaker, playmate, and events coordinator. It is a full-time job. I knew this. I also knew I wanted to finish my bathroom remodel. So, I set up the wet saw and went to work. For the first couple of hours everything went swimmingly. Jude and Simone managed to stay entertained while I made some exacting cuts and laid out the majority of the slate. By lunchtime I was miles ahead of my already ambitious target time. I fed the kids, got them set up in the playroom, and continued to work. My liberal use of the tile saw and the accompanying loud, noxious noise was frightening enough to keep their curiosity at bay. They were content to run around the basement, making a tremendous mess, but mostly ignoring me. The security of my intermittent presence was enough to quell any neediness. This all changed, however, the moment I began mixing the thin-set mortar. There was no scary tile saw to chase off their inquisitiveness.

"Dad, what's that?" Jude asked.

"It's special glue for the floor," I answered, rigorously mixing.

"Glue?" His voice excitedly pitched up. "Can I touch it?"

"Nope," I quickly responded. "You don't want to get this on your hands. Why don't you guys go play in the other room?" Simone giggled and tried to grab the bucket of mortar, nearly getting her hand caught in the electric mixer. "Whoa!" I exclaimed, raising my voice a little. "Jude, take your sister into the other room. I'll come play with you guys in a minute."

They reluctantly exited. The mortar was a very compelling subject of interest. Nothing is more attractive than forbidden fruit. My time was waning, but I still felt confident I could get the project completed. Besides, the cement was thoroughly mixed, reversal impossible. I feverishly applied an even coat to a large portion of the floor. It was aggressively ambitious, but the first few pieces went down smoothly.

"Dad, what are those?" Jude's voice startled me. I had been concentrating so hard I did not hear them return. They had both crept quietly in. Their hands rested gingerly on the mortar bucket rim.

"These are the tiles I'm going to cover the floor with," I quickly replied. "See how great it will look?"

Jude bent down and picked up a piece of slate. The edges were sharp.

"Don't touch that!" I said a bit harshly. The last thing I needed was an injury. I also didn't want him to throw my carefully mapped layout into disarray. He set the tile down with obedient alacrity. This was a good sign. I turned back to my work, but as I precisely placed the next piece, Simone bent down and picked up the tile Jude had discarded, then reached for another one.

"Moners, put that down," Jude chided. He took a step forward to block her and nearly set his foot down onto the wet mortar.

"Guys," I pleaded. "Just give me a second and I'll come play. But you have to get out of here. It's not safe." For some reason I thought appealing to their self-preservation would exact the response I desired. Adult reason and toddler reason are typically not coincident—except in those circumstances when adults act like toddlers.

"Can we watch?" Jude asked.

"Yes," I replied, "but you have to stand in the doorway."

They took a step back, fascinated with the proceedings. I had a piece of slate in each hand, both buttered with cement. I could tell it was starting to dry. If the mortar set up before I could lay my pieces, I would have an enormous mess on my hands. The mortar would need to be chipped away, an aggravating and tedious process, and the whole project restarted. I redoubled my speed and buttered more slate. That's when I noticed a rather pungent effluvium.

"Does someone have a poopy pants?" I delicately inquired while cautiously tapping more slate into place. Simone giggled. The smell grew worse. I tried to hold their attention with inane conversation while placing more pieces. Modern science has made disposable diapers nearly bulletproof. I figured we could hang on through the odor while I completed my task.

"Simone stinks!" Jude exclaimed. "She pooped."

"I know," I replied calmly. "I'll take care of it in a second." I grabbed another tile and attempted to fit it into place. The lines were not faultless, but still manageable. As I tried to delicately finagle the tile edges so they were perfectly parallel, another miasmatic wave accosted my senses—more potent than the last.

"I pooped," Jude laughed. "Oh no! Simone, don't."

Jude's appeal broke my concentration. I glanced across the bathroom and saw that Simone's pants were down and her diaper half undone. Fecal material was running down her leg. Jude started pointing and laughing.

"Stop!" I yelled. "Stand still. Don't move." I gave the tile one last nudge and quickly stood up. Simone took that as an invitation. She giggled and started running towards me, smearing poop with every step. Jude tried to grab her arm.

"Simone! Stop!" he cried. Too late. She was beyond his reach. She was beyond my reach. She slipped on her own feces, falling forward and landing face-first on my evenly spread cement, mixing mortar, feces, hair, and clothes into an evil slurry. I gently attempted to extricate her from the slop, but she was a greased pig. I struggled to gain purchase. Our dance animated Jude, who exuberantly ran around the scene like it was a roller derby.

"Yuck," he exclaimed, hopping about. I could not have agreed with him more. And then, for reasons beyond rational explication, he grabbed Simone's grimy leg and fouled both hands with her creation.

"Don't touch anything!" I cried. "Stand still." The excitement was too much. Simone started crying. Jude didn't know whether to laugh or cry. He danced around on the wet mortar, kicking loose slate about until he tripped on a piece, cut his toe, and fell firmly on his rump. The impact blew his own messy diaper up his backside. He scrabbled wildly, trying to rise, tipping over the bucket of mortar in the process.

I dispensed all pretense of remaining clean. Fortunately, we were already in a bathroom, albeit one that was half torn apart, but thankfully the sink worked. I secured a screeching Simone under one arm, grimacing at the horrendous mess she was making of me, and with my free hand gripped Jude's waistband and tossed him into the empty sink.

"Stay there," I commanded. I ran down the hallway, disgustedly cradling my disheveled daughter, and dove outdoors before Simone started dripping. I began hosing her off, which understandably detonated a verbal cacophony rivaling a sonic boom. We were well past delicacy. I was fresh out of mercy. I stripped her down, in the freezing cold, and hosed her clean, all the while hoping neither the neighbors nor her mother would happen by. When we re-entered the warmth of the house, Jude was howling like a coyote. Thankfully, he had remained in the sink despite the intensity of his displeasure. I dried off Simone, tossed her in her crib, and set to work rescuing Jude. There was mortar, feces, and blood everywhere.

After that day I realized I needed to rework my understanding of what "not slowing me down" really meant. My children deserved better. I was treating them like an inconvenience instead of a gift. That evening, as a cathartic exercise, I spoke with a friend about my adventure. He had a few young children of his own. I was still a little traumatized and put out by the entire affair, so I found little humor in confessing my travails. He laughed for what I considered an inordinate amount of time, and then supplied a bit of advice, which also served as an underhanded admonishment.

"Taking care of your kids is all about expectations," he explained. "You can't expect your day to consist of minding the children *and* something else. It ends at 'and.' You are simply minding the children. That is your vocation for the day. If you manage to get something else done, then hooray for you. But your only expectation for the day must be managing the kids. That is a successful day. They will appreciate you for it, and you will enjoy them because of it."

"Daddy days" acquired a decidedly different flavor moving forward.

LEARNING

"After all, who isn't a survivor from the wreck of childhood?"
NICOLE KRAUSS

It is a testament to the resiliency of the human psyche that more firstborn children do not bear festering scars. They are products of trial and error. One simply hopes that the "error" portion of the equation is not too egregious. I have no capacity to recall how many times I crawled into bed with my wife and, upon reflection on my day with Jude, would hesitatingly state, "Well that didn't work." Oftentimes Jody would just pat my arm and say, "It will be fine." She knows a great deal about relationships and child development. I trusted her. She was usually correct. When you are trying to provide what is best for your child, "fine" is not the goal you are attempting to achieve. I always wanted to be a better parent. But everyone has their first time, and your firstborn child is a product of that experience. Part of your job as a parent is to pray a two-part prayer: First, for parental wisdom. Second, when wisdom proves elusive, implore the Almighty for your child's protection.

I have always enjoyed adventure and novelty. I wanted Jude to develop this same love. I take great pleasure in experiencing things for the first time and am never satisfied with a recapitulation of previous experiences. The problem with novelty is that it is unpredictable. Jude suffered through numerous investigations and forays. Some of them were splendid experiences. Others were terrifying. I suspect this had a long-term impact on his willingness, as he matured, to heartily explore the unknown.

I enjoy hiking. I wanted Jude to enjoy hiking as well. He was going to be my adventure buddy. There was a trail just a few miles from our home that many of the local outdoorspeople would utilize for training. It was relatively short, but rather steep, and the apex of the climb afforded sweeping views of the valley, town, and the Stuart Mountain Range to the north. We were gifted a baby backpack Jude would ride in while I traipsed through the hills. We did this multiple times, and he loved it. He would bounce around, observe the flora and fauna, and try to babble off my ear in absolute glee. With winter approaching, I wanted to maintain this hiking momentum. As the autumn days grew shorter, we continued to climb. What I did not consider, in our relatively new surroundings, was how quickly the seasons changed. We lived in a high desert climate and even on relatively mild days, when the sun set—which it did early—the cold arrived with it. One mid-November we decided (meaning *I* decided, Jude really didn't have a vote) to do our ridge climb. I packed him in the Kidpack and set off. We were dressed the same—lightweight wick-away hiking fabric. With Jude on my back, and walking at a brisk pace, I was concerned about overheating.

As usual, Jude began chirping in my ear. He was always excited to be on the move. He would point out every bird, bush, insect, or make-believe object he thought he recognized. It was all inarticulate baby talk, for the most part. But I could judge his mood through his intonation and prosody. The faster he talked, the happier he was. When his words slowed down, or his voice became deep, I knew problems were afoot. Silence meant he was sleeping, which was always appreciated.

We started later in the day than usual, so I bore down and tried to hustle. About halfway up the hill the sun dipped behind the hills. I soon noticed difficulty with my purchase as my feet slipped several times. The ground was riddled with patches of ice. Balancing a human on your back is different from a static load, so I was keenly focused on staying upright while managing my pace. I knew the temperature was south of freezing, but other than cold hands, I did not think much more about it. Going fast and remaining upright were my only priorities. Consequently, I worked up a considerable sweat.

As darkness encroached, I said a few comforting words to Jude, from whom I had not heard a peep for some time. I assumed he was taking a brief nap. Nearing the apex the ice and frost became increasingly treacherous, and the darkness wasn't helping. After slipping multiple times and nearly rolling down the side of the ravine, I reluctantly halted my progress to assess the value of continuing. I reached behind my ear to provide Jude a reassuring tap when I immediately noticed two things: First, I had a semi-frozen glob of what could only be snot plastered to the back of my head. Second, Jude's cheek, which I delicately brushed with my fingertips, felt like refrigerated Jello.

I quickly removed the backpack to investigate. His lips were blue. His hands were ice cold. He appeared to be gasping for air, which I immediately catastrophized into hypothermic paralysis. As I began freaking out, it became apparent his breathing difficulties were the result of frozen snot. The cold air had made his nose run excessively, and for the past forty-five minutes, it had congealed and solidified all over his face and the back of my head. I deftly pulled him out of the pack and put him under my shirt. In my utter ignorance, I had failed to recognize Jude was not generating any internal warmth from physical exertion. He was sitting still, fully exposed to the crisp night air, in a light cotton onesie. He might as well have been naked.

Keeping him in my shirt, I tucked his head under my chin and moved as quickly down the hill as the conditions allowed. After nearly twenty apprehensive minutes, his hands started to move, and he snapped into action, babbling and struggling like a madman against the confines of my shirt. By the time we safely arrived at the car, he was rather upset, and rightly so. I was just happy he was crying. I cranked the heat and let it blow full throttle all the way home. When we pulled into the garage, he was bright red, like a glowing cherry. He seemed no worse for wear; I was secretly pleased he wasn't old enough to tattle on me. It was, however, several months before he had any interest in crawling back into his carry pack, and he never adopted my love for hiking.

...

Parents are naturally inclined to protect their children. Nothing is more emotionally traumatic than experiencing a child in pain. We also do not want to unduly shelter them and keep them secluded from experiences in life that allow for growth and maturity. Parents will forever be in tension over where to draw the line between protection and seclusion. We tend to label parents "good" if they manage to keep their child safe, and "bad" if something happens to their child which, in hindsight, could have been avoidable. Perception becomes the arbiter of judgment. I suspect the real line between good and bad is mostly drawn by luck.

Jude always had an interest in fire. Part of that is endemic to boyhood. I have yet to meet a boy who doesn't get excited when it is time to make a fire. Part of Jude's journey was accompanying me during projects. As it happened, one such project consisted of torching our burn pile. Unsurprisingly, he was rather excited about this, and I would be lying if I wasn't as excited as he was. There is a reason fireworks are so popular, and it doesn't have much to do with an X chromosome.

The previous spring we had torn out an enormous pile of twenty-year-old juniper bushes and let them dry on an unlandscaped portion of our property. That same spring I had also combed through the outdated and discarded treatment charts in my orthodontic practice. Due to healthcare privacy laws, I could not simply take them to the dump, and there were no shredding services in town. It was a logistical headache to haul them to a larger city and have them professionally disposed, nor did I want to spend the money required to ship them somewhere. So, we decided to burn them.

Jude and I worked through the details. He was only three, so he expressed several opinions but did not have a lot of helpful input. By midmorning, we were ready to go. Jude was the dedicated hoseman. I would get the fire going, and then we would slowly feed it. The junipers had been drying in the desert climate for a couple of months; they also had not been watered when they were living, so it was surprising they hadn't already spontaneously combusted in the summer heat. My boxes of charts were all paper products, cardstock, and cardboard. They had been stored indoors. Flammability was not going to be a problem.

For some reason we could not get our pile going. The charts were compressed so tightly in each box the flame would simply snuff out from lack of oxygen. I did not feel like unpacking all those boxes. I also did not have any diesel or starting fluid, but I did have gasoline. In a fit of undiagnosed lunacy, I decided to use gasoline to help the project along. While I sprinkled a few drops of gasoline onto the boxes, I clearly instructed Jude that this was not the proper way to start a bonfire. During my terse, informative instruction, the nozzle fell off the five-gallon can, and gasoline poured everywhere. Jude discovered a great deal of humor in this, and I'm quite certain he discarded any credibility I may have possessed while watching me fumble in frustration. I finally got the flow abated and discarded the broken apparatus a safe distance away. A cursory evaluation of our environmental disaster revealed nearly all the gas had fallen harmlessly onto the dry, cracked earth, where it was immediately soaked up. While I poked around our unignited pile, assuring Jude we appeared clear for takeoff, Jody came out of the house and stood high above us on our deck to observe the proceedings. She could smell the gas. "Is that safe?" she asked. "Should Jude be so close?"

"No problem," I casually replied. "Most of the gas just poured onto the dirt and soaked into the ground. I doubt we'll even be able to get this thing going without more."

"Okay," she acknowledged. "Is Jude too close?" When my wife asks a question a second time, it's because she's hoping for a different answer.

"No, he's fine. He's on water duty and he's all ready to go. He's been a great helper!"

"Hey, Mommy!" Jude yelled. He had the hose in one hand and a sippy cup of orange juice in the other. He was staring expectantly at the boxes, waiting for something to happen. Three-year-olds are not known for their patience. I grabbed a match and tossed it towards the wet corner of the closest box. It ignited brightly for a moment then died just as quickly. Jude was disappointed. Another flameout. I grabbed another match, stepped closer, struck it, and tossed it onto the pile. For a couple of seconds nothing happened. No flames. No smoke. Jude stood next to me and casually took another sip.

Kaboom! Everything erupted into a searing gout of flame. The violent ignition reverberated with a concussion that knocked Jude through the air, depositing him with a solid thump directly onto his back. His sippy cup ricocheted straight up while the lid popped off, spraying orange juice all over his face. Twenty-foot flames licked the heavens, like we'd opened the bowels of hell. I grabbed Jude and scrambled to safety. Evidently all the gasoline that I foolishly thought the ground absorbed had pooled in the bottom of the tightly packed chart boxes. Some of those boxes were filled with ancient X-rays, the type dressed with cellulose acetate. This made for a wickedly intense bomb. The hose Jude held fell to the ground next to the conflagration and melted instantly. I'd never seen anything like it and didn't know something full of cold water could melt like that. It was fascinating to watch. It also meant Jude was shirking his duty. In his defense, I imagine once he went airborne, he rescinded all responsibility as hoseman. I deserted him and raced around the house to procure more hoses—we lived on the side of a hill covered in sage brush. Fire was a real and present danger.

When I came back with the hoses, Jude was standing safely out of harm's way, covered in dirt and orange juice. He pointed at the flames. "Big fire, Daddy. That's a big fire."

This incident catalyzed his congenital love for incendiary devices. Flames, both physical and metaphorical, were always something he was drawn to.

• • •

Jude loved animals—or at least the idea of animals. From our country home we would go for walks spying on deer, elk, coyotes, and a whole assortment of farm animals. He would read books about animals. He had an entire collection of animal toys that he would manipulate and imagine into all manner of confabulated contingencies. Who knew an ibex and a giraffe could be playmates? The day he and Simone caught a mole was a day of breathtaking excitement. They graciously placed that mole in a bucket and raced into the house just to show their mother. How they managed, through their giddiness, to hop down the stairs without spilling the mole eludes me. They thought they were presenting Jody with an invaluable gift. Their mother was not impressed.

Jude also loved helping me mow the lawn. This consisted of me cutting the grass with Jude traipsing a few steps behind pushing his plastic mower. He pridefully brandished his own ear protection, "gassed" his mower with water, and even went through the motions of pull-starting. It was all very helpful.

Country living came with a hearty supply of "free-range" dogs. We were the only house on our country road that did not own a dog. Most homeowners had multiple canines, but some would be hard-pressed to recognize which dog was theirs. These dogs ranged the entire community, forming a pack, where they would whimsically congregate around different homes and treat them like their own residence.

Jude was fascinated by dogs. I like dogs. I don't like dog poop. If your home was fortunate enough to be selected for a free-range conference, then invariably you would be privy to a great deal of barking, frenzied scampering, and a sinful mess of dog poop. As it turns out children, especially toddlers, have an innate capacity to step on, fall into, and even intentionally handle feces. Jude possessed exquisite talent in this arena. Few things aggravated me more than having to scrape tenacious dog feces off his shoes so he wouldn't track it into the house. This was the primary reason why we did not own a dog.

One summer afternoon we were mowing in tandem when the dog pack arrived. They were especially frisky that day. I desperately attempted to shoo them off my grass, keenly aware of the inevitable gifts they were likely to deposit. My threatening gesticulations only served to work them into a frenzy. I eventually grabbed what I thought was a stick, but turned out to be a deer antler, and started waving it about. They went crazy, leaping, barking, and tearing around the yard like it was a dog track. Our yard had a nifty little infinity edge, which disappeared over a steep, unmanicured hill. I threw the antler as far as I could down that hill hoping it would draw them away and also be impossible to find. They leapt away in an excited rush. I was feeling pretty good about my plan and was about to resume mowing when suddenly they came racing back, even more excited, and I found my antler back at my feet. I had inadvertently begun a game of fetch.

I threw the antler a few more times, with ever-increasing violence and precision. Up the hill, sideways, into impenetrable thickets. It was maddening. They kept returning. In a fit of fortune my last throw caught a gust of wind, cleared the road, and settled in a deep irrigation ditch far below. The dogs raced down the hill with maniacal barking, intent on continuing the game. The ditch thwarted them. The antler was buried and the ditch too steep for the dogs to navigate. The pack appeared to disband. Success.

I quickly finished with the lawn and put the implements away. Jude remained outside to provide some "finishing touches" with his machine. His mowing stamina was legendary. While I sat down on the porch to remove my shoes and appreciate Jude's progress, the cursed dogs returned. In a hysterical craze they streaked across the backyard, depositing the antler at Jude's feet and bowling him over in the process. Jude crawled around, unnerved by the howling pack, but curious all the same. The dogs formed a ring around him, but they were just far enough back he did not feel threatened. And then he picked up the antler. The moment it touched his hand, the dogs went berserk.

Jude was terrorized. He immediately began wailing. He also did what would only seem reasonable to a young child. He brandished the antler like a weapon and attempted to keep the dogs at bay. His strategy consisted mostly of screaming and waving the antler like a madman. You can imagine what this did to the dogs. In their excitement they bowled Jude over, gnawed at the antler, and played a pernicious game of canine leapfrog with my son. By the time I came to his rescue, he was a terror-stricken mess. I cleaned him up and calmed him down, but his wracking sobs continued for many minutes. Eventually he took a deep, calming breath and eloquently characterized his trying ordeal. "Scary dogs, Daddy. Scary dogs."

I have never met a child who did not, at some point in their childhood, ask for a puppy—except one. Jude. Occasionally, careless parenting can work in your favor.

RECREATION

"You are a very special person. There is only one like you in the whole world. There's never been anyone exactly like you before, and there will never be again. Only you. And people can like you exactly as you are."

FRED ROGERS

People gravitate to what they know. This is true of parents as well. First-time parents are most influenced by their own childhood experiences. Your relationship with your parents serves as an initial working template. You may embrace that template or reject it, depending on your childhood reflections. This reflection is vitally important and healthy, especially as it informs your own burgeoning parental plan. It also presents some dangers and pitfalls.

Invariably, all parents tend to cherry pick from their own childhoods. Why would you deny your child the same phenomenological excitement of a traditional Christmas morning, catching a first fish, going on a shopping trip, or cavorting in ocean waves? These experiences are worth celebrating and re-creating. They bridge time and space, shaping successive generations. Unfortunately, when we reflect on those experiences, we misinterpret the event as the culmination, instead of our impression of the experience. We erroneously believe the experience was the critical element, instead of what the experience produced—namely joy, laughter, and bolstered fidelity. When you attempt to recapture the heart of your own precious memory and gift it to your child, the potential exists for your re-creation to become contrived and bloated. All your focus is on the event instead of the product.

The converse is also true. As dedicated as we are to reproducing all we hold dear from our history, we are doubly determined to eliminate from our child's path those experiences we perceived as negative. The awful memories that haunt us—those we would rather forget—we employ as a shield for our child's defense. It was harmful to us, and so we assume those experiences will be harmful to our own child. What a mistake it would be for them to suffer as we did.

Unfortunately, those profound and memorable experiences in our lives that leave the deepest impact often are not the ones we would choose to relive. Even years later, with the privilege of hindsight, we still are not always capable of recognizing how a traumatic event shaped and molded us in a way otherwise unattainable through any other mechanism. It is impossible to understand how liberating forgiveness can be unless you have been truly wronged. And being wronged is a painful affront that may take years, or even decades, to sort out. It is difficult to fully appreciate health until you've experienced sickness. It is challenging to recognize the exhilaration of winning unless you know what it is to lose. Many of the character traits we appreciate in others—humility, graciousness, charity, thoughtfulness, courage—would remain uncultivated were it not for adversity, trauma, misfortune, or hardship.

This doesn't mean we shouldn't try to protect our children from adverse events and caustic encounters. It does infer our perception of the past—how we felt in the moment, how we currently respond in consideration of those feelings, and how we wish it could have been different—may not provide the perfect instruction for how to push and challenge our own children.

When Jude was four, we moved to Lynden, a quaint little town in the northwest corner of the state of Washington. After his brother, Johann, was born, we decided it was in everyone's best interest to relocate closer to both sets of grandparents. I had been close with my grandparents growing up, and I wanted to afford my children a similar possibility. Selfishly, we also wanted the extra eyes and hands it requires to corral three children under the age of five.

Lynden was my hometown. I, also, had moved there when I was four, and desired Jude to value the close-knit, small-town experience the same way I did. I worked diligently to re-create a facsimile of my elementary years, including enrolling him in the same school, living near my childhood home, and surrounding him with the children of my childhood friends.

I discovered very quickly that a re-creation of one's personal childhood experience is impossible. It also is not healthy. There are so many barriers and inconsistencies to overcome. More importantly, you quickly recognize that you are not just like your parents, nor do you want to be, which radically changes the entire operation. But the single most significant barrier to re-creating an idealized past is the simple fact that your child is not you.

Despite my best efforts to harm him as a toddler, Jude managed to not only survive, but flourish. After our move, his unique personality began taking shape. He was becoming Jude. It is exciting and fascinating (and sometimes a little terrifying) observing the maturational intricacies of your child's personality. It occurs at an alarming rate. At first, they are mostly a needful creature, subject to your whims and proclivities, and utterly dependent upon your benevolence for their survival. This quickly evolves. If you are not paying close attention, you will miss it. If you miss it, you will have difficulties understanding it.

I missed it.

Jude was, and always will be, his own person. This seems trite and banal to say. We are all "our own person." What I am trying to convey is that Jude's personality—his attitude, passions, desires, and whims—were altogether different than we expected them to be. As his parents we were not so naïve as to expect, or even desire, a clone. But we assumed some of the character traits we both shared—our enjoyment of education, love for exercise, need to be busy, devotion to faith—would manifest in our child. How could they not? He was, after all, our flesh and blood.

When those assumed traits did not miraculously become patently obvious, we became confused and easily frustrated. Why wouldn't he care to strive for good grades? Why would he be content to slothfully lie on his bed, disengaged from any activity? Why did he love to play video games so much? Why didn't he go outside and shoot baskets or play a pick-up game of football with the neighborhood kids even when they begged him to join? Why didn't he want to play board games with his parents? After all, what could be more fun?

Because of these differences, I thought I was struggling to connect with him. This troubled me. All the activities I had on offer he tended to reject, and all the things he was drawn to I thought were a waste of time. I had no interest in cars. He could read car magazines all day, cover to cover, and recite entire characteristics of different vehicles verbatim. I had never read a car magazine, nor did I want to. If we let him, he could play video games for hours, immersed in that make-believe world, engaged in a computer-generated fantasy far from reality. It was a constant battle to reel him back. We were always putting term limits on his gaming, and he was always pushing back.

"Why do you always want to play video games?" I asked him. "You aren't accomplishing anything."

"Because they're fun," he replied. "It's exciting."

"But it's not real," I argued. "They are a poor substitute for experiencing something real."

"They're fun," he resolutely stated. "That's real."

We were two people speaking the same language, but with no desire to understand each other. I refused to accept that the enjoyment of a video game could be a worthy end in itself. He refused to consider that an even deeper kind of fun might come from an activity that, at first, demands real effort and discipline. We were worlds apart.

What was especially painful for me was the notion that he was wasting talent. In second grade, he was struggling with penmanship. It was maddening. He would bring home papers with failing penmanship grades. A distracted four-year-old riding on the back of a hay wagon with a box of broken crayons could have done better. His work was illegible. We nagged him for weeks about this. His teacher expressed concern. We tried to brush it off as a characteristic of his age (he was young for his grade) and the fact he was left-handed.

One day, he brought home a paper that Da Vinci must have drafted. It was neat, expressive, and symmetric, and so consistent that it looked like a computer simulation. My wife praised him vociferously. On the top of the sheet, his teacher wrote, "Jude, God loves it when you do your best." His teacher knew just how to say the right thing at the right time. He was beaming.

The next day, we were back to the same incompetent handwriting. I was aghast. Jude simply did not care. Handwriting was not important to him. By taking home the one perfect paper, he demonstrated to his parents what he was capable of. It was his way of telling us to get off his back. He was wired so differently than either of us when it came to school. For Jody and me, our feelings about handwriting were irrelevant—we would have put conscientious effort into our task for the purpose of receiving a good mark on the project. For Jude, he was functionally indifferent to the good mark. There was no amount of cajoling, positive reinforcement, or bribery we could implement to make him feel otherwise. When I finally realized this, I knew we were in for some long and difficult days ahead.

He was strong for his age, and decent-sized. But he had little interest in pursuing sports. We forced him to ski, as that was one of my favorite childhood endeavors (even though it only happened once a year). We encouraged him to try different outdoor activities, which he grudgingly obliged but did little self-improvement work. He had an innate musical ability that he had little interest in developing, but even his apathy in that regard was not enough to forestall his mother.

Jody grew up in a musical family. All her siblings were required to play an instrument for a minimum of ten years. She does not always have the fondest memories of those afternoons practicing, but she recognized the value of the love and appreciation those efforts instilled in her. She vowed to provide the same blessing to her children.

Her insistence on having Jude practice both the violin and piano, and Jude's resistance to her demands, have attained legendary status. Fortunately, neither participant was aggressive in their stance. This did not make the war games any less fraught. Jude's ability to contrive any excuse, and Jody's capacity to counter those excuses with patience and reason, deserve their own handbook. Throughout all their thrusts and parries I can only remember one time I felt the need to play the treasonous husband.

One warm, fall afternoon, Jude was outside playing with friends in the creek that ran behind our home. He had his shirt off and was wet and muddy. They were trying to build a dam and were heavily invested in this feat of civil engineering. I was very excited about this. Jude was physically engaged with nature, playing like the proverbial boy, basking in the glory of experimenting his way into a colossal mess.

"Jude!" Jody yelled from the deck, shattering the merriment like a loathsome cudgel. "It's time to come in and practice violin." Her timing could not have been more awful.

"Aww, Mom!" he screamed. "Not now!" The passion in his voice was unmistakable.

"Yes, son," Jody calmly replied. "You know you have to get it done before dinner." Jude arched his back and let out an incomprehensible groan. His frustration superseded the bounds of articulation. The boys were aghast, regarding Jody as if she had just offered them poison. Jude spread his arms and reached to the heavens, letting the mud slowly squish through his fingers, splat off his chest, and lifelessly roll down his legs until they plopped into the running water. He was wracked with a martyr's anguish. I witnessed a Rockwellian painting come to life.

"Perhaps," I interjected, recognizing the need to rescue my son. I too had been in his shoes. "Just this once we could put it off to a later time?" I knew the dangers of getting in between a mother-son confrontation. In this instance, however, I could see Jude's point. Sometimes a parent just has to let their child make mud pies.

Jude did not have the same childhood I did. He did not want it, nor did he need it. Sometimes this is difficult to accept because I am keenly aware of what he missed, and how he could have been positively influenced through similar experiences. What I must acknowledge, and respectfully appreciate, is that he traveled a road uniquely suited to him, and the experiences which molded and influenced his character were just as powerful and profound. Jude was not born to be an improved version of me, or a mirror of his mother (who needs no improving), or a facsimile of a cousin or Grandpa. He was called to be Jude, and the Being responsible for Jude's journey has much more wisdom at His disposal than I ever will.

COLLISION

*"Education without values, as useful as it is,
seems rather to make a man a more clever devil."*

C. S. LEWIS

Mischaracterizing a relationship is a fantastic way to purchase a one-way ticket to trouble. Tales of courtship are replete with examples of these misunderstandings: The young man, emotionally stirred through his infatuation with his breathtaking companion, impulsively blurts, "I love you!" They have only gone on a handful of dates, and she has revealed no indication she regards him as anything but a friend. Her lack of reciprocation is awkward. The wonderful evening the man has planned unravels, and any chance of a developing relationship evaporates.

A close friend of mine once divulged an experience he shared with his wife. One evening, as they relaxed in their living room, his wife interrupted his reading. "Is it okay if I ask you a question?"

"Certainly," he graciously replied.

"How well do you feel like we are operating right now, as a couple. What do you think about us?" She sat up a little straighter in her chair and leaned forward.

"Fine, I think." He smiled for a bit, and then briefly raised an eyebrow. "Why? What's up?"

"How about on a scale of 1–10." She stretched her arms apart to mimic a gauge. "What number would you give us?"

"Oh … I don't know exactly. Depends on what you want to compare it to? But I would say probably a 9. Sometimes maybe an 8.5, but usually at least a 9. Don't you think?"

"Oh, buddy." She shook her head menacingly. "I'd say we're a 3, tops. We've got some talking to do!"

* * *

By the time Jude entered his freshman year, our relationship, from what I could ascertain, was no better or worse than any other father's with their fourteen-year-old. Young teenage boys can be characterized as a "hole about an inch deep." Jude was very average in this regard. There were so many aspects of his personality I found trying, and I worked very diligently to polish off the parts I could only perceive as "rough." I remember retrieving him from a church function when he was eleven. He came out of the room red and sweaty, boisterously shouting with a deafening intensity. I placed a hand on his shoulder to calm him down and peered through the open doorway where there were several other boys running around in what appeared to be controlled mayhem. One of the leaders pulled me aside and asked, "How is Jude doing at home? Does he spend a lot of time out of control? Is he treating you okay?"

"Yeah, yeah … everything's fine at home."

He must have noticed my overtly quizzical expression, because he chose to elaborate.

"Well, he's burning off a lot of energy here. Extremely rambunctious. Can't be quiet. Interrupts all the time. I could barely handle an hour of it. No idea how you put up with that daily."

"Hmmm … must have been a bit of an anomalous night," I pondered. "School can feel a little suffocating to these young boys."

"Perhaps," the leader agreed. "But the other boys don't quite push the edge like Jude. Good luck!"

This was not a pleasing report. At home, Jude was mercurial but never unhinged. In my estimation, this conversation only encouraged me to redouble my efforts towards "polishing." This meant I would take extra time and care to point out instances when his behavior was less than admirable. I tried to be both fair and kind. I also learned the importance of choosing the right moment. Unfortunately, what I thought was insightful and persuasive, Jude perceived as oppressive and critical.

He continued to push back against doing his schoolwork. Keeping him on task was a constant struggle. He gravitated towards friends who, while not unsavory, tended to lean into the same impulsive and energetic behavior he was developing a reputation for. He loved music, which was positive, but he was very attracted to rap music, especially rap music with abusive language.

This became an ongoing battle in the home. Jody and I were, in our estimation, exceptionally lenient with the music we let him listen to. He ignored all our parameters. We set restrictions on his device, so he worked around that by procuring a separate iPod, which he subsequently hid. We had him draft a behavior contract and let him argue for conditions which appeared, to our sensibilities, absurdly tolerant and forgiving. After signing that contract, he proceeded to rapidly turn it into a mockery. We countered by having him write an essay on integrity. He surprised us with his fluency but completely ignored the point of the exercise.

All children need boundaries. It is the unenviable task of every parent to discover where those boundaries should reside. Every child has different needs and variable receptivity to resistance. No child should be unduly suppressed or smothered. By the same token, no child should be granted absolute sway. Finding the tipping point unique to each child is a true gift. That is the place where the child is most apt to flourish, can appreciate their circumstances, and have the rough edges polished without excessive recoil. For Jude and me, an understanding of those limits, and his perception of those limits, were positioned on different parts of the playing field. Sometimes I wondered if we were even in the same stadium.

What distressed Jody and I the most was his frank pushback and even outright antagonism to faith formation. He had no interest in developing a relationship with God. Churchgoing was extremely bothersome, and while polite, he tended to eschew dinnertime devotions and prayer.

Parents always want what's best for their child. And while parents can sometimes become misguided in their understanding of what's "best," or be forced to make concessions which depart from their ideal, some characteristics are simply inviolable. The faith of our children was one such item. When we imagined how each of our children would develop, we never once considered a child wracked with Christian antipathy.

It is extremely difficult, if not impossible, to nurture your child by instilling qualities consistent with righteousness when there are no agreed-upon ethical or moral foundations. How do you encourage the fruits of the Spirit in someone who instinctively resists anything rooted in Christian principles? Jude's rejection of faith squashed our appeal to absolute morality. He tested us severely in this regard.

"Why do you want to keep listening to that trashy music?" Jody would ask. "It's just a pile of swear words. They get in your head and then you start to talk that way."

"I don't really listen to the words," Jude responded. "And besides, why does it matter how I talk?"

"Because it's impolite and offensive, for starters," she reasoned. "And it makes you sound ignorant. And it's not appropriate behavior."

"Appropriate for who?" he snapped.

"Appropriate for anyone under this roof. Appropriate for anyone who goes to a Christian school or to church," Jody answered with slightly more intensity than she intended.

"Those rules are dumb. They don't need to apply to me." Jude jutted out his chin and half rolled his eyes. It was all I could do not to climb over the table and smack him. I am very proud to say I never beat my kids. We did spank them occasionally, emphasis on occasional, but were never overly physical. This does not mean, however, I didn't desire to knock some sense into him on occasion.

"Sometimes we do things that are difficult or hard simply because they are the right things to do. We grow through them, and they make us better people. Sometimes rules are there, even when we can't see it, to serve as guardrails to keep us moving along the right track." Jody smiled reassuringly at Jude.

Thank you, Jody, I thought. *You could not have said it better. Perhaps we should frame that quote and hang it over the dinner table.*

Jude blurted his response before the echo of Jody's wisdom even threatened to fade. "Well, I don't like rules. I just want to do what I want to do."

There was the rub. Any rule tinged with a Christian ethic made him bristle. Any impediment to his perceived freedom was deemed unfair and oppressive. Nothing is more aggravating to a parent than recognizing your own shameful character flaws manifesting in your children. A perceptive parent will work overtime to annul those flaws, usually with more aggression and fervor than required. Jody and I were both fiercely independent. We possessed the capacity to rationalize and defend our own poor choices and actions with a readily defensible logic, regardless of its wrongheadedness. Jude was demonstrating the same capacity. This panicked us.

During Jude's early teenage years, the three of us danced on thin ice. There was a constant, pervasive tension generated by Jude's antagonism and our desire. Jody and I alternated between the carrot and stick, forever confused about which to employ. I felt like we did a decent job navigating the tightrope. Judging by Jude's attitude and response, my perception and Jude's reception were wildly incongruent.

On Good Friday, Jude ran away from home. For a moment, Jody had to peel me off the ceiling. After a quick discussion and situational assessment, our apprehension diminished. We knew he was trying to send a message. We also knew most of his complaints were grossly inflated. More importantly, he was leaving a wonderful home which provided for all his needs in abundance. His quest for a better alternative was, in many ways, laughable. But we also recognized there were problems that required attention, and not all those problems stemmed from his attitude.

We attended services that evening without our oldest son. It was a touch embarrassing when people inquired as to his whereabouts, and our answer was a frank, "We don't know." Unfortunately, that was the truth—temporarily. The beauty of modern technology is that children do not think they can live without it. We had the capacity to track his movements through his phone, so we could rest in relative ease knowing he was safely under the roof of a friend's house. Had he turned his phone off, a manhunt would have ensued, and it is very probable Jude's journey would have launched down a rather tumultuous tributary.

The next morning, I was tasked with collecting him. He had spent the night about five minutes from our home. It was one of the longest drives I've ever endured, and I spent that time in fervent prayer, seeking wisdom and guidance. What would be the best way to handle this? What words were at my disposal that Jude would be receptive to? Was there an ethic to which I could appeal that would resonate? Did a compelling, reasonable social contract exist that aligned with his attitude?

While I rang the doorbell, my mind roiled with confusion. The father of Jude's friend opened the door, completely oblivious to the tension of the situation. He thought Jude had been participating in an impromptu sleepover. I did not disabuse the man of his belief. My burden was strictly between Jude and me.

I politely asked him to rouse my son. Jude arrived at the door tired and grumpy. He attempted to forestall his departure but could recognize from my expression that this was not subject to discussion. Jude was always perceptive and empathetic, even if he did not always deploy those attributes to the advantage of others. I reached out, put my hand on his back, and said, "It's time to come home."

We cautiously walked to the car and climbed in. I wanted to erupt and decry his foolishness. I opened my mouth several times to berate his selfishness and insolence. I attempted to formulate a biting diatribe which would cut him to his heart, to shame him into obedience or some degree of thoughtfulness. No words came. I remained mute. It felt like a powerful hand had wrapped itself around my venomous mouth like an impregnable muzzle.

Instead, I drove. Very slowly. And we both sat in the car, silent, expecting the other person to say something. The silence introduced a calm, and the sanguine fever which had so heatedly gripped my sensibilities evaporated. In that blessed stillness, the temperature changed between us. My approach was all wrong. I had been misguided in my attitude and posture. A wordless, peaceful epiphany quietly thawed the icy frustrations driving our interactions. I had been desperately trying to work on him instead of myself. In that moment, when Jude and I discovered each other at the bottom of the pit, I learned the most important lesson in being a father: *I must first love Jude for who he is, not for who I want him to be.*

Enacting the power of this epiphany injects a liberating beauty into any relationship. It is a profound experience when a father begins to learn from his son. Jude has been teaching me ever since.

FOOTBALL

"We are our choices."
JEAN PAUL SARTRE

Most of us can reflect on our personal history and identify significant pivot points. These pivot points are choices, circumstances, or incidents we encounter which profoundly influence the trajectory of our lives and the shape of our character. Some pivot points are contrived and rather obvious. When my wife graduated from high school, she was unsure what she wanted to do. This is not unusual, nor is it bad. Which eighteen-year-old has the self-awareness and maturity to qualitatively assess their strengths and weaknesses so accurately they can unambiguously confine themselves to a single-track, lock-step vocational program without ever doubting their choice? A rare few.

Jody decided to enroll in art school. Weeks before she was set to matriculate, she had a change of heart and instead decided to attain a four-year degree at a liberal arts institution. To this day, I have no doubt my wife would have been a talented artist, likely a clothing designer with her own line of fashion. Except for SCUBA diving, she succeeds at almost anything she throws her heart into. Instead, she became a world-class neuropsychologist. Radically different tracks. Wildly different outcomes. That was a pivot of singular importance.

Most pivot points are not so radical or obvious, but they may be just as significant. One such point for Jude was his decision to play football. On the face of it, this seems rather trite. Why would something so simple as football be so influential? For some children, it likely would not. For Jude, it made all the difference.

Jude's personality straddled many poles. He loved physical activities but was saddled with inertia. He enjoyed reading but didn't have the patience to let a story develop. He loved community but enjoyed isolation. He loved to learn but despised the effort required for understanding. He was, in many ways, a person in conflict.

His first opportunity to play football came in second grade when he enlisted in a flag football program. He loved it and was successful. He was not quite as enamored with playing with children he did not know, especially against other teams that operated with breathless intensity (Jude lived in a sports-oriented town, and even lower competition could get rather intense). He also had difficulties adjusting his attitude towards being on a schedule. Jude wanted to do what he wanted to do. If he did not feel like practicing football at that exact moment, then he saw no need to participate.

The following year, he decided not to participate. I was a little disappointed, but he was still young. This decision would not preclude him from participating in later years. I did, however, want him to find something to become passionate about. Anything that would spark some ambition, whether it be music, school, sports, hobbies, whatever—the subject didn't matter, he just needed some passion. Even I was wise enough to know that pushing him into something would be a disaster.

To my joyful surprise, Jude chose to play tackle football in fifth grade. This was quite a commitment for him, as the season lasted nearly four months with multiple practices a week and games on Saturdays. I was proud of him for stretching himself. I was also very nervous. Jude was not an aggressive child. Although he was physically healthy, he was hardly a specimen to be reckoned with. He was young for his age, and not at all precocious. He was also notoriously resistant to hard work. Not the best recipe for a football player.

Fortunately, his practices were held in the field behind our backyard, so travel time and inconvenience were insignificant. He also had some school friends on the team whose presence was compelling. That year, he learned what it meant to play a role, how to function within the broader framework of a team, that the better you practice, the better you perform, and that he had the physical gifts to adequately compete with his contemporaries. His team had more successes than failures, and Jude was able to impact the outcome of many of those games. Most importantly, since I was already a coach and passionate about football, it gave us something to connect over. In my estimation, his first full campaign was a success.

He chose not to play the following year. I thought this was foolish and shortsighted. I also knew anything beyond mild encouragement would be met with recalcitrance.

I have undoubtedly created the impression that Jude and I spent much of our time at loggerheads, in constant conflict and strife. Yes, we had tensions and frustrations, which ultimately came to a head. But like any maturing relationship, we also had beautiful moments of encouragement, laughter, and peace. Our relationship was complicated, but not one-sided. We were a father and son finding their way together. I saw football as one vehicle through which we could relate and strengthen our bond. Jude was eleven. He only saw the composite of work and rigor that comprises any athletic endeavor.

In seventh grade, inspired by friends, he elected to participate in the school football team. This was a distinct step up in both intensity and requisite skill. The year was a challenge. I coached the eighth-grade team so I could observe him from a distance. He evinced some skills, but his lack of focus or passion and physical hesitancy were not advantageous. He did not receive much playing time, and this was frustrating for him. Fortunately, he understood why. Unfortunately, he did not want to adopt the moxie or motivation to address it.

Before the start of the eighth-grade season, he decided he was not going to play. I could tell he was nervous and unsettled about his decision. I was conflicted. That was the team I was coaching, and I wanted him to be part of it. I was also apprehensive of the family strife which would undoubtedly prevail if his year went sideways. My wife quietly intervened, and with some well-timed motherly wisdom and delicate prodding, encouraged Jude to approach me and have a discussion. At the time I found it rather cute. In hindsight, appreciating the significance of that conversation, I should have been crippled with anxiety.

Jude approached me rather contritely, as if he had a confession to make. I knew what was coming. I wanted him to take ownership of his decision. "Dad, I don't think I'm going to play football this year."

"Why not?" I asked, trying to keep my tone light. "I thought you had fun last year?"

"I did," he agreed. "But I didn't play very much. My friends were better than me. It's not that fun if you don't play."

"There is more to football than just your playing time," I answered.

"What do you mean?" he blurted, as if I was an idiot. I regarded him patiently and let his wheels turn. He was confused by my statement, and I could tell he did not want to wrestle with its implications. I tried to nudge him along.

"What about the time you get to spend with your friends? Think about the fact you will be learning a skill. What about the idea of being on a team? It takes a lot of players to make a football team click. Even if you don't get in the game, it doesn't mean you aren't valuable." He regarded me quizzically, but I could recognize he was pondering these thoughts. This was his maiden attempt at making a personal decision based on peripheral, overarching outcomes instead of simple, immediate gain. His burst of inchoate wisdom encouraged me. I tried to fan it into life. "Perhaps you can think about this season as an investment."

"An investment? How does that work?" He was bewildered, but also intrigued. It appeared he wanted an excuse to play but was having difficulty fabricating an individually compelling reason to participate.

"You aren't that big right now, and you haven't played as much as your classmates. If you don't play this year, they will get another year of experience behind them, and they will be that much more improved. You will be further behind. What are the chances you will get an opportunity down the road if you don't develop some skills now? Remember, we all change. Just because you aren't the biggest or fastest now doesn't mean you won't be later. In fact, I will bet you right now that in three years you will be taller than a number of the kids on your team."

"That's not going to happen," he laughed. "There's no way I'll ever be taller than Levi, or Davis, or—"

"Don't be so sure," I disagreed. "You might be surprised. How tall and big are your mom's brothers?"

"I don't know," he shrugged. "Why does that matter?"

"Just wait," I answered. "You will likely be as big as they are. Do you think you'll regret not playing football if that happens? But even if it doesn't, and you never get any bigger or better and never get on the field for a single play, do you have other plans for your time?"

He chewed on our conversation for a couple of days. I patiently waited for him to draw his own conclusions. Whatever he decided, I was pleased he was giving his choice the attention it deserved. Most eighth-grade boys lack any capacity for introspection. The fact he didn't make a knee-jerk decision was a positive development. Ultimately, I am not sure what convinced him, but he chose to play, and that critical choice transformed him.

⋯

Athletic competition is a powerful tool. It can be motivating, inspiring, and gratifying. It can also be imposing, intense, and terrifying. The adversity inherent in any competition serves to expose both the best in our nature, and the worst. Jude went into the season not knowing if he would ever get a chance to play in a game. He worked hard, improved, and became competitive. There were five kids vying for two available cornerback positions. As a coach I felt a great deal of trepidation engaging in the deliberations, ultimately deferring to the other coaches regarding Jude's placement. In the end, Jude earned a starting position. He had a tremendous season. As he competed, he learned an enormous amount about perseverance, competition, friendship, and the value of hard work. He also learned a much harder lesson.

The final game of the season was against the crosstown rival. Our town had two schools, with a highly competitive history between them. The Lyncs and the Lions. Recently, because of the growth of the Lions' district, the schools only played football against each other through eighth grade. Jude played for the Lyncs. This was his last opportunity to claim a lifetime of bragging rights.

Both teams were undefeated, setting the stage for some rather intense and palpable drama. For an objective outsider, understanding the breadth of the rivalry is impossible. For those eighth graders who had grown up competing alongside each other, the ethos was severe. Jude was so nervous he could not stay still. I think he peed five times within twenty minutes before kick-off. While humorous and quaint, it was fun to see him take something so seriously. He also was justified in his concern, because their opponent was a team that liked to throw the ball, and they had one fantastic receiver Jude would be responsible for covering.

The game was hard fought and well played. With under two minutes remaining, the Lions were marching down the field. They were behind by a touchdown and growing desperate. The Lyncs managed to make some solid defensive plays, putting their opponent in a difficult, long yardage situation. A downfield attack was imminent. Jude knew. I knew. The crowd knew. Sure enough, with the game on the line, the Lions attempted a long pass play to Jude's side of the field. The receiver raced down the sideline, with Jude running stride for stride, as the ball was heaved in their direction. Jude's opponent had three inches and thirty pounds on him. The throw was elevated, a perfect toss designed to benefit the receiver's physical advantage. Inspired by the intensity of the moment, adrenaline coursed through Jude's veins, and with an explosive leap he outjumped his opponent and knocked the ball away.

His teammates went wild. The crowd was screaming. Jude was so delirious with excitement I thought his helmet would pop off. It was our ball, with the lead. We were going to win.

If only real life came with a script we could control. We had possession and the lead. All the Lyncs needed was one first down to secure victory. Instead, we fumbled, the other team recovered, and they quickly scored to tie the contest. They then attempted an onside kick, improbable at best, and somehow managed to recover the ball. With just seconds remaining, they scored again to win the game. The Lyncs were devastated. A once-jubilant Jude was devastated. It was a magnificent season tainted by two minutes of poor play and bad luck. I was so disappointed for them. Jude sat in the middle of the field, not even sure how to respond. All that time, all that work, all that effort trumped in mere seconds. How does one tie a bow on something so bitter?

I was very proud of how far Jude had come in just one short season. He had committed himself, stretched his boundaries, and risen to the challenge. He turned a maturational corner and had no reason to hang his head. When I met him in the middle of the field after the game, I relished the opportunity to let him know how proud I was of his efforts. A tear or two ran down my cheeks when I hugged him, surprising both of us. My reaction demonstrated to Jude just how much I cared for him, and for the person he was becoming. Of course, Jude knew this already. But this was the first time he felt it. There is no substitute for experience. Unfortunately, I was also keenly aware that Jude had learned, however bitterly, that sometimes in life, regardless of your best efforts and intentions, the outcome is not what you hoped or dreamed.

※ ※ ※

Despite his eighth-grade success, Jude was still conflicted about playing his freshman year. He was still a maturing adolescent, working hard to manage inconsistencies at war in his personality. Thankfully, he had friends who were encouragers. Never underestimate the power of a group of friends. He elected to play and continued playing all four years. As he matured and gained confidence, he grew to love football. He thrived on the competition, enjoyed practicing with his buddies, and reveled in the improvements practice and exercise made to his physique.

He also learned something many high school athletes fail to recognize: A great team does not always consist of only elite athletes. A great team is a complicated organism that develops synergy. The sum becomes greater than the parts. This can only happen with selflessness, respect, and trust. It requires encouragement, time, and intentional effort.

Jude's sophomore year showcased what it meant to have talent but no synergy. His teammates never found a rhythm, and it turned into a long season. The one upside to that season, however, was that I moved to the varsity staff, and so Jude and I spent three hours together every afternoon. Even though the season was arduous, our relationship blossomed. Our nadir, his flight from home, was behind us. Now we were participating in a joint project, working together for a common goal. Those afternoons allowed us to peer into each other's personalities and witness how we functioned together and within the framework of a larger group. Shared experience drew us close. And every single practice—even the dark, miserable, wet, loathsome practices—I will cherish forever.

By his junior year, it was apparent the players were on to something. They gelled, and the synergy ignited. The Lyncs had not been to the state football playoffs in fifteen years. During Jude's junior campaign, they reached the semifinals—a glorious season fraught with surmounted challenges and magical moments. It was the product of all the hard work he and his teammates had put in over the previous years. Their investment was paying off.

His senior year, expectations were high. This is always dangerous, as nothing dashes hope quicker than assumptions about success. But the synergy remained. The theme for the season was family, and that is what they became. Each player recognized the value of their partners. They became football junkies, competing in practice, trying desperately to outwork their companions. They loved to practice because they simply loved football. They were a pleasure to coach. The excitement on Friday nights was like a firestorm. Even Jody, who evinced little interest in sports, was swept along by the fanfare. Simone became a cheerleader, and she and Jude's joint participation fueled a family interplay that was emotionally nourishing and socially dynamic.

The run through the playoffs was difficult. The Lyncs played some great teams, managing to pull through each time. Much of the team's success was a simple refusal to fail. And this was brought on primarily through wholehearted encouragement. Regardless of the size of the role, each player brought value to the team. They stood on each other's shoulders. They demanded much from each other. What set them apart was their rejection of individual blame. Success was a team effort, as was failure. It was family at its best.

Jude's ability to articulate extemporaneously made him a favorite of the media. He was constantly asked to do postgame interviews. This makes a parent exceptionally nervous. Teenage athletes are not always known for their diplomacy or thoughtfulness. The first few times Jude gave an interview, I was a tense wreck, waiting for him to spew colorful invectives or stumble and stammer with jumbled, cliched banalities. He did neither. We went from being apprehensive over what he might say, to what he might become. He enjoyed the public interview process. Suddenly we were worried this experience would catapult him into a life of politics!

The Lyncs made it to the championship game. The growing faithful evacuated town to see it. None of the pundits gave us a chance. It was a David and Goliath scenario, as the Lyncs had not won a championship in twenty-two years. The team they were playing, Royal, had won the state title five of the last seven years, and had only lost one game during that remarkable stretch. The Lyncs were predicted to lose by three touchdowns. Some of Jude's teammates were so nervous they puked before the game. Jude did not. He was working hard to avoid having his father kill him. When we got off the team bus and started to dress for pregame warm-up, Jude approached me with a stricken look on his face. "I don't have my cleat," he said. His face was ashen.

"What?!" I erupted. "How can you lose a cleat? This is the most important game of your career! You realize it's too late for Mom—" Then I shut my mouth and took a deep breath. He already knew it was a problem. He didn't need me to remind him or make him feel worse than he already felt. "Okay, no worries. Let's figure this out. I'm sure there is a solution."

So, while everyone dressed and started warming up, we scoured the locker room for his missing cleat. It was nowhere to be found. Not on the bus, another player's bag, or anywhere on the grounds. How do you lose a single cleat? The only thing we could surmise was it had fallen out somewhere between hauling his gear from the school to the bus. Incredible.

Finally, we found a sophomore player who, barring a blowout, was not going to see the field for this game. He had the same shoes as Jude, albeit a half size larger. Jude borrowed a single cleat. He spent the first twenty minutes of warm-ups trying to cut and plant with a larger shoe. The first attempts proved intractable, as he kept tripping over the elongated toe. I quailed at the absurdity of the circumstance, wanting nothing more than Jude's and the team's success. I also chuckled at how this predicament personified my son. It was the most important game of his career. He was so excited, nervous, and impassioned about this event. And yet he still managed to lose a critical piece of equipment.

With a fully packed stadium and the players' intensity thrumming at a fevered pitch, the game evolved into a tense and dramatic tug-of-war. Neither team could secure a credible advantage. Jude made a crucial, momentum-turning interception in the second quarter, allowing the Lyncs to enter halftime steady and confident. Somehow, the second half ratcheted up in tension, with equally great teams battling for supremacy. When the fourth quarter commenced, Jude's team truly recognized and believed victory was attainable. It is one thing to dream about participating in a championship event, it is something altogether different to perform in one. For some, the moment becomes too big, and they crack under the pressure. But Jude's team was a family, dialed into one purpose. They may have been playing the role of David to the proverbial Goliath, but they had a sling with five smooth stones, and they wielded it without fear.

As the fourth quarter dwindled, the crowd's encouragement became so raucous the coaches could barely hear each other in their headsets. The Lyncs were behind 20–14 with three minutes remaining. Our implacable defense stiffened, forcing a punt. Royal fouled the snap, and we pounced on it, a tremendous opportunity. Three plays later, we scored, surging ahead 22–19. There were only two minutes left in the game. While the players celebrated the go-ahead touchdown, I glanced at Jude, something I had assiduously avoided until that moment, and noticed he was jumping up and down with tears streaming down his face. I had never seen him so ecstatic. It was wonderful to see him so impassioned. But I was a coach first, so I grabbed him by the shoulders and shouted, "Now, you must get it together and play your best football yet. They get one more chance. Don't let them take this moment away from you!"

He nodded his head and regained his composure, rallying the defense for one last stand. After a tremendous kick, Royal was pinned deep in their own territory. They had two minutes to negotiate eighty yards against a ravenous and confident defense. The Lyncs' defense had proven to be the best in the state that year. We were two minutes from a championship ring.

Jude's responsibility was locking down their number one receiver. For the first time all season, the inherent dichotomy of being both a coach and father jostled my composure. I was suddenly so nervous for Jude I could hardly watch, but only because I was his dad. As his coach, I knew Jude had the skill and talent to accomplish his task. On the second play of Royal's drive, for reasons unclear, two of our defensive backs miscommunicated. They became confused about their responsibilities—very uncharacteristic for that season—and as fate would have it, Royal's quarterback recognized the breakdown and took advantage of it. In an ugly, jarring twist, defeat was snatched from the jaws of victory. One mistake. We lost.

Having a front-row seat to Jude's—and his team's—emotional devastation was gut-wrenching. I knew exactly how much that game meant to him, and to his teammates. I knew the hours of sweat he had poured into that opportunity, how he had dreamed it into existence and watched it twist into a nightmare. Jude was again painfully reminded that despite your best efforts and intentions, desired outcomes are not guaranteed. He had already learned that lesson. It proved galling a second time. There are some lessons you only need to learn once.

After the game he stayed to do interviews. I was very proud of his composure, giving the media his best insights and congratulating the opponent. I patiently waited for the reporter to finish. We were the last two team members left on the field. They kept asking him questions, and I recognized Jude's growing frustration. He wanted to be with his teammates. His grief needed company. I signaled the reporter to wrap it up, and he gratefully obliged. Jude caught his breath, turned towards me, and our eyes locked for the first time since the buzzer was blown. "I'm so very proud of you," I said, knowing there were no words that would take the sting away. "There is nothing I enjoy more than watching you play." We both burst into tears.

* * *

Jude loved football. We loved it together. He cradled that final loss, holding it deep and tight. Football is just a game, and high school football is short-lived at that. But there is something altogether powerful about battling with a band of brothers—a football family—that weds itself to the core of your being. The ache that accompanies defeat is shared by all.

A month later, we were gathered with our extended family for a Christmas party. Jude's little cousin, Elias, six years old, had drawn Jude's name for the Christmas gift exchange. I cannot recollect what he gave Jude as a present. What I do recollect was the handcrafted card accompanying the gift. It was a portrait of Jude playing football in the championship game with the caption, "You tried your best. I'm sorry you lost." Jude was so moved he wept in front of everyone. Teenage boys are extremely resilient. They can recover from a host of insults. They have short memories and even shorter attention spans. But Jude's spontaneous flood of emotion served to prove that for even the sturdiest, there are some broken dreams which never truly die.

COVID

*"Whether it's the best of times, or the worst
of times, it's the only time we've got."*
ART BUCHWALD

Up until the point Jude and I collided, we had an acceptable, serviceable relationship. There was love there, albeit somewhat disordered, along with appreciation, respect, and joy. Compared to the relationship between many fathers and sons, it may have even been characterized as wonderful. It was not exceptional, however. It was not all it should have been or could have been. Jude's flight had triggered a mutual epiphany. This invoked a particular clarity and insight for each of us. Fully cognizant of our nadir, a response was demanded.

There is a vast gulf between *recognizing* the importance of loving someone for who they are and not for what you want them to be and *actualizing* this insight. The advantage of colliding at the bottom is there are no more holes to hide in. Guile, subterfuge, selfishness, and resistance are stripped away. Unless your heart is laid bare, it cannot be remodeled. The strongest foundations are erected from the deepest pits.

Jude and I were at a crossroads. We could elect to patch and glue our relationship—in essence, continue to live within the framework we had already established—or we could rebuild it. At the time, neither of us overtly confessed plans to rebuild. It is likely neither of us could even articulate our intentions. Hindsight always brings clarity. But the Lord used that moment to grant us the wisdom to recognize what was necessary and the willingness to pursue it.

Now, there is an erroneous notion in our current culture that has done more harm than any anachronistic custom, institutional misstep, or religious perversion. This is the ubiquitous belief that love is an independent, self-willed sentiment capable of whimsically exerting its influence on whomever it chooses. We are at the mercy of its desires and the subjects of its fancy. We have no agency over love's machinations. In one moment, love may open like a clandestine trapdoor, which we unsuspectingly fall into, and in the next, it may heartlessly discard us, coldly excluding us from its embrace. The ideas of "falling in love" and "falling out of love" could not be falser. Love is a choice. It always has been, and always will be. Nothing degrades and demeans love's beauty more than to believe it is beyond your control.

True, unconditional love is difficult, if not impossible. Some relationships make love relatively easy, while others make it seem impossible. Some people have a certain gift for loving that not everyone possesses. Regardless of your capacity or inclinations, love requires intentional, continuous effort. Ultimately, love is an achievement.

Choosing to love Jude was easy. Granted, he was my son, my own flesh and blood, which carries with it a nearly irresistible, preternatural pull. Yes, he had personality quirks that made me bristle, and he made decisions I sometimes disagreed with. We did not always see eye to eye on the language he used, the friends he kept, or his social comportment. I was still his father and had the responsibility of being his parent. Loving him for who he was did not release me from my duty. It did not demand my approval or acquiescence. But now I was freed to recognize the beauty of his unique personality and could begin to cultivate his talents and distinctive character in a manner which I hoped was edifying and God-glorifying, while simultaneously enjoying him in the moment. Jude was empathic. He had an insightful and satirical sense of humor. His wit was infectious, and his laugh captivated. His reactive guffaw rolled through the house like thunder, ineluctably altering the moods of all who were present. I never witnessed Jude erupt in a full-throated laugh without carrying bystanders with him. The expression of his personality was large. He could drown a room with his energy. But he could also be sensitive, kind, and benevolent. He was intimidated by no one. Sometimes this trait was perceived as arrogance or pride (which he also possessed in abundance). What it really meant was that whatever your predilections, social station, or ethnic class, he would discover an aspect of your personality he could appreciate. No one taught me better how to value others more than my own son.

Once we realize love is a choice, relationship-building becomes much easier. You are allowed to be proactive instead of reactive. You are not passively waiting for something to happen to you. Instead, it happens because of you. This also means you have a deep, personal responsibility to make it happen. Just like planting and tending a garden, unconditional love requires foresight, planning, and sweat. You will have to pull weeds, apply fertilizer, and water appropriately. A garden left untended will never flourish. Love neglected will eventually become disordered and adulterated.

Football was a wonderful vehicle for Jude and me to learn to love each other. Shared activity is always important, especially for a male relationship, and so we pursued interests that stretched us into new shapes, shapes that fit better together. I learned to talk with him about cars and taught him how to properly shop for cars. He read some of the books I enjoyed and even languished through the horror of discussing them—however briefly. We chose programs we could watch together. We discussed relationships. We battled through ping pong tournaments, built Legos, and even played family games. When Jude was a freshman, I had imagined common ground was irretrievable. Freed from the fetters of relationship anxiety, discovering common ground became immaterial. Common ground found us.

This was not because we had a radical transformation in our personalities or discovered an endeavor previously unrevealed. Rather, it was possible now to enjoy engaging in these activities because we appreciated the personality we were engaging with. The activity was simply the vehicle. The quirks were still there, peccadillos abundant—we both had a long road to travel in realizing our potential as image bearers. But if you are focused on recognizing and acknowledging the best in someone, it is much easier to forgive the worst.

Remarkably, the one event that served to catalyze these endeavors was the Covid pandemic. The ills, frustrations, and absurd, incongruent responses to Covid have been discussed ad nauseum. For many, the pandemic was a source of immense frustration and sadness. Our family was not immune to some of those feelings. Jude was a senior when the pandemic hit. I rue the fact he was unable to finish his high school career with an official graduation. The culminating events that seniors remember for a lifetime—banquets, concerts, senior skip day, awards ceremonies, and all the rest—are just a void. Covid isolation undermined some of his relationships, which were inchoate yet budding. Who knows what unique friendships he missed out on? His senior soccer season was taken away from him. Soccer was never his first love, but losing the opportunity to enjoy one last senior experience fighting as a team, striving for a common goal, was like ending a concert with a discordant note. I could appreciate the value of what he lost, but as his father, the forfeiture of his soccer season is infinitely more haunting. I desperately wonder if, while the season progressed—forcing Jude into the intensive action of running and jumping on his two powerful legs—the insidious ill that was brewing inside those rigid bones would have been exposed earlier.

Despite those misgivings and losses, Covid was a blessing.

If asked what "family" means, many of us reflect upon our childhood and conjure an idyllic, quintessential picture, a snapshot framed from our perspective that epitomizes, in a single tableau, what that word represents. Hopefully, the picture is pleasant. For many, it may be a scene during Christmas, sitting together opening presents. Or possibly a favorite summer vacation, full of mutual exploration, laughter, and relaxation. Undoubtedly, the images are personal and nearly infinite in scope. Whatever the case, whenever we reflect on the word *family*, an image appears. As parents, we strive to re-create and enhance this picture. It's not until you've raised your own children that you realize this idealization is really a simple snapshot taken in a brief sliver of time. And for most of us, that snapshot is compressed between the chaos of breathlessly running after young kids, oblivious to anything but the trying vicissitudes of each day, and commencing the ritual of shooing them out the door as they stumble into their first travails as adults. Assuming your children live fully under your care for approximately two decades, it is likely your quintessential notion of "family" encompasses less than a handful of years.

For our family, Covid enhanced and protracted this snapshot. Jude, Simone, and Johann slowly evolved into a sibling cabal. They fed off each other's personalities. They discussed, teased, and investigated each other's choices and motives. Covid supplied the time and space for this organic family enterprise to mature. At the dinner table, instead of checking with everyone's schedules, figuring out where we had to rush next and hurriedly eating our meal so we could participate in the next engagement, we could sit and enjoy each other's company. How novel!

Our dinners took hours. Jude and I are notoriously slow eaters anyway, but we set records for deliberately sluggish consumption. Jude would tell a story, with dubious embellishments, purposely neglecting to take any bites throughout the process. He drove his sister and mother mad. They both possessed a supernatural capacity to adroitly devour any meal, regardless of the circumstance or setting. Since they had nothing else to rush off to, however, they remained. And so "Covid mealtime" was born. This transformed our family from a network of related individuals, pushed and pulled along parallel paths, to a unit intertwined and invested in each other. When I recollect "family," the picture I conjure will always be the five of us sitting at the table, three plates empty, two plates full, with Jude seated at the head, surrounded by laughter.

* * *

For those of us fortunate enough to experience the joy of a summer break, we can likely point to one summer that stands above the rest as the "golden summer." Responsibilities were limited, friends plentiful, and shenanigans abundant. Jude's "golden summer" began at the inception of Covid. Technically, school was still in session, but the requirements were minimal, and his investment even less. This was a perilous path to navigate as a parent. Jude was simultaneously enjoying friendships and the liberation associated with a lack of institutional oversight. Jody and I struggled with how much to expect and press. Knowing he was destined for college and many more potential years of education, we erred on the side of complacency.

Every day turned into a master class of time-wasting foolishness. Jude thrived in this element. One day, he was making TikTok videos, the next was an all-day *Call of Duty* extravaganza, followed by an evening recap with friends who would hang out in the basement laughing and talking until all hours of the night. And just when I thought the party would break up, allowing for some blessed sleep, the energy would be redistributed. After leaving our house, Jude's buddies would fire up the next round, gather online, and play into the wee hours of the morning. I don't know how often I stumbled downstairs in the dead of night and told Jude to "wrap it up." His online play was a sonic detonation. I marveled and envied Johann's capacity to restfully sleep adjacent to Jude's mayhem.

Just when I would get frustrated with his reliance on technology for fun, he would head into the mountains with a group of buddies and build ski jumps and snow caves. They would practice stunts, take pictures, and undoubtedly imbibe an illicit substance or two. The bedlam was nonstop. While many children and parents were languishing under the thumb of Covid, Jude thrived.

As parents, we reaped the fruit of his pleasure. Regardless of Jude's daily activity, or lack thereof, we always retained our "Covid dinner" engagement. These never grew stale. One evening, we might all dress in formal attire. The next, we would play a family game. These dinners had two constants: First, everybody had to help clean up. Second, Jude always played the informal role of the *middler*.

The *middler* is the position at the dinner table responsible for directing and massaging the conversation. A good *middler* must follow multiple threads of conversation, be witty, sustain a myriad of subjects, and be capable of transforming a reserved patron into a paragon of volubility. This was Jude's wheelhouse. Conversation was never livelier and more engaging than with him at the helm. We learned more about each other during the short stretch of Covid dinners than we had through the entirety of our family's existence. Jude's playful and extravagant melodrama, coupled with his natural empathy and keen insight into the human condition, served as a social epoxy. He was the cornerstone of our collective architecture. At the odd dinner he was absent, the silence was deafening.

* * *

Jude's summer before college saw him working days at Lynden Door Factory. This was a large fabrication facility, and he quickly learned the travails and monotony of line work. He slung around sheets of plywood, running a glue machine or sander or some other heavy piece of equipment. The beauty of factory work is that he was forced into a rigid structure, something he needed. He also made good money. More importantly, he was exposed to all different sorts of personality types. This was a place where grown men worked. They were supporting families and making this a career. Conversations ranged the entire gambit of possibilities. Fortunately, Jude enjoyed bringing these conversations home with him, where we could dissect these novel perspectives and attempt to bring some insight and perspective to bear.

Those discussions helped me recognize Jude's profound capacity to approach new relationships with an open hand. Any personality type would pique his interest on some level. Even if he shared no common interests and was on a wildly different life trajectory, Jude was willing to learn something about, or have fun with, just about anyone. This was refreshing to witness. It also taught me a great deal about appreciating others. Somehow, when approaching a relationship, he managed to jettison any temptation towards preconception. I would love to take credit for his technique, but this was something he adopted despite his upbringing. Few aspects of his personality were more impressive to me, or more foreign, than watching him walk into a room of complete strangers and make friends. His social network was immense.

The summer before Jude's departure to college was the moment Jody and I wanted to freeze in time. Everything worked. Our idealized notion of family was realized. Our children were maturing. They were enjoying life, each other, and us. Every day was a joy. We were also wise enough to recognize that no family dynamic is static. So, we relished each moment, pinching ourselves as we crawled into bed, thanking God for his manifold blessings.

. . .

The danger of living within an idyllic moment is believing—mostly on a subconscious level—that it is something your hard work and intentionality created. You deserve this. All the effort invested in parenting, all the hours cultivating your children, have come to fruition. Because of your foresight, it really could not have gone any other way. Families that were not thriving obviously had issues with their operating mechanism. You had worked through the difficulties, been diligent during affliction, and faithful when family life was stressful. God's blessings were not a gift, but an obligation.

In late July, Jude was holding court at the dinner table when he mentioned his leg had ached a great deal while at work. We surmised it was likely due to the fact he was standing on concrete floor for nine hours each day in totally inadequate footwear. He refused to change his footwear, and despite his stubbornness and my cajoling, the leg pain vanished. He could not reproduce it when he worked out, and even though we had gone on numerous hikes and he routinely played basketball in flip-flops, it did not reappear.

August saw us prepping him for his next phase in life. He had been accepted to Whitworth University. We were very excited about this prospect. He would have an opportunity to play football, experience dorm life, move to a midsize city away from small-town life, and most importantly, receive a liberal arts education from a Christian perspective. After our collision, Jude had done a lot of maturing. We could see the man he was becoming and were excited to bear witness to this revelation. He also had a long way to go. For all the positives he possessed, there were still aspects of his personality that needed refinement. Like most eighteen-year-old boys, his issues were not unique. He could be thoughtless, selfish, impulsive, and irresponsible. He loved his family but did not fully realize the value inherent in that relationship. He felt entitled, lacked motivation, and could be mercurial with his integrity. He wore pride like a designer jacket. What troubled us most, however, was his faithless recalcitrance. He had very little interest in pursuing a personal relationship with Christ.

Jude had always been resistant to a spiritual calling. For Jody and me, our Christianity was the bedrock of our relationship and the foundation on which we built our family. Jude's opposition was baffling to us, and frustrating. He hated the idea of having religion "shoved down his throat." We never understood what he meant by this. Yes, he was required to attend church with us on Sundays, and yes, he was enrolled in a Christian school. Out of sensitive deference to him, we were cautious in conversations about faith and certainly did not demonstrate an overtly charismatic Christian culture in the home. He was not afraid to talk about it. When pressed about his resistance, his remonstrations focused on two issues. First, he did not want to adopt someone else's faith. Parroting those around him was anathema. If he was going to participate in the Christian life, he wanted to take full ownership of a faith that was all his own. He was looking for a true conversion experience. Second, he had no patience or tolerance for hypocrisy. Unfortunately, when you live in a Christian community, you are surrounded by hypocrites. The most difficult obstacle the church must overcome is the fact it is populated by imperfect people. Jude could not get past this. He was making the category error of assuming participating Christians would lead blameless lives.

And if he wanted to join them, he too would have to lead a blameless life—and he had no interest in that. He still "wanted to do what he wanted to do."

It was our prayer that Whitworth would be revelatory and expose him to aspects of the life of faith that his upbringing could not. Jody remarked numerous times that it would require something substantial, a significant life event, to reorient his understanding. Perhaps it would be a charismatic friend, failing at school, or a romantic relationship that would produce the desired effect. She even went so far as to surmise the necessity of something happening to her—an illness or an accident—to ignite his faith. I adamantly refused to pray for a catastrophe. Her audacious conjecture and our rejection of that possibility made us laugh.

. . .

Nowadays, it seems families spend a great deal of energy attempting to build community through contrived experiences. I have seen the colloquialism, "Making memories," dominate a family's architecture to the point where the means become the end. I never wanted our family to function this way. We discovered early on that the most refreshing, intense, and merry family moments were those that happened spontaneously. This did not stop us from planning all manner of vacations and outings, but it tempered our expectations. Sometimes our outings flopped, sometimes they did not. The important aspect was spending time together, whether it was enjoyable or catastrophic.

The weekend before Jude was set to leave, we decided to have one last event. He and I, along with his little brother Johann, decided to do a backpacking trip into the Mt. Baker backcountry. My expectations were low. Jude was not an outdoorsman. We had dragged him on all manner of hikes during his lifetime, and before each one, there was always pushback. Interestingly, after dragging his feet for nearly every hike, he usually thanked us afterwards, expressing how much he enjoyed the view and the exercise. This did not stop him from resisting future outings, however. His resistance to hiking bordered on instinctual. Unsurprisingly, my aspirations for an overnight trip were met with acquiescence, not excitement. Summer had been exceedingly rewarding and wildly busy, so I thought this would be a good way to pull him away from friends, technology, and all the hullaballoo surrounding his departure. This would be our one last male family bonding experience before he entered his next phase of life.

The weather could not have been more perfect. The trail was well-kept and easily navigable, and Jude and Johann dialed into the beauty of the mountains immediately. At the top of the pass, we ditched our packs and hiked to the apex of the mountain that demarcated the border to the backcountry. Normally I would never be able to convince the two of them to expend extra effort, but that weekend was different. The panorama was splendid. The investment paid off. From our vantage, we were afforded a bird's-eye view of our destination, the Chilliwack Valley. This valley contained a picturesque river, a thin blue ribbon meandering far below, tightly squeezed between two sharply ascending ridges. The combination of tranquility and majesty evaporated any anxieties we carried into the trip.

To prepare for college football, Jude exercised most of the summer, including time on a StairMaster. This added significantly to his enjoyment of the trip, as he was not suffering the ravages of fatigue that can so easily drain the joy from the experience. It also ensured a rapid pace. This provided an opportunity to explore the river and the surrounding forest before making camp. Sitting alone in an old-growth forest, feet dangling above a glacier-fed river, was mesmerizing. God's imagination was on full display, and I thanked Him for it. Much to my surprise and joy, Jude acknowledged this. I found this encouraging and somewhat revealing. It added even more joy.

This wonderment, however, did not stop us from vociferously complaining about the no-see-um biting gnats accosting us at sunset; the fact we had pitched our tent on a subtle slope, which slowly pulled us into a corner, making sleep nigh impossible; and the frigid morning that greeted us with frosty breath and numb fingers. All standard fare for the accomplished backpacker. For two boys who spent little time in the woods, it was grounds for breaking camp early and seeking respite in their comfortable home.

As we trekked our way out of the valley, the hike turned majestic. The warm glow of the early-morning sun reflected perfectly off the river—like a golden cataract—and pierced the evergreens, brightening the impenetrable foliage. Spider webs hung like gossamer tapestries, sparkling with dewy iridescence. We hiked through the morning scenery and our share of spiderwebs, serenaded by birds and reveling in the splendor. It was difficult conceiving our proximity to civilization. We felt as if we were exploring a different world.

Late morning saw us crest the top of the pass. The sun's intensity redoubled, and the packs grew heavy. We took a short break and soaked in the beauty of the valley a final time before commencing the five-mile descent. Thankfully, it was downhill the rest of the way. Nonetheless, the heat was daunting. We wanted to hurry along before it became oppressive.

The first half-mile was a shallow grade requiring minimal effort. Then the trail steepened significantly, punctuated with variable and rocky terrain. Jude was walking ahead of me, letting the hill propel him downward. As he took an exaggerated step over a misshapen boulder, he let out a shout.

"What happened?" I asked. "What did you do?"

"I don't know," he replied. "I just stepped over this boulder and my knee popped. It's killing me." He sat down and started to rub the side of his left leg, just below his kneecap.

"Did you lose strength?" I inquired. "Does your knee feel wobbly? Did you feel something give?" I had seen him make the step. Nothing extraordinary appeared to have happened.

"No." He grimaced. "I just felt shooting pain, like someone stabbed me in the side of the leg. I don't know if I can walk."

My heart sank. We were four and a half miles from the car. Jude and his pack weighed 220 pounds. Johann and I could not carry him out. We had no cell service or emergency beacons to notify Mountain Rescue. My mind started to race. "Can you take off your pack and stand up? Maybe try to put some weight on it?"

He wriggled out of the pack and pushed himself up with one leg. Tentatively he put weight on his left side, testing for pain and strength. After a few seconds, he stood up straighter and took a deep breath. "Yeah, I can put weight on it. The pain is diminishing." He took a few cautious steps, ambling about. "Okay. I think I can keep going. That was weird."

I breathed a sigh of relief. "Why don't you take my hiking poles so you can take some of the downhill pressure off your leg as we go?" He accepted them gladly. I took some of the items out of his pack to lessen the weight. We started on our course again, albeit slower and with a bit of trepidation. Somehow Jude managed to continue, half hopping on his good leg, while placing much of his body weight over the poles when he stepped on his bad leg. It made for jaunty, awkward progress. I could see he was in visible pain but also determined to get off the mountainside. There was very little I could do for him other than be encouraging. It maddened me being helpless while he struggled. As a father, this was not a pleasant experience, and my euphoria from our overnight experience drained away in seconds. It was quickly replaced with pride, however. Watching him grit out those four miles was remarkable. I had never seen him show such perseverance. It was obvious that each step sent shooting pain down his leg, causing his entire torso to stiffen with every impact. I cringed with each impact. Somehow, he soldiered on.

When we reached the truck, he fell onto the seat exhausted. The relief gained from sitting was therapeutic. I had never been so happy to complete a trail than I was at that moment. Jude was even happier. I was also very perplexed about what might have occurred. Eighteen-year-olds don't typically have debilitating, shooting pain in their leg from minimal insult. I was baffled.

It took us an hour to drive home. When Jude stepped out of the truck, he flexed his leg, placed weight on it, and walked around. "Hey, it eased up a bit," he proclaimed. "Doesn't hurt as bad."

"Okay," I responded. "Just keep me posted. That was weird."

"Yes," he agreed. "It was weird. It hurts when I press on it, but it's definitely less pain than a few hours ago."

"Why don't you ice it," I suggested, "and we can reassess in the morning?

You also have football to think about. Practice starts in a week. You need to be in good condition when you arrive."

"I know." Jude nodded his head gravely. The prospect of college football was exciting and intimidating. He really didn't want to start his career hampered by an injury.

The next day saw some improvement, and surprisingly, subsequent days came with rapidly diminishing pain and discomfort. At the week's end, when we began packing his car, he moved around like nothing had ever happened. And in typical Jude fashion, he forgot what was behind him. Instead, he greedily consumed the college adventure poised squarely before him.

JOURNEY INTO NIGHT

*"For these attacks do not contribute to make us frail
but rather show us to be what we are."*

THOMAS À KEMPIS

Entering college during Covid was a unique experience. Jody and I were extremely grateful that Whitworth elected to move forward with in-person classes. Jude needed this. He was ready for college life. We packed up his Subaru and drove across the state. It was our first time dropping a child at college and we were rather unsure how to think or feel. Jude's complete absence of anxiety helped settle our emotions. Jude proved his unpredictability daily. We honestly had no idea how he would fare. There were too many variables to consider. Our hopes and prayers—excessive prayers—were for Jude to encounter extraordinary, Christ-centered students who would become lifetime friends. We wanted him to engage with professors capable of stretching and challenging him. We wanted him to acquire a faith he could take ownership of. We wanted him to pursue a myriad of interests capable of propelling him down a road of self-discovery that would serve to motivate him as the hands and feet of Christ. We prayed for him to recognize and appreciate what he had been blessed with, and to return that gratitude with service towards others.

While these grand, worthy desires swirled constantly through our minds, they were subtended by the reality of college logistics. There is something awkward and uncomfortable about leaving your child for the first time. What do you say? What constitutes a grand farewell? You've had eighteen years to impart wisdom. Is there something you can express in the last sixty seconds which will counterbalance all the parenting mistakes you've made?

Because of Covid, entrance into the dorms was on a rigid schedule and rather secluded. Jude could not move in at the same time as his roommate, and the entrances and thoroughfares were heavily monitored. Instead of the typical chaos associated with dorm life, his move-in was sedate and rapid. After a few trips to the car, everything was in the room. His mother, perhaps the most organized person extant, unpacked and arranged all his items. In the time it took him to unpack his computer, we had the rest ready to go.

So, we idly sat and killed time for a bit, unsure how to shape our leave-taking. I mentally fidgeted with words I thought would be profound but crashed into roadblocks at every turn. We were marooned in his tiny dorm room, looking at each other like strangers at a bus stop. Finally, Jody suggested we walk through campus and try finding his classes. Covid made every endeavor solitary. We felt like we were dropping him into an isolated internment camp. For a social dynamo like Jude, this was crippling. Fortunately, as we ambled about the campus, we encountered a few of his football coaches. They were so excited and ebullient that our trepidation evaporated rapidly. They enveloped Jude with the magical energy we were hoping he would experience on campus. He was provided a personalized locker, and we toured the rest of the facility and had a meeting with the head coach. I snapped a commemorative photo of him in the locker room—tan, 175 pounds, fit and ready for action. It was then Jody and I knew he was in good hands. Those men would gather him into the Whitworth football family.

We walked back to his dorm room, much more relaxed, prepared to say goodbye. We could sense the ease in him also. We all felt good about his decision to attend Whitworth. This was going to be a great year. I placed my hand on his shoulder and prayed, "May the peace of the Lord Christ go with you, wherever He may send you. May he guide you through the wilderness, protect you through the storm. May He bring you home rejoicing at the wonders He has shown you. May he bring you home rejoicing once again into our doors."

* * *

We were less than twenty minutes down the road when the phone rang.

"Hey, Jude, what's up?" I answered.

"Uhhh..." he mumbled. "I can't find my keys."

"What do you mean?" I asked, a bit incredulous. Jody was trying hard not to laugh while we simultaneously nodded our heads knowingly. We both covered our mouths, stifling the guffaws from echoing over the phone. It was much too early to shame him. The funniest part to us was that he had lasted as long as twenty minutes without needing some help. Organization and planning were not his fortes.

"I don't know where they are," he answered, a bit exasperated with my unhelpful response.

"I get that," I responded facetiously. "What do you expect us to do? We are on the freeway driving home."

"Well, do you know where they might be?" He was actually being serious.

"Have you checked the pockets of your shorts?" Jody asked. "Or did you leave them in your car?" She'd had this conversation with him so many times her questions were a reflex.

"No... they aren't there. Do you think they're in your car?" he asked.

"Not likely," I said gruffly. "But we will check." Jody did a quick perusal of the vehicle while I continued motoring down the highway. "Nothing over here, son. Sorry."

"Well, how am I supposed to get around without keys?" he whined.

"Great question," I answered. "Just keep looking. I'm sure they will turn up. We will check back with you in a little while." He abruptly terminated the call, obviously displeased.

"You think he's ready for this?" I asked Jody, raising an eyebrow and smirking.

She laughed. "No. But he better be. Does any of this surprise you?"

"Are you kidding?" I laughed. "Not at all. But I thought we might get a couple of days into it before our first 'need mom' crisis. This has to be a collegiate record."

We continued to head for home, laughing and shaking our heads. That was our beautiful boy.

...

Snapchat is the app of choice for communicating with our children. Their choice, not mine. I hate it. There is no memory built in (intentionally), which means a historical account of communication is impossible. I'll Snap one of my kids a question, and a day later I'll get a reply. By then, I've forgotten what I even asked, making the answer completely irrelevant. When Jude was at college, that was how he chose to interact with us, so we followed along.

According to his coaches, his professors, and my uncle—who happened to be a professor at Whitworth and our lone, de facto investigator—Jude was not doing *well*. Two weeks in, he still hadn't bothered to open his biology textbook. His coach noted he was skipping mandatory lifting sessions. His professors reported a few missing assignments.

I called him to talk about this. He was not particularly forthcoming. I got the impression he was having a great deal of fun, but socializing appeared to be the sum total of his college experience. We encouraged him to get on track. He assured us everything was under control. Even from three hundred miles away, I could smell his dishonesty.

Snapchat, 2 a.m.

Jude: *My leg hurts*

Dad: *From lifting, or football?*

Jude: *I don't know. It wakes me up at night. It aches so bad I can't stand it.*

Dad: *That sounds serious. Did you have the trainer look at it like I suggested?*

Jude: *Yes. He said to give it a week of no lifting and reevaluate.*

Snapchat the next night, 2 a.m.

Jude: *My leg is killing me. I'm dying.*

Dad: *What does it feel like?*

Jude: *It hurts. BAD*

Dad: *I get it. But like what? Does it ache? Sting? Sharp pain?*

Jude: *It feels like a grenade went off inside.*

Dad: *Does anything help?*

Jude: *A whole bottle of Advil*

Dad: *Let's get you in to see a doctor. Talk to the trainer tomorrow and set it up ASAP.*

Jude: *Okay*

Jude followed my suggestion and was evaluated by a physician the following day. The doctor noted some swelling on the outside of his left leg, just below and off to the side of his kneecap. It appeared to be near the head of his fibula, the smaller of the two lower leg bones. The physician prescribed rest and more Advil. This diagnosis did not sit particularly well with me, as his intense pain appeared insidious. I was concerned about a deep infection, or something worse. Something I was not ready to say out loud. We decided to give it a day or two more before exploring further, likely pursuing a specialist.

Two days after his appointment, Jude spent his Saturday at my uncle's house doing laundry, and, in a fit of responsibility, he opened a book and studied. He also did not complain much about his leg. When I talked with my uncle later in the day, he was cautiously optimistic and happy that Jude was starting to settle into Whitworth. Jody and I felt some minor relief but were still anxious. His leg problem was not wholly solved, and it was obviously affecting his mood and capacity to function properly.

> Snapchat, 1:30 a.m.
>
> *Jude: My leg blew up*
>
> *Dad: What? Is it getting worse again?*
>
> *Jude: It's so bad I think I'm going to die.*
>
> *Dad: Okay. I'll make some calls. Hang in there.*
>
> *Jude: Thanks dad*

We got Jude an appointment with an orthopedic group the next day. They did an initial evaluation and prescribed prednisone. They thought the muscle had pulled away from the bone and filled with fluid. They were hoping to reduce the swelling and reevaluate it in a week. The doctor assured Jude she had seen this before and that it could take a long time to get better. Her confidence was reassuring. While neither of us was pleased with the diagnosis, it bore the weight of professional validity. At the very least, we both hoped the prednisone would give him some relief.

Every family can point to a date in their history that lives in infamy. September 23, 2020, is our date. Jody and I were busy people, both with practices, heavily involved in church and school, in addition to all the craziness inherent in managing three children. We were not strangers to stress or the myriad vagaries a heavily invested life carries with it. We existed in a concoction of organized chaos. When my phone buzzed in my pocket on Friday afternoon, I answered it reflexively, never once imagining the call could be anything but benign.

"Is this Doctor Veltkamp?" blurted a breathless voice.

"Yes," I calmly answered, assuming it was a patient emergency.

"Hi, I'm glad I caught you. Johann crashed his bike and he's not moving. He's hurt. We called the ambulance."

This news caught me sideways. Jude was the one who had been dominating my "worry box." I never once considered Johann might have an incident. "Whoa, where is he?" I tried not to sound concerned, as the stranger speaking was rather panicked. We didn't need two people anxiously speaking past each other. The introduction of an ambulance, however, was not a positive symptom.

"He's by Bender Field Park," she answered. "He's just lying there."

"Lying there?" I prodded. That description was not particularly helpful. "Lying there" could run the gambit from "taking a brief rest" to "deceased."

"Yes. He may have broken his arm. We're not sure."

"Thanks. On my way," I all but shouted while I ran to get my keys.

I sprinted out of the house, hopped in my truck, and went searching for my youngest son. After some frantic driving, I saw the flashing ambulance lights and followed them into the ballfield parking lot. I ran past the EMTs, wanting to get to Johann before they did. I found him, surrounded by his friends and some very kind ladies, face down in the dirt, straddling the bike path. His right arm was in the shape of a U. I breathed a sigh of relief. This was a broken arm. After working in the ER and coaching football for fifteen years, I had seen plenty of broken arms. It looked ugly but it was going to be fine.

"Hey, buddy," I said cheerily. "No worries. Looks like you did a real number on your arm there."

"I don't want to move," he groaned. "Is it bad?"

"Well, it's broken. But it's fixable. Let's just figure out a way to sit you up without doing more damage." His eyes got wide, but I could tell he was tired of laying in the dirt. He also had some significant road rash on his arms and cheek. I found no need to bring that to his attention. Fortunately, the EMTs arrived and provided a temporary splint. We all agreed I could take him to the ER and get it cast. "Ready for the longest walk of your life?" I asked. He nodded his head and cradled his arm. I was glad the splint disguised his arm. It looked terrible. We had to walk nearly half a mile back to the truck. I did not want him staring at his hideous appendage the entire time. Fortunately, he toughed it out. We both knew he was in for a long evening in the ER.

After an uneventful drive to the ER, the two of us hunkered down and prepped ourselves for an interminable evening. As we waited, Jody arrived to check on her baby. Other than being impatient, everyone was doing fine. Of course, Johann grew discouraged as he recognized he would not be engaging in his usual life until his arm healed, but we were all happy it did not turn out any worse. Breaking an arm is nearly a rite of passage for boys. We all sat together, trying to relax through a lame situation.

Jody's phone broke the silence while we waited. Jude was calling from Whitworth.

"Hey, Jude, we're in the ER. Johann broke his arm," Jody told him.

"Oh, buddy, that sucks. Hang in there!" Jude hollered through the receiver. He sounded lighthearted, which was very encouraging.

"So, what's up?" Jody asked.

"Well, I can't lift my leg," he answered.

"What?" we asked simultaneously. "What does that mean? Your whole leg?"

"No, my foot. I can't lift up my foot. I can raise my toes a little bit, but I can't lift up my foot." Jody and I looked at each other. If there was ever a time to capture a portrait of two worried parents, that was it. I felt the blood drain out of my face. My brain rapidly cycled through all the maladies I could list on a differential diagnosis that could potentially be the culprit. I did not like the options one bit. I also did not want to create consternation and anxiety for Jude, nor did I want to neglect Johann. The water was rising.

"That's getting serious," I replied as blandly as possible. "We need to get some pictures. I will get you into imaging, and we can get to the bottom of this." Just then, they called Johann back to have his arm set. I promised Jude I would talk to him later and that he didn't need to worry.

I hate lying to my children.

○ ○ ○

After getting Johann fixed up, we turned our attention to Jude. His doctor wanted to start with X-rays, and, depending on what they revealed, order an MRI. I vociferously objected that X-rays would be inconclusive and mostly a waste of time. Thankfully, she relented and ordered the MRI.

The following Tuesday, September 29, Jude was scheduled for his follow-up appointment. We debated whether one of us should drive out to be with him, but he assured us that was not necessary. He did not seem particularly worried, even though his leg hurt and his foot was partially paralyzed. Were I in his shoes, I would have been reeling, but Jude possessed a unique gift. He could live squarely in the moment. Even though he was suffering through an enigmatic health event, waiting a couple of days for a diagnosis was in no way debilitating. He very consciously eradicated any thoughts of his potential diagnosis and spent the entire weekend hanging out and partying with buddies. As usual, very little studying occurred. I did not blame him.

Tuesday afternoon, Jody joined a conference call with Jude and the doctor. I anxiously awaited news and checked my phone every couple of minutes. Information was not forthcoming until Jude sent me a picture via text. He provided no words or comments of his own, just a hastily snapped picture of the MRI his doctor had pulled up on the computer monitor. When I opened the text, my heart stopped, squeezed, and exploded inside my chest. I tried to take a deep breath—to calm my heart—but my diaphragm froze. Everything distorted. I gripped the corner of my desk, desperate to stay upright, and as my fingers clawed desperately for balance, my vision narrowed to a single point of light. It felt like a giant hand was crushing my skull while the room spun wildly around me. My phone clattered on the floor, and as it bounced away, the photo on the screen mocked me, as menacing as a demon's cackle. Forever burned into my mind's eye was a picture of the ugliest tumor I had ever seen. No amount of blinking, rubbing, or squeezing could make the image go away. I still cannot make the image go away.

I slumped into my chair, absolutely crushed. It was crushing to have the truth revealed. It was crushing to know my son was isolated, receiving this devastating news without my presence. It was crushing to recognize how, in an instant, our family's trajectory had been derailed. It was crushing to know my son would never be the same. I suffocated under the weight of it.

As parents, we all tell our children we love them. We know this as a fact. We know in our hearts the truth of that love, and we know that love runs deep. I can assure you there is a mighty chasm between knowing, and experiencing, the true depth of love. The image of Jude's leg elicited an immediate and visceral response. Without hesitation, devoid of any competing thought, I bowed my head in utmost reverence and pleaded desperately, "Dear Lord, if this cup must be borne, place this burden on me, and me alone. I implore you, spare my son." I lay my forehead on my desk, begging for an answer. My pleading was ineffable. I poured the entirety of my soul into that blunt request, desperate, hungry, and willing.

God was silent.

The next hour at work was a tumultuous blur, and I took my leave as quickly as possible. There were so many unanswered questions, so many variables to attend to, it was impossible to gauge a starting point. The enormity of what lay before us overshadowed my capacity to envision a workable path. I never imagined I would encounter a moment too big to handle. And yet this rendered me incapacitated. I had an impassable, monolithic block of despair pressing against my consciousness, making my limbs so heavy it hurt to move, yet remaining still was impossible. I ran to my car, anxious to be home, and felt like I was swimming up a waterfall. The steering wheel of my car was a bar of iron. The road that took me away from my office was all too familiar, but I felt lost, like I was driving into the unknown. I was as terrified as I'd ever been.

As I settled into my commute, I forced myself to accept this new reality. Despair was not a solution. My son needed me more than ever before. My family needed me. Selfishness is an easy posture to fall into, but it is never admirable, and it is always harmful. Jude's plight demanded my unadulterated and unequivocal support. While I drove home, I realigned my attitude, recognizing the only possible solution to this predicament was to serve my son with inexhaustible fervor. I committed myself, then and there, to seeing his journey to fruition with every ounce of love and passion at my disposal. Unconditional love could not demand less.

My wheels began to spin, formulating a plan of action. The length and breadth of the journey Jude was going to take was beyond me, but I possessed enough clarity to recognize what step one must be. I needed to talk to my son.

"Hey, Jude. It's Dad," I said as cheerily as possible. "Thanks for sending the pictures. What did you think?" I nearly gagged when I asked him that. There is a fine line between encouragement and authenticity.

"Yeah…" he blandly responded. "That was a little surprising."

"I know," I agreed. "Certainly not anyone's first choice. Did the doctor elaborate?"

"Not really," he answered. "She just said it needs to be addressed immediately."

"Well, that's hardly astounding advice!" I responded jokingly. "It's a good thing she went through all that training." Jude chuckled, but it was purely a courtesy laugh. He was not a particularly serious kid. This revelation was chewing through his insides. "Did she give you instructions for the next steps?"

"Not really," he said. "Just that they were not equipped to handle it there, and they would send the images wherever we wanted."

"Did she have any suggestions?" I asked. Jude remained silent. I so wanted to be with him. It was impossible to ascertain the severity of his emotional state over the phone.

"Well, buddy, I think—" My voice broke. I cursed silently for not being stronger for his sake, but the tears started to flow. I struggled to create words. My silent sobs squeezed my lungs, choking my voice. I knew Jude needed me to be in charge, to guide and buoy him. He needed to rely on my confidence and knowledge. But my first response was as a father terrified for his child. "I'm sorry, son," I sobbed. "I'm so, so sorry this is happening to you. No one deserves this, least of all you. If I could take this away right now, I would do it instantly. I love you." Those were the first tears I spilled over Jude's plight. Every ocean begins with the first drop.

• • •

When I arrived home, my wife was standing in the kitchen, bewildered and forlorn. She had the stricken look of an abuse victim. When you have been married for twenty years, words are sometimes unnecessary. They muddle emotions and poorly represent the language of the heart. We had no words. Our hug was rife with anguish, terror, sorrow, and despair. We both wept, clinging to each other.

"Not our son," she murmured into my ear, through the tears. "Not our son." She squeezed me tighter. "Why did it have to be Jude?" she sobbed again while I gripped her firmly. After a long moment, we disengaged, and I looked her squarely in the eye while cupping both her cheeks in my hands.

"You were made for this," I whispered fiercely. "There is no mother alive who can handle this better than you." My wife is resilient, brilliant, motivated, and undeterred. She loves her children fiercely. She also possesses an incomparable work ethic.

"Yes." She nodded her head. Her movements were wooden, distant. "Yes," she whispered a second time, pulling herself into the present. She stood before me quietly, like a mannequin determined to animate. "Yes," she repeated a third time, with conviction. "I was made for this." She nodded again, life returning to her eyes. With a force of will both admirable and profound, she burned away the anguish, supplanting despair with duty and mission. It was the true arming of the warrior. I hugged her deeply and released a very deep, tense breath. We prayed briefly and then began to speak in earnest. We were going to war.

OPENING CHARGE

"The true soldier fights not because he hates what is in front of him, but because he loves what is behind him."

G. K. CHESTERTON

Wars are not won by accident. Victory requires sound strategy and flawless tactics. It also requires resources, conviction, and a willingness to stretch beyond expected capacity. Sometimes much beyond.

Because Jody and I had worked in healthcare for decades and had family members and many friends in similar fields, we had resources aplenty. I have a friend who is an accomplished orthopedic surgeon, blessed with the training, insight, and contacts to guide us directly towards experts in the field of bone cancer. We knew Jude's cancer was either going to be one of two types: osteosarcoma or Ewing sarcoma. Both options were poor. Both were rare. This limited the number of experts available, but it also meant it did not take much time to discover them.

We knew how to navigate our cumbersome healthcare system. The same day Jude's tumor was revealed, Jody flew directly to Spokane, Washington, and packed up Jude's dorm room—eight months too early—and prepared to leave. After interviewing and evaluating different facilities and sifting through a myriad of details, it was apparent the hard tissue oncology team at Seattle Children's Hospital would be Jude's best option. Fortuitously, one of the physicians on the pediatric oncology team was renting a room from Jody's sister. He was informed of Jude's plight and graciously sliced through many of the bureaucratic hazards notoriously embedded in many hospitals. Jody and Jude drove directly from Spokane to Seattle and were greeted by this generous physician at the door. He whisked them through the facility, providing a firsthand education in navigating the complexities of Seattle Children's Hospital. The information proved invaluable.

The key element in fighting any battle is understanding your enemy. Jude had bone cancer, and the initial imaging looked terrible. We needed verification. We needed to understand the extent and type of the disease. Had it spread? If so, where? How virulent and aggressive was it? How long had it been hiding?

Some of the answers we would never know, but type and extent were absolute necessities for creating a battle plan. Upon arriving at the hospital, they immediately began the diagnostic process, subjecting Jude to all manner of imaging, blood work, and scans. This is also where, as a parent, one learns anxiety comes in many different forms and intensities. Each diagnostic procedure carried with it the weight of revelation. Success or failure depended on the outcome of each of those tests. When the yardstick for success is measured by life or death, the gravity becomes infinite. As results poured in, anxiety feverishly burned.

Jody and Jude were a beautiful pair. Jude is anxious about nothing. He laughed and smiled through most of the tests, thankful he was not sitting in class, intrigued by the novelty of it all. He also chose to remain blissfully ignorant. Not in a dismissive fashion, or in an effort to ignore reality. Rather, he was the complete realist, recognizing his situation was dire, but choosing to focus purely on the immediate. He did not let his mind or attitude become consumed with conjecture. Jody is not one typically saddled by routine anxiety either. However, the depths of a mother's love are immeasurable, and so was her unease. She knew exactly what each test purported, and as a realist, she could not emotionally deceive herself. It was tempting to retreat into a

Pollyannish fugue and recite the mantra, "Everything will be okay." The simple fact is, it wasn't okay. It was bad. And it was scary. Jody took care of the planning, communicating, and worrying. Jude took care of making sure the providers tending him were having a pleasant day.

Texting is a horrible communication medium. It is exceptionally convenient and well suited for conveying utilitarian information, but that is where its positive attributes end. It would be beautiful if there was such a thing as a sarcastic font, or a perturbed font, or a joyful font. Instead, we attach silly emojis to short lines of text and hope for the best. Jody's concern was so high she somehow managed to convey her worry even through the sterile medium of texting. Every word dripped with fear. While the two of them tested, I became a slave to my phone.

The most significant test of that arduous day was the CT imaging of Jude's lungs. If the disease had spread, the lungs were the most likely destination for metastases. If he had any growth in his lungs, his chance of survival dropped by over 70 percent. It was just a short test. A quick picture. So much hinged on that picture.

Anxiety grew like a rolling crescendo as we waited for Jude's imaging results. I sat poised by my phone, nervous and sweating, fully cognizant of my helplessness. For each minute that passed, my heart rate elevated. The wait was interminable. Finally, my phone blinked. As I reached for it my heart was beating so strongly I could not even take a full breath. I peeked at the bland text, intentionally blurring my vision like a protective blanket of insulation against the inevitable. Miraculously Jude's lung imaging came back negative. I felt the collective release of anxiety from over a hundred miles away. For the first time on that difficult day, and the first time in the previous thirty-six hours, we were granted the one intangible gift necessary to survive any tribulation: hope.

Anxiety and hope are funny playmates. They ebb and flow together. As hope builds, so does anxiety. When hope is taken away, anxiety withers. Their intertwining creates an odd, tenuous emotional state. We were given a first taste, and after just a small morsel, we were spent. Little did we know this was merely a simple hors d'oeuvre before the entire smorgasbord of emotion that a battle with cancer elicits.

True prayer serves as an antidote to anxiety. It is amazing what one prays for when confronted with something so overwhelming that the breadth of it is difficult to comprehend. In the blink of an eye, my prayers transformed from simple, nebulous utterances of thanks, praise, and supplication to very intense, pointed pleas.

"Thank You for this home and food. Thank You for Your amazing creation and our place in it, and please help my children to know You and become gracious, compassionate, and healthy… Oh, and help them glorify You in their game tonight, and if it be Your will, allow them to win…"

My common mode of prayer was discarded as vacuous drivel. What value was there in recitation of half-hearted requests and thoughtless, nearly rote incantations? The fight was on. The need was real. And that is where one starts to recognize the true state of one's prayer life.

In my experience, the intensity of our supplicative prayers seems inversely proportional to the request. "Please eliminate hunger in Africa." "Please stop the war in the Ukraine." "Please be with all the missionary families in Japan." These prayers are uttered with almost heartless desire, as if we know the request is so grandiose God will discard it as an absurdity. But when the focus narrows, and the plea becomes tangible, the intensity meter dials up at an alarming rate. Is this a measure of our faith? Do we only pay lip service to the all-encompassing miracle because we really do not trust God? Do we pray harder for the smaller things because we are not willing to believe in an active, all-powerful God and instead leave some wiggle room for luck or coincidence? Do we pray with limited conviction, attempting to protect God, providing Him with an "out" if the prayer is not honored the way we prescribe? Are we afraid if the prayer is not answered, our faith isn't real, so we don't dare pray for that which is unattainable through other methods—like our own hard work or perseverance?

When I began praying for Jude, the need sharpened my focus. I'm not sure it sharpened my faith. A deeply faithful, convicted father would have simply prayed for the cancer to be eliminated from Jude's body. There would be no vacillation or compromise, only trust. For me, the cancer was already there, its instantaneous removal impossible. I could not bring myself to pray for the impossible. I wondered then, and I wonder still, if I really believed in miracles. Does the supernatural occur? Does God intervene? Are miracles accessible? Praying for one seemed like wasted breath. Or was I afraid to trouble God with too large a favor? Perhaps I could sneak a small favor past Him, one ultimately explicated with multiple options. Despite my misgivings and fragile faith, what I knew I could do was pray for the improbable. Those prayers began in earnest.

Not having cancer in the lungs was huge. Considering the size of Jude's tumor, this appeared, for all intents and purposes, to be miraculous. Our first prayer had been granted. The second prayer that day was for the diagnosis to come back as Ewing sarcoma and not osteosarcoma. Ewing is another form of bone cancer, which is also awful, but more receptive to chemo, and the chemo is not as harsh. There is also a higher survival rate. It felt very surreal to get down on my knees and plead with the Lord to gift Jude Ewing sarcoma. Who does that? Could I have imagined myself, just three days earlier, begging God to curse Jude with a horrible cancer and see it as a mercy? Yet there I was pleading on Jude's behalf that his affliction would be Ewing.

The diagnosis returned as osteosarcoma, depleting the small bubble of hope created earlier in the day. Jude's itinerary was bleak. Why had God not listened a second time? Are blessings finite? What good is one positively answered prayer if its value is dependent on subsequent offerings? Is God's mercy whimsical? We were only minutes into this crisis, and my theology was already taking a beating.

* * *

Osteosarcoma is a rare bone cancer diagnosed 700–1,000 times a year in the US. Compare that to the nearly 300,000 cases of breast cancer and 270,000 cases of prostate cancer and that provides a picture of how rare it is. Rare is not always bad. It is rare to win the lottery, but I would not mind if it happened to me. It is also rare to be an astronaut, but that is a proud accomplishment. Osteosarcoma does not fall into either of those categories. The problem with being rare is that little is known about it. In addition, its rarity precludes the research and funding many of the other more "popular" cancers receive. Osteosarcoma is mostly unknown, little researched, and not likely to garner any financial or institutional push to be studied as a result. The only thing going for it (which is a macabre and grotesque phrasing) is that it mostly happens in adolescents, and it is disfiguring and deadly. Those are symptoms people rally around.

The moment the diagnosis was confirmed, I needed to learn as much as I possibly could about it. This took about half a day. I had access to all manner of textbooks and primary research articles including unpublished studies and international data. The total amount of information on the disease was scant. It should not be that easy to become an expert in a particular field. I found this unsettling. What was more unsettling was learning that the strategies employed to fight osteosarcoma were little changed in the last half-century. We were about to battle an advanced, aggressive foe with ordinance and technology from the dark ages. Never bet on the person holding a knife in the middle of a gunfight.

When I explained this to Jude's oncologist, she did not necessarily disagree. However, she did insist that the incidence of death from osteosarcoma had dropped in this century. Statistically she was correct. However, it was not because they had discovered novel and favorable treatments. The only reason the death rate had diminished was because oncologists had improved their capacity to attenuate the caustic effects of their chemotherapeutic agents. They were using the same poison but keeping the poison from killing their patients. This was not particularly reassuring.

In the case of osteosarcoma, "chemotherapy" is very much a euphemism. In other cancer fields, chemotherapy has made great strides. We now have agents that are tumor-specific, can be deployed at therapeutic doses directly to the target, and are void of many of the noxious side effects associated with older forms of therapy. I know some cancer patients who, after receiving their diagnosis, have continued with their daily routine throughout their entire treatment regimen. Other than the inconvenience of some doctor visits, lifestyle choices and engagements remained unaltered. There are patients able to tailor their regimen to be type-specific, intense, and quick. The therapy is unpleasant—but manageable and short-lived. Osteosarcoma could not be more different. This is old-school cancer. This is the kind of cancer that only responds to carpet-bombing, and if the carpet-bombing is ineffective, there is no alternative except to drop a bigger bomb.

Jude's chemotherapy was simply poison. There is no other word for it. We all hoped the poison would be strong enough to kill his cancer without killing him. In addition to keeping him alive, we also hoped for limited collateral damage. Anything on Jude's body that was growing or changing would be susceptible to significant alterations. We knew the chemo would hurt his heart; we just did not know how much. We also knew it would hurt his ears; we just hoped he wouldn't go deaf. We also knew that this chemo regimen would quintuple his susceptibility to getting other cancers later in life. The long-term sequelae of his regimen were depressing. The short-term effects were hell.

INTO THE VOID

*"In sickness the soul begins to dress herself for immortality.
And first she unties the strings of vanity that made her
upper garments cleave to the world and sit uneasy."*

JEREMY TAYLOR

Seattle Children's Hospital is one of the best hospitals in the world. It is very organized, efficient, and holistic. The people working there want to take care of you. When they have a patient like Jude, they redouble their efforts. Jude's world had been turned upside down. He went from a carefree college freshman, who was taking advantage of every opportunity life presented, to a chronic care patient in a hospital ravaged by the Covid pandemic. He was completely sequestered. He was poked, stabbed, and prodded multiple times each day. As a defense mechanism, he elected to remain ignorant of all the micro procedures foisted upon him. Instead, he projected affability, appreciation, and thankfulness for the efforts his caretakers levied. Even when he was tired or irritable, he always engaged with his doctors and nurses, asking them about their day or what they enjoyed about the work they did. His demeanor and personality were so attractive that nurses not even assigned to him would come to his room simply to say hello or assist Jude's caretakers in streamlining procedures. He even had nurses from other departments pop in just to meet him. All the patients at Seattle Children's Hospital are treated with profound dignity and respect. Jude became a minor celebrity.

Between Jude's initial introduction to the hospital and his first treatment, he was able to return home for a long weekend. I had not participated in his retrieval and had not seen him since his diagnosis. When he walked in the door, I was greeted by his massive, curly coiffure which jovially adorned an energetic smile. He burst through the door with all the exuberance of a man returning from a blissful holiday. I bravely put on a smile and gave him a hug. I was so happy to see him, but terrified for the reason. It was October. He was not supposed to be home until Thanksgiving. It all felt so out of place. When I walked with him to the car to retrieve his belongings, the full force of what was happening to him caught me with renewed vigor. This was the first time I had seen him since his diagnosis. His plight, however grievous, had retained some degree of clinical detachment. Now he was here in the flesh, his victimization obvious. Jude was limping. The nerves in the front of his shin had been displaced and damaged, preventing any muscle activation. He elevated his knee and performed an awkward shuffle-hop so he would not catch his toes when he walked. His maneuver was no different than the videos I had seen of final-stage syphilis sufferers with drop foot. Jude had only been gone five weeks, but he had already lost twenty pounds. The tumor was growing so quickly that it hijacked all the calories he could put in his body. The transformation of his robust frame was shocking. What had happened to the tan, muscular man I had hugged goodbye just weeks before? The reality of his predicament was undeniable.

"You ready for this?" I asked him.

"Do I have a choice?" he responded.

I contemplated his question and responded succinctly. "We always have a choice. It's our choices that define our character."

He regarded me seriously, focused on the conversation. A few weeks ago, he was a boy just out of high school. How quickly he had transformed. I could sense his receptivity, which made me desperate to say something motivating and encouraging. Positivity erodes quickly when options are marginal. And I knew Jude was not one easily inspired by platitudes or the trite snippets of jargon found on the back of a bumper sticker. He was hungry for the truth, and that is what I supplied.

"It isn't your fault you have cancer, Jude," I continued. "You weren't responsible for this. What you are responsible for, and what you have complete control over, is how you respond to the hand you've been dealt."

"The people at the hospital were upbeat. They seem to have a good plan. I'm not afraid." He flashed me a winning smile. "I don't want to do it!" he laughed. "But this is my current reality. So, let's get it over with."

Jude was not an optimist. He was, however, quick to accept his present reality and contentedly live within its confines. This was a gift for which I was jealous, and a skill I wanted him to teach me. He spent his free weekend soaking up life. He met with friends, laughed with his family, and raced around the county in his car. His car was a manual transmission. His partially paralyzed leg made it trickier to drive, but he still managed. He loved to drive that car.

The following week Jody took him back to the hospital. The entire weekend she and I had made battle plans. Jude's cancer team had supplied a schedule of events based on his treatment needs, surgical interventions, and likely dosing repertoire. His chemo administration day would be Wednesday. Because the chemo was so harsh, he was required to stay in the hospital until his doctors deemed his constitution hardy enough to go home. This was usually four to five days. Jody and I planned our practice schedules around these dates, creating enough buffer for flexibility in case something went awry. Our initial plan was for Jody to take him down to Seattle mid-week (we lived in a small town a hundred miles away), and then I would relieve her in the hospital Thursday night or Friday morning and take Jude home when he was released on the weekend.

No sooner had Jude checked in for his first treatment than we learned that "home" meant a location within thirty minutes of the hospital. At first, we attempted to argue. We had already set up his room and had the house "chemo ready." Jody and I were medically savvy. My sister was a chemo nurse. We were prepared for the challenge. Unfortunately, because the chance for infection or any blood dyscrasia was so high, and the reactions so common, Jude's proximity to the ER was critical. We lived two hours away. An infection, fever, or clot could kill him sooner than that. The situation was nonnegotiable.

One simple misunderstanding was all it took for our battle plans to unravel. Reality, already topsy-turvy, crashed around us. As difficult and daunting as the next nine months appeared, we had been resting in the assurance we would battle together, as a family, with the support of a broader network of family and friends to aid us in our struggle. Now Jude would be isolated and the rest of us separated.

We needed to find a place to live in a big city in the middle of the Covid pandemic. The pressure was absurd. He could hardly walk, and we knew that would get worse. He was certain to have extensive surgery, the nature of which was yet to be determined, necessitating a wheelchair and extended time on crutches. He would be convalescing. Our new home needed to be quiet, on the ground floor, and close to the hospital. Options were limited, as was our time frame. The mounting pressure to get this arranged was absurd.

My wife has never been one to dismiss a challenge. Never underestimate a determined mother. Her resilient heart and determined spirit outshone my despair. When I drove down to the hospital to relieve her, she went on a housing crusade. Within hours, she discovered some serviceable options. House hunting in Seattle is not something we ever imagined we would do as a couple. And yet here we were.

None of the options fully fit the necessary criteria. Any one of them would have been workable but not ideal. As providence would have it, however, Jody employed an agent to aid us in our struggle. This lady grew sensitive to our plight and began working overtime, lending expertise and insight. She uncovered a condominium in a retirement community less than two miles from the hospital that was available for rent. It was not currently being advertised. The only problem was that we were not old enough to live there.

When I contemplate my future, I have a broad imagination. I can see myself engaged in any number of activities, living various lifestyles, pursuing varied hobbies and service projects. I had never envisioned myself making an appeal to a planned retirement condominium association for premature instatement. The process was maddening. On the one hand, I am deeply grateful and thankful they even considered us. The facility was ideal for our needs. On the other hand, the fact they felt the need to take hours of our time to ensure compliance with their bylaws and association minutiae stretched my patience beyond repair. My son was in the hospital alone, sick, scared, and miserable. I sat in a lobby with a three-ring binder while the superintendent and association president read to me, verbatim, the rules for elevator etiquette—including how to hang padding from the handrails if I ever used the elevator to move freight. Perspective defines our experience.

Fortunately, after the appeal and rules shakedown, they granted us access. The only issue was that we could not move in until mid-month, so we would need a temporary landing spot until that time. My sister-in-law, Leslie, discovered a home only a few blocks from the hospital that friends from church owned. They agreed to vacate during the week of our need. We were only days into Jude's chemo travail and already people we did not know were bending over backwards with exceptional benevolence. It was humbling and much appreciated. It was also very instructive. We were being taught the meaning of hospitality.

* * *

Jude's first chemotherapy treatment was every bit as awful as one can imagine. He started off with a double dose of doxorubicin and cisplatin, colloquially known as the "red devil" and "splat." The names speak for themselves. In addition to their harshness, Jude received a child's dosing schedule. Because children are physically more resilient, and they metabolize chemicals quicker, the dosing regimen they can tolerate is typically higher than an adult's. So, children usually receive a higher percentage dose relative to their body weight. Physiologically, Jude was an adult. They dosed him like a child.

Jody and I both have private practices. It is incumbent upon practitioners in a private setting to be efficient and productive. This is a courtesy to our patients and employees. In addition, we are also punctual. If my wife is on time, she operates as if she is five minutes late. Hospitals do not work this way. Less than a week previous, we were told Jude's situation was dire and chemotherapy treatment required posthaste. Every minute the cancer grew unchecked was another minute his odds of survival decreased. We were desperate to begin.

Understandably, chemotherapy treatment of the style Jude received has many moving parts. It is difficult to organize and requires a concerted effort to maintain. Jude checked into the hospital on Wednesday after completing surgery for port placement as well as a deep biopsy of the tumor. His pain was mounting. Sleep was hard to come by, walking nearly impossible, and the constant, deep bone ache was torturous. He grew desperate for relief. Before we could start therapy, we needed the final pathology report to finalize the treatment plan. This arrived Friday morning. Osteosarcoma was confirmed. The terms *aggressive*, *invasive*, and *proliferating* were included in the report. Nothing about the description was reassuring. But the last barrier to treatment was removed. We were assured that once chemo started, the agonizing pain would diminish.

We waited. And waited. The Friday day shift came in and explained Jude's sequence of events. He was reevaluated by all his doctors. His oncologist prescribed the order. Everything was in place. And we waited. Jude was miserable. His leg throbbed so profoundly he was nearly incapacitated. Conversation slowed dramatically. So did time.

By dinner, I was beside myself. We had been assured for the past ten hours that chemo treatment was imminent. An entire day passed, and nothing happened. Then they had a shift changeover, and everything started all over again. More questions, more reviewing of orders, more confusion. Apparently, it was unprecedented to start chemotherapy on a Friday. The nurse suggested we consider commencing the following week. I heard Jude sigh.

Nothing exposes character flaws like trauma and anxiety. I was tempted to go ballistic when that suggestion was made. With a deep breath and an appeal to the Holy Spirit, I very calmly left the room, located the chief resident, and quickly, yet forcefully, described our situation and desire to move along. She capitulated and assured me she would run it up the chain of command.

At midnight, they started chemotherapy. Jude was eager. He was in so much pain, very frustrated with just sitting helpless in a hospital bed, and desperate for anything to happen. Starting at that time was atypical, but we were quickly learning that hospitals are isolated, sovereign spheres. Within that sphere, there is objective time, personal time, and *hospital time. Hospital time* has an entirely different set of conditions than the time most of us are used to. We did not care. We were just happy we were starting the process. Before they began the infusion, I grabbed Jude's arm and said, "Here we go, son. The first step on your road to victory." He tried to smile, projecting an air of nonchalance, but his discomfort got the best of him. He looked ill, like he belonged in that room. He also appeared uncommonly anxious. This unnerved me. Pain has a way of stripping away veneers. Jude was exposed. At that moment, he would have succumbed to any treatment if it would relieve his pain.

The moment they pressed "start" on the chemo infusion and the first chemical dripped into Jude's vein, I excused myself from the room, found a private alcove, and just sobbed. The die was cast. There was no retreat. He was receiving a torrent of chemicals that would irrevocably change him. We knew it was the right thing to do. This did not make it any less traumatic. To understand you are intentionally harming your own child, regardless of the greater mission, is emotionally debilitating. The son I loved was being poisoned in that room. I was his witness.

. . .

Jody and I made a promise to each other and a promise to our son that he would not suffer or fight alone. We would be with him every step of the way. The culture of Children's Hospital was conducive to this, as they encouraged and even expected parents to be there. Covid was not. The rules and regulations surrounding safe practices handcuffed nearly every aspect of our experience. Only one caretaker was allowed in the room, so Jody and I could never be together with our son, except on rare occasions. Only two caretakers were officially allowed access to the hospital, so it was nearly impossible for any other people to visit. All the healthcare providers wore double masks and face shields. This compromised communication, but it also meant no one was recognizable. I essentially lived in Children's Hospital for nine months, had numerous meetings with his oncology team, countless exchanges with his nurses, and at least a dozen private, extensive conversations with his treatment coordinator. If they stood before me today, I would be hard-pressed to identify them. Covid strove to impersonalize a process that was deeply poignant and emotionally unique. It was imminently frustrating and added another layer to the misery of treatment.

Jude's initial chemo treatment hit him like a sledgehammer. He had some intense nausea to start, but that settled down in a matter of hours. His second infusion finished around six in the morning. Neither of us got any sleep, but Jude had so much medication swirling through his system that measuring time through normal human rhythms was irrelevant. He had steroids to counteract swelling and immune response, opioids for brutal bone pain, a chemo cocktail, and every anti-nausea medication extant. This included any medication that had anti-nausea properties, even as a side effect. For a single human body to function with such a swirling cocktail of poison, opioids, anxiolytics, steroids, antipsychotics, and anti-nausea medications seemed to exceed the organic limits of endurance. Jude retreated into himself. He worked hard to let the medications sweep him away and give him the opportunity to chemically retreat from the horror ravaging his body. For the first twelve hours, he remained semi-comatose and non-communicative. That reprieve disembarked much too soon, however. By the following evening, he was very well aware of how miserable he really was.

It all became decidedly worse when he stood up to urinate and his leg cracked. The cancer had broken his leg when we had gone hiking six weeks prior. Somehow, the bone had managed to knit together and remain functional. But with continued tumor growth, the entire area was compromised. The pain felt like someone carved open his leg and filled it with molten lead. He fell back onto the bed in a rictus of pain. Unfortunately, his quick reflexes also triggered his pending nausea. He clutched his smoldering leg while I held his barf bag. I knew, in that moment, just how trying this entire affair would be. You can mentally groom yourself, imagine some of the unpleasant scenarios you will encounter, but there is no substitute for experience. Neither of us was prepared for the exacting distress his ailment initiated.

I was desperate to dispel his agony. No parent can tolerate the suffering of a child. This was extreme. I pleaded with God to place the burden on me, to provide some relief. It did not come. Even with the medication, acute discomfort from the break synergized the deep bone pain and chemo nausea. Jude's misery crescendoed. He rolled on his bed simultaneously retching and rocking. I wanted to scream in frustration, to lash out at his doctors, nurses, and even God—anyone who would listen—to mitigate the suffering. Instead, all I could do was sit stolidly and whisper encouragement while applying aid where appropriate. I've never felt more useless.

Eventually, the pain from the fresh break retreated back into the constant thrum of agony defining his existence. The opioids exerted influence, and the waves of nausea subsided. Jude toweled off his sweat and stink, laid back in his bed, and started thanking the nurses for helping him through his trauma. After brushing his teeth, he surfed the internet, looking for cars, and chatted about everything, from soup to nuts, as if the last three hours of his life were a distant memory. He cracked some jokes and told stories about the fun he had at Whitworth. His capacity to live purely in the moment, to discard unpleasantness and not allow it to define his mood, astounded me. I was so traumatized I could not sit still. I paced the room, reorganized his clothes, arranged his barf bags, folded his blanket, and then did it all over again.

"Dad," Jude called impatiently. "What are you doing?"

"Just preparing," I replied. "Making sure you are okay. How are you doing?"

"The same as I was doing four minutes ago, the last time you asked me," he answered, obviously exasperated.

"That's great." I feigned cheeriness. "Hopefully it stays that way. You were struggling a bit ago," I said, cringing at the understatement.

"Yeah, that was pretty miserable," he agreed. "But that's behind us. So let's not worry about it."

Jude steadfastly decided not to worry. I discovered I could worry enough for the two of us.

CARETAKING

"You gain strength, courage and confidence by every experience in which you really stop to look fear in the face. You must do the thing you think you cannot do."

ELEANOR ROOSEVELT

Checking out of the hospital after receiving chemotherapy treatment may be the single most arduous process any person can endure. Every one of Jude's caretakers needed to be notified—and many were notoriously difficult to locate—and then sign off on his departure. Prescriptions needed to be filled, with requisite instructions. There was always an excessive gap between when the nurse said you could be discharged, and when you were actually discharged. Jude and I became professional "dischargers" as his time in treatment progressed. We streamlined the process, and it became something of a game to us. Our first discharge, however, was a mess. Not because the hospital did anything wrong, but because we were so ignorant.

Jude had been hospitalized for five days. He'd had very little sleep outside of the chemically induced slumber following his infusion. I couldn't even consider sleeping in that madhouse of activity, with beeping alarms, rotations, and bed checks. We were emotionally frayed. Jude felt abysmal. The chemo combo was wreaking havoc on his GI system, and his leg pain, while not exquisite, was no small matter. They could do nothing for the broken bone other than to suggest weight-bearing limitation. This meant a wheelchair, crutches, and the occasional hopping—the latter doing nothing to quell his nausea.

We began the discharge process on Sunday afternoon. The list of instructions seemed limitless. The potential side effects to be on guard for filled volumes. I received an enormous tome, a three-ring binder essentially filled with "what ifs." What do you do if your fever rises above one hundred? What do you do if you are unable to drink sixteen ounces of liquid in the prescribed time? What do you do if you vomit blood? What do you do if there is uncontrolled diarrhea? None of the scenarios were appealing. The solution to these "what ifs" was nearly always the same: Come to the ER immediately or call the oncology emergency line so that they can tell you to come into the ER immediately. There was a great deal that could go wrong.

The most difficult part to manage was the medication. We were given a spreadsheet listing all of Jude's pills, dosages, timing, and duration. It looked like a military requisition order. The first time the nurse showed it to Jude, his eyes glazed over. Without hesitation, he turned to her and said, "My dad will take care of it." I was honored he placed so much trust in me. I just wished I felt the same.

The discharge process concluded around 8 p.m. The hospital was very quiet. I had a homecare kit that filled an entire suitcase. I dragged it, and the rest of our gear, down to our car, which I parked in the exit circle. I scrambled for a bit, trying to locate a wheelchair for Jude. I rolled that empty wheelchair silently through the long corridors, taken aback by the lack of activity. It was pitch black, cold, and raining outside. I felt very alone and very unsure. The last five days seemed surreal. I dreamed someone would intercept me as I strolled along and say, "You don't belong here. Resume your normal life." But there was no interception, just my own forlorn footsteps trudging grudgingly back into my son's nightmare.

When I entered Jude's room, he did not notice me at first. He was sitting on the bed, wrapped in the fleece blanket he's slept with since childhood. He looked very much like someone checking into a hospital, not checking out. His skin was sallow and pasty, his eyes glazed, with tubes connected everywhere. He gripped the emesis basin on his lap as if it were a life preserver. Intermittent shivers wracked his body, and he huddled to stay warm, yet there was sweat gathering about his temples. My grief blossomed. Jude had been tortured for the last thirty-six hours, and his journey was only at its inception. The future was overwhelming.

He looked at me and grinned, shocking my melancholy. "You ready?" he asked.

"I think so," I replied. "I think I have everything. You up for moving?"

"I'm not sure," he answered. "I don't feel very good."

"Something tells me that's an understatement," I quietly joked. He smiled briefly and took a slow, deep breath. His positivity was his lifeline. If that was abandoned, he would sink quickly.

"No, I can do it." He gritted his teeth and swung his legs over the bed, somehow managing to get his shoes on. If he bent over too long, waves of nausea would sweep through him. His movements were judicious and cautious, a stark contrast to how he typically approached life. His slow movements were also hampered by all the tubes, needles, and monitor leads attached to all parts of his body. Thankfully, when the nurse returned, she began disconnecting everything—our last hurdle to freedom. Jude looked like he was being extricated from a fish net.

"You're lucky," the nurse explained while she worked. "Usually they don't let people out this late. You must really be doing well."

"I think 'well' must be a relative term," I responded. "I'm not sure we're comfortable leaving."

"Why not?" The nurse seemed puzzled. "He's doing great. How many times have you puked?"

"Just a couple," Jude answered. "But I really don't feel well."

"I get it." The nurse tried to be encouraging. "But you're really doing great. It will only get easier." Thankfully, Jude took the nurse's comments at face value. I knew there was no "easy" in Jude's future. In fact, quite the opposite was in store. Chemo treatments have a cumulative effect. The toll would magnify.

We got him in the wheelchair and headed for the exit. I had to move cautiously, as any bump or abrupt change in direction twisted his intestines. Somehow, we managed to situate him in the passenger seat without a serious nausea attack. But his leg started screaming, and every time he moved it sent jolts of pain through his body. He sat next to me in the car, holding his throbbing leg off the floor with one hand, a barf bag in the other.

"I will drive slowly," I told him, "but you need to tell me if you're going to barf. I love you, son, but I really don't want you to barf all over my car."

"Yeah, yeah... I don't want to barf in your car. I don't want to barf at all. I feel terrible though." He took a gulp of air. It appeared a retching episode was imminent.

"I get it," I said. "I know you do, and I'd do anything to take that away. Let's just find this house we're supposed to stay at and get you to bed."

Jude's aunt had graciously procured a temporary house for us to live in for Jude's first week out of the hospital until we could move into our condominium. It was only a few blocks from the hospital, which was fantastic, but it was wedged into an old residential district that made for tricky navigating. Between the hills, one-way roads, and weekend streetside parking, I felt like I was navigating an obstacle course. The wet, inky blackness added to our difficulties. Every time I turned a corner, Jude groaned. He clutched his barf bag like a rip cord. We had to drive down a street under construction with the asphalt pockmarked and broken. I could hardly see the myriad imperfections, and the bumpy asphalt spared no mercy on his broken leg.

We eventually located the residence. For some reason, there was a pile of dirt in the narrow driveway, which the rain inauspiciously eroded into a slippery, muddy mess. Parked cars lined the street in both directions, as far as I could see. Walking was out of the question. I delicately wedged the car alongside the dirt pile, creasing it between the mud and a concrete retaining wall. Jude was just staring at his lap, panting. His hands were shaking so badly he could hardly grip his barf bag. His personification of abject misery was so horrific that for a moment I seriously considered backing out and returning to the hospital. Jude would never forgive me for that insult, however. He was suffering, but the act of returning to a hospital bed would only exacerbate his feeling of helplessness. Unfortunately, after I dismissed that thought, I noticed the next hurdle. The house was built on the side of a hill. The entryway was twenty-two variegated concrete steps above us. I was an exhausted mess. Jude was poisoned, sick beyond compare, and he had a broken leg. The trek appeared unscalable.

My brother-in-law exited the house and met us in the driveway, pointing to the doorway which, from our vantage, could have been on the moon. I roused Jude, gripping his shoulder, and gave him a knowing look. "One last hurdle, son, before you can go to bed. Can you do this?" He looked out the window and squinted with discomfort.

"I have to go up that?" he whispered incredulously. "I can't make it up that."

"You have to make it up there, son. We don't have any options." My heart was racing. Jude looked completely defeated. "I will help you. Once we get in the house, it will be easy." Jude nodded his head. I could see he was trying to psych himself up for the challenge. It was the last thing he wanted to do. Neither of us wanted any of this. The injustice of the entire affair threatened to erase the last vestiges of my determination. Despair's grip squeezed hard, capturing both of us. "You've surprised me before, my son. Now it is time to surprise yourself."

He grasped the door handle, gulped more air, and pushed the door open. He managed to swing his legs out of the vehicle and, as fate would have it, plunk them directly into the mud.

"Shit!" he exclaimed, hanging his head. He regripped the door handle and handed me his barf bag. The driveway was so tight I had to wriggle my way out of the driver's side and squeeze between the retaining wall and the side of the car before I could aid him. My brother-in-law came down the stairs and supported Jude on his right side. I managed to get Jude's left arm around my shoulders, thereby taking the weight mostly off his left leg. We warily lifted and attempted to delicately pull and semi-drag him to the stairway. The pavement was wet and slippery, the stairs uneven. We began inching ourselves at a graceless trudge up the staircase, each step looming like a giant's hurdle. We navigated the first fourteen steps with an awkward, hopping gait. Jude was panting and sweating, his body so frail and weak he could hardly support any of his weight. We nearly toppled many times, and I strained to keep him upright. We stopped to rest on that fourteenth stair when he doubled over and retched. His hands shook violently.

"I can do this," I heard him whisper. "I can do this." He hopped once more with our support, but his toe caught on the lip of the next step. We both stumbled forward. To avoid smashing his face into the concrete, he halted his descent with his left leg. As his leg buckled from pain, I frantically attempted to break his fall. His mouth opened in a twisted rictus of agony, but the expected scream was just a tormented gargle. I was mortified. In desperation, I leaned down, wrapped both arms around his torso, and heaved. I staggered up those last eight steps, through the rain and darkness, clutching my son with as much care and love as I had in his infancy. He clung to my neck as a little child. I fought my way onto the threshold and gently deposited him in the entryway—the mountain finally conquered. We both stood there, arm in arm, shaky and sweaty, unsure if we should feel relief or trepidation. My in-laws courteously directed us down a hall to the bedroom where Jude could lie down.

His leg was shot. He was desperately ill. So with a final effort, I carried him down the narrow hallway towards an unwelcoming, foreign bedroom—a gruesome foreshadow of Jude's future. There was nothing inviting about it.

I tried to gently set him on the bed, but my arms gave out and we both fell onto the mattress in an exhausted clump. As we lay there together panting, Jude reached over, fumbling in the darkness, and grabbed my arm. He clutched it tightly, squeezing it as if he was searching for safety. Suddenly, he sat up, dry heaved, and put his face in his hands. His abject despair permeated the room. I had never seen him, or anyone, so lost and forlorn. I delicately placed my hand on his forehead, wrapped my other arm around him, and drew him close. The terror of what he had endured, and what he must still endure, haunted us like a grisly specter. All the fortitude we had worked so hard to buttress over the last five days crumbled into rubble. We both started to sob.

"I can't do this," Jude whispered. Tears ran down his face. There was fear in his eyes. For a moment, he had let himself look to the future. It was the first time I'd seen him appear truly defeated.

"Yes you can, my son. I know you can. You are stronger than you know. And I will be with you every step of the way." I clutched him tightly. Our tears intermingled. We stayed locked together for many minutes.

"I love you, Dad."

"I love you too, son."

I have never uttered anything truer in my entire life.

EROSION

"'The times are bad! The times are troublesome!' This is what humans say. But we are our times. Let us live well and our times will be good. Such as we are, such are our times."

AUGUSTINE OF HIPPO

Cancer is the ultimate parasite. It hijacks the body's resources, using the physiology of the host to grow and multiply, slowly depleting reserves and overrunning repair mechanisms until the entire system collapses. All it does is take.

Cancer's greed extends far beyond physical boundaries. Part of the joy of parenting is witnessing your child's maturation from utter dependence to complete independence. Sometimes this is a painful process, replete with setbacks, disappointments, and frustrations. No one matures in a perfectly linear fashion. As our children zig and zag towards maturity and the possession of an autonomous self, parents shift as well. We transition from primary caretaking to leading, enabling, nurturing, and actualizing. Ultimately, we move from a position of complete authority to a position of no authority. The role of a parent is one of constant transition. Parenting a uniquely autonomous adult is radically different from parenting a fully dependent infant. The beauty and joy inherent in participating in that transition is a gift from God.

With the advent of Jude's cancer, we had the horrible experience of watching this transition reverse. When we moved Jude into Whitworth University, he was reaching the pinnacle of autonomy. Physically, emotionally, relationally, spiritually, and financially, he was becoming his own person. Granted, eighteen-year-old men still have a long way to travel, but the progress was evident. He emerged from the cocoon of adolescence ready to approach life as an independent adult. We were excited for him and proud of him. Considering his history and numerous struggles, we were also nervous for him. Our anxiety did not mean he was not ready, however.

The moment he was diagnosed, that independence eroded. The first thing cancer took was his college experience. You only get to be a freshman once. There is nothing quite like being thrust into a new life, surrounded by others just as wide-eyed and inexperienced as you. You must learn to navigate your immediate surroundings without the handholding of a parent. Your daily choices are not constantly evaluated or assessed by an authority. Your actions, and the consequences of those actions, are borne strictly by you. This is exciting. It is also played out in a protected environment. University teaches you how to be independent, without the rigors or travails associated with true independence.

Suddenly, Jude was at the mercy of his doctors and his treatment plan. His parents swooped in to help guide and manage his treatment. His life had regressed. He had very little say in how he would function as treatment progressed. In the blink of an eye, his autonomy vanished. Losing something you have earned and achieved, through no fault of your own, is immanently frustrating and exceptionally maddening. As a parent, it all seemed so unnatural. Time can't reverse. Our trajectory flipped.

Within hours of leaving the hospital, Jude transitioned from an independent, adult student to an infant. Once again, Jody and I became the proud parents of a six-foot-one newborn. And just like leaving the maternity ward for the first time, we were suddenly on our guard and fully responsible as round-the-clock caretakers. We had to check him at night, help him with food and clothes, and closely watch for any changes that fell into the "what if" category.

Jude's medication list was three pages long. The hospital printed a spreadsheet of every pill he had to take and when he had to take it. Much of his medication was titrated over an extended period, meaning one day he would take three pills, and the next day he would take two, and then the next day he would take one and a half and so forth. We dedicated the kitchen table to all his prescriptions. The bottles alone took up half the space, and then there were pill cutters, pestles for grinding, measuring cups, and a weekly calendar to aid in distribution. Some pills he took every day. Others he took only on Mondays and Tuesdays. Some he took only when he was feeling nauseous. Others he took to help him not feel nauseous. Some pills were there to help him stave off potential infections, while others were there in case of infection. He was a mobile apothecary. Deciphering the when's, why's, and how much's took immense fortitude. We became slaves to his medication routine.

The first night Jude and I spent away from the hospital was more stressful than the first night we took him home after he was born. With every twitch, grunt, or sob, I was on my feet at his bedside, assessing his status. All his pills were laid out in sequence, with multiple alarms set to get the timing correct.

After my third or fourth foray into his room, around two in the morning, we experienced our first curveball. I gave him a handful of pills which he struggled to ingest. His nausea roller coaster ride reached the pinnacle, and he was hanging on to the sidecar handles for dear life. Fortunately, his medication curtailed excessive vomiting, emblematic of this chemo regimen decades previous, but there is a vast gulf between incessant, projectile puking and feeling tip-top. The idea of putting something in his mouth for the purpose of ingestion was unbearable.

After three or four attempts, he finally managed to swallow his pills. I sat with him for a few minutes, making sure he was comfortable, and then dragged my way down the hallway to a makeshift bed, which was really just a sleeping bag on a mattress in the playroom adjacent to Jude's bedroom. It didn't matter where I laid down, though—restful sleep was only a fantasy at that point. Despite knowing I would not sleep, I still went through the routine of getting comfortable in my sleeping bag. Just as I got situated, I heard him puking.

"Hey, man, you okay in there?" Silence. Then the sounds of more retching. "Do you need anything?" More heaving. I crawled out of my sleeping bag, wondering why I had even bothered getting in.

"I feel terrible," Jude moaned. His entire body was bathed in perspiration. I nearly gasped when I saw his eyes, which appeared to be bleeding. Then I realized they were bloodshot from the trauma of heaving. Jude sat cross-legged on his bed, panting with exertion as his body convulsed with silent heaves. He was miserable, and I was miserable for him. We also recognized he had puked some of his medication into his barf bag. There were the remnants of multiple pills in the swirling mess of bile, mucus, and Gatorade. The question was which pills, and how many? Did we have him take all the pills again? Did we assume some of the medication was absorbed, and if so, how much? I certainly did not relish emptying the contents of his bag into a receptacle that could enable proper assessment of both amount and type. It also did not help that it was three in the morning, neither of us had gotten any sort of rest for days, and our emotional fatigue stunted any efforts toward rational thought.

"Looks like there are some pills in there," I told him. "Some of those pills are pretty important. Some probably don't matter much. Either way, we have to figure out what to do. What do you want to do?"

I asked Jude that question because I wanted him to feel like he was in control. I did not want him to think cancer had the only say in his life, and I wanted him to cling to his own sovereignty. I believed the more empowered he felt, and the less at the mercy of his malady, the stronger his resistance. "I don't know," he stammered, obviously exasperated. His patience was frayed. "You decide. I don't want to think about it." He slowly eased himself out of bed, hobbled to the bathroom, and brushed his teeth for what must have been about the tenth time. I realized then the best gift I could give my son was to bear the burden of daily decision making. He was the one waging the war. He was the one suffering the ravages of chemo. He was more than happy to relinquish the burden of tactics. Just like a small child, his agency was best served by being told what to do and when to do it. He wanted his mind free to deal only with his immediate struggle, and when the struggle was relieved, he wanted his mind clear so he would not have to worry about what lay ahead.

This incident marked the beginning of my relationship with the oncology on-call team at Children's Hospital. It had only taken us eight hours before we were forced to call in with our first conundrum. They were both patient—and champions of patience. I like to understand why something is happening and the reasoning behind directives. They had to deal with innumerable questions from me, and they did their level best to assuage my concerns. That night was no small matter. They supplied a simple algorithm for how to manage pill taking after an emesis event. I cannot remember all the details now, but we followed them closely. Unfortunately, this meant rearranging our entire medication countertop to deal with pill fragments and adjusted dosing. It also meant modifying our timing and resetting all alarms. We became very efficient at this. Jude crawled back into bed while I managed the apothecary. I lay on top of my bed and stared at the ceiling, wondering how soon we would have to do this all over again.

* * *

I was hopeful morning would bring relief. We quickly learned day and night were irrelevant at this stage in his treatment. Time was measured purely in relation to when his last chemo treatment was finished. You could set your watch to what he would suffer through, what medications would be needed, and how we would function based solely on that timing. If chemo was finished at noontime, then we could expect X around midnight. If chemo was finished at 6 p.m., then X would not occur until 6 a.m. Life was hijacked by the chemo calendar. Jude's independence was hijacked by his treatment.

His therapy decimated his immune system and his metabolism. Between the tumor growth and the poison, flesh peeled off his frame. His oncology team had a nutritionist, who kept very specific tabulations of his weight. Jude's decline was shocking. Before chemotherapy even started, the team suggested Jude receive a nasogastric tube that would supply a slow calorie drip into his queasy stomach. This would ensure he was receiving proper nutrients, and since it was a slow drip, his stomach volume would not be pressured or triggered. It also meant his vomiting would not be cataclysmic. Jude was not particularly keen on this idea. The thought of having a tube hanging down the back of his throat, running out of his nose, and taped to the side of his face was not attractive. His nascent foray into the life of a chemo patient still demanded he hang onto some old habits. He tried to trump nutrition with fashion. I let him maintain hope.

We worked hard, from day one, to keep his weight up. His nutritionist had any number of suggestions and feeding itineraries. He supplied us with several samples, all of which contained high-density products of fats and proteins. This diet was radically different from what Jude was raised on. Jody and I, while not extreme, are fitness enthusiasts. Jude's diet consisted primarily of lean meats, vegetables, and complex carbohydrates. Outside the confines of his home, he did not eat particularly healthily. He was no stranger to Big Macs and Taco Bell, and he was forever sneaking bags of chips and crackers into his room. This was a far cry from what was suggested, however.

On our first day, I tried to get him to ingest a protein shake consisting of high-fat yogurt, flavored protein, fruit, and heavy cream. It was absolutely delicious and tasted like something concocted at the Heart Attack Café in Las Vegas. Jude had no chance. Even if he was not suffering the ravages of chemotherapy, there was no way his constitution would allow such calorie-dense products to enter his digestive tract. It was much too rich, like eating a stick of flavored butter. He was not accustomed to that sort of diet. One or two swallows was all he could manage.

We tried nearly everything suggested. He struggled to keep anything down, and what he could keep down he could only manage a scant bite or two. For the consummate food lover, I am sure it would all sound attractive, but the reality was quite different. A bite of cereal drenched with half-and-half is quite tasty. Four or five bites is revolting. There is a reason why classy restaurants only serve tiny ramekins of crème brûlée. A jug of such exquisite dessert is unpalatable. Can anyone really eat more than three small squares of fudge without feeling sick?

We finally decided to return to what we considered to be his regular diet. We achieved some degree of success with this, but his caloric intake was less than half of what he typically ingested. What was also problematic was that something that tasted good one day would be repulsive the next. He was like a pregnant woman. We were forever running around town trying to find something attractive to eat that he could not only keep down but continue to enjoy in the ensuing days. It was an ongoing struggle.

After thirty-six hours, I was beside myself. He'd managed to eat a few hundred calories. It was doubtful any had been absorbed. Cancer had already stolen pieces of his independence, now it was starting to steal pieces of his flesh. On day four after his initial chemo treatment, he had already lost ten pounds, and we had no way to pump the brakes. He could hardly eat, and his intestines could barely absorb nutrients. Jude was so robust when he left for school—the epitome of health. Now he was sickly and frail. It was as if a giant, life-squelching insect had entered our home and sucked the vitality right out of him.

Jody arrived the following day. When she saw Jude, her heart clenched. There was no hiding what we were up against and what this sinister parasite was capable of. Jody put on her bravest face and donned the mantle of the positive, smiling nursemaid. She was determined to nurture him through this campaign. But she could not hide her concern from me.

Selfishly, I did nothing to assuage her apprehension. I was just relieved to see my wife, knowing she would grant me a reprieve from the nightmare. For five days, I had suffered under the irrepressible weight of Jude's malady. It felt like I had been at it for decades. The stress of managing his new existence, combined with constant worry and anxiety about his future, exacted a toll. Later, I would grow hardened by these travails, but the initial shock of that first round was overwhelming. I was desperate for a respite.

...

Before I could leave I needed to educate my wife. Now, Jody is an extremely competent administrator. She is gifted with a surfeit of executive function. I know few people with her capacity to multitask. However, when I revealed our makeshift apothecary and elaborate medication dosing schedule, she quailed with concern.

"Wait, wait ... What is this again?" she asked for the fourth time.

I patiently re-explained the systematic dosing itinerary and walked through the entire process a second time. I had been immersed in it for days already, and although it was not routine, it was becoming manageable. It was also fortuitous for Jody that some of Jude's meds had been curtailed.

"That's the dexamethasone. It reduces swelling and nausea. He needs a tapered dose. See, it's written right here." I flipped the page and showed her where it was displayed on the hospital discharge sheet. "So, for his next dose, you give him two and a half pills."

"Half a pill? How do we manage that?"

"With this nifty little pill cutter right here," I explained. I pulled out a small green box. Inside, there was a graduated channel for multiple-sized pills and a razor blade embedded in the lid for cutting. "Just place the pill in the channel and press. Make sure you keep both halves and place the unused piece in a safe place other than the container. You will need the other one later." I smiled knowingly. I had already made the mistake of tossing the other half into the bottle where it fell to the very bottom, making retrieval difficult.

"Okay. I think I got it. Let me run through it again with you." We patiently went through his directives one more time. They were important. The list seemed interminable. Taking care of Jude was daunting and a full-time task. Jody spread all the instructions neatly on the table and rearranged every bottle.

"You got this," I encouraged her. "He needs you." And that was the truth.

Jude and I had walked through fire. He needed his mother. More importantly, she had brought his Xbox with her. His mother was critical. A distraction doubly so. As a family, we were starting to be enticed by the one danger that is the death knell of the infirm: wallowing in your own misery. Fortunately, our beautiful son, through an unimaginable depth of character and strength of will, started modeling how to resist this compelling temptation. He began growing in ways unimaginable.

AID

*"Bear one another's burdens,
and so fulfill the law of Christ."*

GALATIANS 6:2

My father-in-law is a prayer warrior. He is a pastor and evangelist by trade, but a true connoisseur of prayer. When Jude was originally diagnosed, Jody and I knew we were in for a busy season, and we mentally prepared and planned. As independent personalities who are pridefully self-reliant, we did not entertain the idea of asking for help. It isn't that we didn't want help or would have refused help if it was offered; we simply did not think about it. We did, however, turn to Jody's father for spiritual aid.

Christianity influenced all aspects of our lives. This would be no different. Jude's circumstance was dire, and who better than the Almighty to support us, and Jude, through this journey. We had been praying for our children since before they were born. We would now increase our efforts.

Jude was in the hospital for only a handful of minutes when the gravity of the situation revealed my limitations. His situation was life-altering. It was family-altering. Jude was going to need help, and likely more than the provisions of his parents alone. It was then that I elected to turn to social media. Now, I am not a Facebooker, Snapchatter, Instagrammer, or any of the rest. I occasionally dabbled, primarily to stay connected to my own children. I certainly did not possess any compelling need to use them further, but Jude's predicament helped me recognize the potential value of social media. His grandfather was a single prayer warrior. Jude had an entire community of believers out there willing to join the fight.

With trepidation and deep humility, I posted Jude's diagnosis on Facebook. I made a simple appeal for prayer. Namely, that Jude's life would be saved, his leg would be spared, and that his feeble, nascent faith would take root. The response was overwhelming.

Most of us tend to take for granted what it means to live in a faith community. I will never make that mistake again. The number of people committing themselves to pray for my son exceeded my imagination. I was contacted by literally thousands of people. This outpouring of love, and the sustaining prayers that followed, became our first antidote to despair. I shared many of the comments with Jude, and with each one, I watched a flicker of determination blossom in his spirit.

It is always difficult to know how much to share. Neither I, nor my wife, are particularly open people. We certainly did not desire the issues and problems in our lives to become a burden to others. I am sure our Caring Bridge and Facebook posts did not always accomplish their intended purpose—to thank, acknowledge, and inform. When one is in the midst of a crisis, it is difficult to apprehend objective thought and detached perspective. We tried our best. We thank everyone for their grace with our communication endeavors.

Jody and I thought this would be enough. Now that we had an army of people praying, we assumed we could handle the rest. But I will never know if we could have managed, because our community did not allow us to make the attempt. Within days of that initial post, offers of help poured in. We dismissed them. That was when people took it upon themselves to provide despite our recalcitrance.

We needed to move into our condominium in Seattle. This was a difficult logistical project, made even more difficult by the fact one of us was constantly tending to Jude. Friends and family stepped in, procuring furniture, dishware, groceries, trailers, and the manpower to settle us into our new accommodations. The wife of my dear friend was currently fighting colon cancer. She was going through chemotherapy herself and was taking a year away from her teaching career for her campaign. With her free time, she managed to organize a meal train. This was a lifesaver. Another group of friends decided Jude would never go a day without receiving a pledge of support. Hundreds of people were organized to send him at minimum a card, and oftentimes a gift, every single day. Those served as a continuous, unbreakable lifeline. The prayers were constant. They say it takes a village to raise a child. We learned it takes a community of Christians to save a child. What a blessing.

I would love to write that this outpouring of support turned the tide and Jude's journey became smooth and routine, but then this narrative would be fiction. Jody stayed with Jude for a few days in our temporary housing until we settled into the condominium complex. With everyone's help, this took less than a week to accomplish, and we were feeling confident with our arrangements. Jude had managed to start eating again, albeit meekly, and our working knowledge regarding what the vagaries of long-term caretaking would consist of were beginning to take shape. Jody and I had our work schedules modified, our new home was stocked, we were buoyed by prayer—we felt ready for the marathon.

A few days after settling, Jude spiked a fever. This is always problematic with chemotherapy, doubly so in his case. One of his chemical agents possessed the unfortunate side effect of obliterating bone marrow production. This meant most of the cells Jude's body needed to fight infection were not being replenished. Much like an AIDS patient, he was dangerously susceptible to any invasive organism.

Antibiotics were introduced. He had already taken some as part of his medicating routine, but now they changed the type and dose. After twenty-four hours his fever continued to rise and his general malaise increased. No sooner had he pulled out of the well of misery than he was being dragged back in. His next chemo dose was not due for two more weeks. This was supposed to be his time of respite. Instead, his nausea and pain were returning with exacting force. Something was off.

Jody took him into the Children's ER. They could not ascertain the source of his symptoms. They thought perhaps he was getting an infection at the biopsy site. His white blood cell count, a measure of infection, was quite high. They put him on IV antibiotics. His fever held steady for a day, and then his leg erupted. One moment he was in a hospital bed suffering from a fever and general malaise—nothing unexpected with a serious chemo patient—the next he was writhing on his side in intense agony. The doctors were baffled. Yes, he had a horrible, bone-swelling tumor in his leg that was prodigiously painful, but much of that had been mitigated after his first blast of chemo. Pain of this stripe was wildly different than the typical ache of tumor growth. They thought it could be an acute neural reaction due to tumor impingement, but medication to quell that symptomology had no effect.

His fever rose, his pain intensified, and they pumped him full of antibiotics and pain meds, still mystified. I relieved Jody at the hospital two days into Jude's attack. I was fatigued from the trials of the previous week, so I couldn't imagine how Jude was doing. Surprisingly, when I arrived at the hospital, Jude was obviously uncomfortable but upright, mildly talkative, and fully engaged with the staff and constant bustle surrounding him. The pain meds and antibiotics appeared to be working. Jody said her goodbyes.

That night it all went sideways. What had been a four or a five on the pain scale jumped to a ten. Jude curled into the fetal position, clutched his leg, and just moaned. He was rigorously inspected, but no one could make any sense of his agony. They continued with the pain meds. I sat by his bedside in a vain attempt to keep him comforted. He rolled in and out of sentience as the pain meds ebbed and flowed, dampening his system. Every time he fell into a troubled, semiconscious state, I would bow my head and pray.

By morning, nothing had changed. The pain remained intense. Jude was a sweaty mess incapable of carrying on any sort of conversation or interacting in any meaningful way. He just lay on his side with his eyes clenched, writhing and moaning. I had never felt more helpless. I begged God to let us trade places. I pleaded to remove the misery. Nothing. It only continued to mount.

By the middle of the following night, Jude was physically ill from the agony. His fever rose, his leg burned, and in fits of strained conversation, he described the sum total of his existence as if someone was taking electrified daggers and carving them into the back of his thigh. His left leg was an inferno of torment.

We brainstormed various options. Amputation surfaced at the top of the list. This solution was so grossly abhorrent to me that I would not even entertain it. Just two weeks previous, Jude had vowed he would rather endure four years of chemotherapy before surrendering his leg. Despite his heavy discomfort and desperation for relief, he was not ready for extremes. In their bafflement, the team elected to perform a battery of diagnostics, including another MRI and an ultrasound. We wheeled Jude into imaging that very evening. Unfortunately, we had to get him to lie still and keep his leg straight or the images would be useless. After sliding onto the imaging bench, he gripped the sides with white knuckles, determined to get it right, but suffering uncontrollably. It appeared at times like he was having a seizure. I sat in the room with him, wiping his brow, utterly useless. It was absolutely emasculating. Seeing one's child suffer is heart-rending. Witnessing his relentless agony slayed me.

After imaging, the pain managed to intensify even more, and Jude retreated into a shell. He lay on his side, gripped his leg, and panted. He willed himself away to a fantasy land of his own design, a full-on psychological retreat from the growing torment. I watched the clock tick ever so slowly. Time grew so heavy I was afraid the weight of it would freeze us in place. I have never wanted to get past a moment faster than this. His suffering was intolerable.

By early morning, the results came back. We discovered there were multiple issues at play, all contributing to his suffering. First, Jude had developed multiple blood clots scattered the length of his entire leg. Some were rather large, and all were serious. They were also intensely painful. Second, his tumor had swollen even more, elevating pressure against both the bones inside his lower leg, like a lever threatening to separate them. Bones are not particularly flexible. Bones with calcifying cancer in and around them less so. He had a self-produced and constantly growing internal torture device in full operation. Finally, the one piece of good news was that parts of his tumor were starting to necrotize, or die, and Jude's immune system was having a strong reaction to this dying tissue. Unfortunately, this reaction was causing a great deal of swelling and edema in an area already pressed and stretched to its limit.

When we received the report, I squeezed Jude's hand, leaned over his bed until my lips brushed his ear, and whispered encouragingly, "It's working, son. Just hang on." It was all I could give him. Tears of hope and frustration welled at the corners of my eyes. We'd been immersed in this nightmare for two weeks and finally we had a tiny shred of hope to cling to. His tumor was responding to the treatment.

Jude could grasp the news, but it did not alleviate his immediate situation. The prescribed treatment strategies were to begin blood thinners for the clots and steroids for the swelling, along with more pain meds. Jude would have to hang on until those remedies were effective. There was no guarantee they would work. It could be days. It could be never.

He stayed in a shell the entire day. Other than pain meds, there was nothing to be done. I sat by his bedside and tried to get him to drink something. Eating was out of the question. Conversation was nonexistent. My words were simply an appeal to hang on. We carried this routine into the night. He would take a sip or two and then retreat into himself. I would clutch his hand and pray, fantasizing an angel would stride through the door and sweep us away from the hell Jude was living through. Deep into the night, I continued my vigil, hoping and praying, my pleas growing ever more desperate. In the middle of one of my appeals, I started feeling terrible. I thought I was becoming ill. The last thing I wanted to do was pass something on to Jude. I left his bedside to splash some cold water on my face and figure out what I should do. I took a few unsteady, discouraged steps and was overcome with nausea. The room started to tilt. The next thing I remember was Jude talking. "Dad! Dad!" he yelled. "Are you okay? Dad, get up. What's wrong?"

I could not figure out why I was lying on the floor. "I'm fine," I reassured him.

"No, you're not fine," he argued. "You passed out."

"What?!" I exclaimed. "Don't be ridiculous."

"Something crashed," Jude said. The strain in his voice sounded like torn sandpaper. His effort to roll over and talk to me was an intense struggle, frightfully illustrated by his lustrous hair matted from perspiration while all his bedding was a mess of soaked sheets wadded around his torso. He looked awful and likely felt worse. His IV monitor started to squawk. "Dad, you don't look very good."

"That's not very reassuring coming from you," I replied with a much-too-strained smile. I attempted to sit up. Jude's face scrunched with worry. Once I was upright, he clutched his leg and rolled back over. Just then the nurse walked in to check his IV.

"Are you doing okay?" She shook Jude's shoulder. He sat up, looked her squarely in the eye, and said something I will never forget.

"I am doing just fine," he told her confidently. "You need to check on my dad. He just passed out. I think something is wrong with him." He had been suffering from acute pain for nearly a week. His world had been turned upside down. His doctors were threatening an emergency amputation. He was sick, fighting for his life. Minutes before, he had been writhing in his bed, curled in a rictus of pain. He had every reason to ask the nurse for a quick bolus of pain meds, a wet cloth, or something to drink. Instead, he was worried about me and put my needs above his own. It was the bravest thing I had seen him do. I was shocked.

"No, no, I'm just fine. Please get him his next bolus." She looked at me quizzically. I was still on the floor.

"Why are you on the floor?" she asked, obviously perplexed. I quickly got up and resumed my position in the chair at Jude's bedside.

"Not sure," I replied sheepishly. "I was just using the bathroom."

"He passed out," Jude interjected. "You need to make sure he's okay." The nurse pushed a button. The next thing I knew, someone was slapping a blood pressure cuff on my arm.

"Look," I explained, "I'm fine. I just got a little faint. I'll rest here. No more bother." I took the cuff off my arm and settled everyone down. Eventually the nurses vacated. I felt terrible. Jude kept staring at me like I was an alien.

"Dad, you're really pale," he said.

"How can you tell? There aren't any lights on in here."

"You look like the moon." He groaned again. I grabbed his shoulder. The sudden movement made me lightheaded. What was wrong with me?

We sat in silence for nearly thirty minutes. His last bolus of pain meds seemed to put him out. I was queasy, anxious, and completely wrung out from watching him suffer. And that's when it occurred to me: I had had nothing to eat or drink for nearly three days. I had not left his room. I had not gone to the cafeteria, I had not ordered any food, I had not taken a sip of water. Nothing. The only time I had held a beverage was to try and get Jude to swallow something. Nothing had entered my system.

I grabbed an apple juice and drank it. Then I drank another one. Then I drank a liter of water. I was still thirsty. I took Jude's Sprite and drank that. Fifty ounces of liquid later, I started to feel like a person again. Jude was sleeping and clutching his leg, but the deep strain that had so obviously marked his existence appeared, to my increasingly practiced eye, mildly ameliorated. I laid my head back and took a very deep breath. For the first time in three days, I closed my eyes.

I called Jody the next morning. She adjusted her schedule and rescued me. My father came with her and drove me back to Lynden. Jude had suffered like no person should. My anxiety and helplessness for his plight had taken me to my limit. Somehow, with astounding resilience and an immense reservoir of fortitude, Jude had yet to reach his.

IGNOMINY

"Some of us are walking around with full ornamentation, but not much else. It's not the decoration that makes us."

EVE ENSLER

Jude spent thirteen days in the hospital. When we finally secured a release, he was ecstatic. Lying in bed for an extended period is demoralizing. The exit of Children's Hospital is hardly a panoramic vista, but Jude soaked it in like he had been released from a thirty-year incarceration. The cold, dreary, slate-gray sky, framed with drooping evergreen trees, was Shangri-la.

Chemotherapy is never routine. Each day is accompanied by novel trials. One hopes those trials run smoothly, making for a predictable process. Until now, Jude's journey had been the opposite. Most days were train wrecks. Part of it was the harshness of the chemotherapeutic agents, part of it was his physiology betraying him, and part of it was the fact that osteosarcoma is so rare that words like *routine* and *predictable* are complete misnomers.

Every day was an adventure. Some of the events, at the time, were absurdly traumatic. Thanks to Jude's upbeat attitude and irrepressibly insouciant personality, they acquired a flavor of humor that appeared, to my sensibilities, sacrilegious.

During our frenetic move into the condominium, Jude received his first methotrexate infusion. He was handling it with much aplomb. Compared to cisplatin, in his words, this was "a walk in the park." His assessment, however favorable, was a touch premature. He did not realize that his first few days of methotrexate would include manageable fatigue, malaise, and nausea, but it was the next couple of days after that—after the lining of his intestines would slough—when the roller coaster would leave the station.

We were both oblivious to this timetable. Together we hung out, whiling away time, waiting for his kidneys to clear the poison so we could be released from the hospital. Compared to our previous nightmare, the current affair seemed like a vacation. So, after a brief conference, he assured me it would be acceptable to leave him alone and run some much-needed errands. Of primary importance was the acquisition of internet access for our new abode. For reasons unknown, the technicians could not connect remotely, requiring me to physically gather materials from their store. So, much to my chagrin, I traded waiting alongside Jude to wait in a Comcast service center. After an interminable delay, my name was called. As fate would have it, just as I made my introductions to the servicing agent, my phone buzzed. It was Jude.

"Dad," I heard him whisper on the other end. "Dad," he whispered again, with real urgency.

"Hello—Why are you whispering? What's going on?" I asked. The agent watched me impatiently.

"Dad, I have a real problem here." He sounded very put out, but not afraid or in pain.

"What kind of problem? Do you need me to come back? Is this something the nurses can handle?" Our interpretation of a "problem" was not always coincident. For Jude, a "problem" could range from a missing charging cord to a catastrophic car wreck. For me, a real problem would mean the hospital was on fire.

"I don't want the nurses to handle it," he replied sheepishly.

"Well, what is it?" I honestly did not know where he was going with this, but I also knew he would never bother me without significant concern.

"I pooped on my pants," he answered. The resignation and embarrassment in his tone was palpable.

"Oh man, that's no good. Wait a minute. What do you mean you pooped *on* your pants. Don't you poop *in* your pants?" I realized I was standing in a crowded, public facility and I had responded much too loudly. I also noticed many patrons politely trying rather unsuccessfully not to look in my direction while simultaneously straining to follow my conversation. I excused myself from the agent, who happily obliged, and jogged to my car while I continued to talk.

"Yeah, I know," he half-laughed, half-wailed. "I was standing up to go pee, balancing on one leg, and my sweatpants dropped to the floor. And then my intestines just heaved and there was nothing I could do to stop it."

"What are you doing now?" I inquired.

"I'm just standing here on one foot. I'm a mess. My clothes are a mess. The floor is a mess. I don't know what to do." His distress and discomfort were obvious.

"I hate to say this, son, but you're going to have to call the nurse."

"I can't do that to her," he interjected. "There is no way I am going to have people I don't know come in and clean up this disaster. I'm disgusting."

"Jude," I argued, "I am on my way. But you need to realize these nurses work on a pediatric oncology ward. They see this every day. They will not be shocked. In fact, they will be happy to help you out. It's what they do."

"That may be true, but this is embarrassing and it's gross. I really don't want them to deal with it," he pleaded.

"Okay, I'm driving as fast as I can. Hang tough and I'll be there soon."

I raced to the hospital, parked the car, and sprinted up to his room. I knew his predicament was a grim reality of this treatment, but foreknowledge did not alleviate the grisly details of the very thankless task I was rapidly approaching. I was prepared to do anything for my son, but that did not mean I had to look forward to it.

I grabbed some towels and washcloths from the sanitary cart sitting next to his room. After pulling the door open, I pushed the curtain aside and was greeted by a sight I had never imagined. Jude stood next to his bed, balanced on his good leg, with his pants and underwear at his ankles. Feces were everywhere. And, true to his word, it was on his pants, not in his pants. He looked at me and smiled. There were two nurses and a custodian working feverishly around him. Jude jovially teased them, and everyone laughed, not at all taken aback or threatened by the mess. How they could make this situation palatable, let alone comfortable, was a testament to their professionalism and good nature.

"They arrived before you did," he said. "I told them not to come in but they didn't listen."

"So, you didn't call them?" I asked.

"Absolutely not," he answered.

One of the nurses interjected, "I already chewed him out for not ringing us. He knows better now." She patted him appreciatively on his shoulder, unfazed by his naked state, and continued to mop around him with all the casual indifference of a custodian at an after party. "What we do need from you, however, are some new pants and underwear."

I responded with alacrity, secretly pleased and grateful I was not the one doing the dirty work. It would have taken me five times as long and I would have done a worse job. Amazingly, Jude stood there through the entire operation as they cleaned up his bed, his floor, and his body. He thanked them profusely and managed to keep the scene lighthearted. He had every right to be embarrassed and frustrated. Instead, he accepted the incident with a certain grace and flair that left everyone involved pleased with their performance. It is a rare gift indeed to enable those around you to feel both pride and a bit privileged cleaning your poop. It would have been easy for the staff to become resentful, annoyed, or even bitter. Jude's magnanimity created a certain ease and welcoming grace that gave his nurses and orderlies pause for thought. To remain charitable and courteous in the face of distress requires immense fortitude and intentionality. My son humbled me.

As fate would have it, however, the gruesome specter of feces remained present. After Jude's discharge, I became keenly aware that there were no more nurses or sanitary staff hiding in our condo closets poised to come rushing to our aid. Fortunately, by the time Jude was released, the worst of the repercussive effects were behind him. Nonetheless, his body could still betray him at any time. After one infusion, his diarrhea became so intractable we were at a loss. Jude couldn't leave the bathroom. He was dehydrated, miserable, and growing frightened. After numerous consultations, the doctors finally determined we would have to bring in a stool sample in order to test it for certain rare bacteria strains that could manifest in an immunocompromised person's bowels. The only problem was that the feces needed to be deposited at the laboratory within thirty minutes of capture. They suggested Jude be admitted so that they could take the sample on the spot.

Jude refused. He wanted no part of being in that hospital any more than necessary. He also wasn't sure he could make it to the hospital without an accident. We both knew what this meant. Now, parents will do anything for the health of their children. There are some things we expect to do, others we hope never to do, and some things we can't imagine we would ever do. This fell into the latter category. After Jude's next bout, I carefully captured some of the noxious material in a special receptacle and delicately prepared it for transport. The instructions were to "keep warm and not to jostle." One would think I had been instructed to care for a Fabergé egg. I wrapped the specimen in an insulating cloth, hopped in my car, and held the prize aloft to not jostle it while I sped to the hospital.

When I arrived, there were some construction issues near the regular parking, and two of the entrances were closed. Because of Covid and hospital security, the line to enter was both exceedingly long and stagnant. It was cold outside. I placed the feces in my coat pocket, enclosing it with my hand, keeping it warm. I felt like a hen responsible for one precious egg. As the clock ticked, I grew impatient and worried. This was not an enterprise that demanded a repeat performance. I fully intended this to be a one-time operation.

The line remained static. People in front of me hopped from foot to foot, trying to stay warm. The clock kept ticking. I only had a few minutes remaining before they would reject the sample. Desperation supplanted social niceties. "Excuse me, please step aside," I boldly announced while attempting to squeeze past the line. People turned and looked at me like I was a disheveled vagrant, which was not far from the truth. Reversible jogging pants, an oversized coat, and a worn baseball hat do not convey authority. "Please step aside," I firmly repeated. Nobody moved.

I waited another minute. The line was in stasis. My frantic and frustrated mind started to churn. I could not believe I was about to be thwarted by a logjam of people waiting to get into a hospital. I pulled the vial out of my pocket and yelled, "Biohazard! Need to get through! Make way for the biohazard."

I strode forward with the diarrhea held before me like a radioactive shield. The presence of the vial parted everyone like the Red Sea. The security guards waved me through, and I sprinted across the atrium and up the stairs to the after-hours laboratory—gingerly holding the feces above my head so it wouldn't slosh about. With minutes to spare, I deposited the precious cargo with the lab technician, gingerly handing it over like it was a newborn infant. The tech regarded me with incredulity and not a little concern. I suppose it's not every day someone's dad desperately sprints into your laboratory cradling a fistful of feces.

• • •

The parasitic monster of cancer remained insatiable. It had already consumed Jude's independence. It was consuming his dignity, and it was gnawing on his will. It was threatening to consume his leg and had designs on Jude's very life. Some of these morsels were acceptable casualties. Certainly, independence and dignity could be re-cultivated, weight regained, and energy restored. The fight was unfair, but it was still a fight, and Jude was pushing back gallantly. The first significant blow to his determination was the loss of his hair.

Now, this may seem rather silly. Nearly everyone who has any working knowledge or experience of cancer recognizes hair loss as a rather trivial sideshow to the serious war raging on other fronts. But for Jude, his hair was a crown jewel. As an infant, he was born with a dark, dense, unruly mane. For a moment, it lightened, threatening to become blond. This turned out to be a unique and fleeting iteration of his hair saga. By the time he entered school, his hair had taken on the consistency of a beaver pelt. It was impenetrable. When he took a bath, he would dip his head underwater for as long as his breath allowed, then re-emerge with all the water sluicing off the crown like a surprised cataract. Despite total immersion, his hair remained perfectly dry. A magician would have paid a mint for such capabilities. To properly wash it, we would have to dig our hands into his scalp and first knead water, then shampoo, deep into the roots. And with soap acting as a chemical sponge, attracting the water through his formidable thicket, it would take multiple dunkings and liberally applied buckets to rinse everything away.

Puberty brought another drastic change. Until his growth spurt, Jude's hair had been arrow straight, void of any body, wave, or curl. In just a few months' time, it softened and developed abundant, graceful ringlets. Had I not witnessed the change firsthand, I would have assumed it was fabricated. Alas, it was a true metamorphosis. Completely unpredictable. He wore the change with the pride and dignity of a monarch's crown.

Shortly after our return to the condo, following the second round of chemo, Jude took a shower while I read a book. The day was sunny, we had no hospital obligations, and it appeared for the first time in a long time we would be blessed with a simple respite.

"Dad!" Jude yelled from the shower. I immediately jumped to attention, ready to attend a disaster. His call was not aggrieved, however. He sounded whiny, even petulant.

"Is everything okay?" I yelled back, strategically stationing myself next to the bathroom door.

"It's happening," he cried.

I sat in silence, waiting for an explanation. What was happening? Was he puking again? Had he expelled his gastric tube while vomiting? Would we have to make another run to the ER?

"Ummm, would you care to elaborate?" I was almost afraid to ask.

"My hair," he gasped. "It's happening, Dad. It's starting to come out." His forlorn expression was gut-wrenching but also endearing. This was a known casualty and not a source of worry. For Jude, however, it was like murdering his cult of personality.

"Hey buddy, we knew this was going to happen. It's okay. You can rock any style!" I tried to sound upbeat. "Is a bunch of it falling out? Is it plugging the drain?"

"Not yet," he replied, "but my hands are full of the stuff." That was likely an understatement. He possessed much more than a handful. We could measure his hair in bushels.

"Well, what would you like me to do?" I asked.

"I think it has to go. I don't want to shed like a dog." His tone was simultaneously resigned and depressed—like he was giving up a baby for adoption.

He appeared in his bathrobe, moving with all the gravity of a funeral dirge. I set up a chair on the deck and organized the clippers. We took one last picture and ran our hands through his unkempt mop, savoring the springiness and astounding density. A few curls let go, torn free by our touch. I started to get choked up. The ongoing diminishment of my once-robust son continued to chisel chinks from my emotional armor.

"Alright," Jude chirped, shaking the hair from his hands. "Let's have some fun with this!" He flipped a psychological switch, instantly jumping from sullen and morose to jubilance. Here was another opportunity to have a unique experience, to be frivolous, to playfully stand at the trailhead of an untrodden path and investigate a new vista. His capacity to embrace positivity and delight was infectious. I was supposed to be the one supporting and guiding, lifting him through his darkest trials. Here I was, glum and angered over his hair. So Jude buoyed me, displaying an unimaginable selflessness. He refused to focus on what he didn't have or what was being taken away. Instead, he worked with unflinching diligence to open any gifts available.

We had fun. I shaved a line right through the middle of his head. We laughed hysterically. I could barely hold the clippers. We debated the merits of attempting a perfectly coiffed tonsure, or something less refined. Eventually, after a few more "artistic" cuts, we shaved one side of his head. He looked like a cross between Cyndi Lauper and Mike Score from A Flock of Seagulls. We played with this for a few minutes until the hair clippings grew itchy and the cold air settled in. Eventually, I shaved the other side, leaving just a few beautiful curls in the front for the purposes of saying goodbye. We performed the last rites on his hair, and with a fanciful flourish, I zipped away the remaining sacred locks. I took great care with those last ringlets, however. They were going home to his mother.

HOLIDAY

"Work to become, not to acquire."

ELBERT HUBBARD

Using words like *blessing* or *luck* are ghastly absurdities when chronicling the vagaries of chemotherapy. In Jude's case, it turned out that every fifth weekend his white blood cell count would elevate to the point where he could convalesce in his hometown, two hours from the hospital, and see both friends and family. Granted, we were embroiled in the heat of the Covid-19 crisis, so large get-togethers were problematic, but because of his radically depressed immune system the circumstances appeared to work in his favor. Providentially, those fifth weekends happened to fall on Thanksgiving and Christmas. Thanksgiving was Jude's first trip home since the commencement of chemotherapy, and we were all excited.

The holidays acquire an urgency when your family is in crisis. When life is simple, or uneventful, the holidays can possess any type of flavor you inject into them. In 2020, we were desperate for Thanksgiving. Our celebration that year was a far cry from our typical Thanksgiving experience. It consisted only of our immediate family, we were in our own home, and Jude looked like a ghost. His skin was flaccid, bone white, like someone slathered him with curdled milk. He was bald, except for a few stubborn patches desperately resisting the ravages of his treatment. Their presence cultivated a macabre appearance to his countenance, but he resisted parting with them for they represented a treasured part of the past he was reticent to relinquish. Perhaps the most difficult change was his lack of energy. Jude always sat at the head of the table, holding court, serving as a liaison between his younger siblings and their parents. He was the conversational glue that kept mealtime lively and engaging. His personality catalyzed the rest of us, fueling the emotional synergy necessary for a vibrant Veltkamp ethos.

He attempted to reprise his role, but the shackles of his circumstances handcuffed our merriment. Behind every witticism and guffaw lurked a tension which could not be teased apart. We all did our best to ignore it, to recapture the flavor of past Thanksgivings, but the tyranny of the present possesses a morbid talent for continuously reminding you that reality is not an illusion, a personal fiction, a fantasy one can whimsically discard. Reality does not lie. The volume of Jude's circumstance screamed the truth with such stentorian solemnity that conversation proved difficult.

Jody and I worked hard to fabricate normalcy. Jude did not want special treatment. His gaze was always leveled outward, never at himself. He could not abide pity. So, we obliged him. That Thanksgiving, we made him pick up his room, put away his clothes, even help clean his bathroom. All five of us squeezed into the kitchen with a moratorium on departure until the dishes were finished. He went out with friends, stayed up late, and got out of bed when we asked him to. He did not receive any special favors, and it seemed to energize him. His old high school football coaches came to visit and in a blessed moment of prescience, interacted with Jude like colleagues, casually reminiscing about the glory days. For a moment, the ever-expanding balloon of tension compressed, and Jude repossessed his assuredly mischievous glimmer. To see that spark, however fleeting, was like a beacon of hope. My son was still very much himself—a consumer of life, and lover of people. That was something to be thankful for.

DECISIONS

"Trust in the Lord with all your heart and do not lean on your own understanding. In all your ways acknowledge Him, and He will make your paths straight."

PROVERBS 3:5-6

The bitter pall of Jude's unfortunate circumstances crashed rapidly into the foreground when the Thanksgiving holiday ended. Jude had a decision to make, and it was a choice I wish for no person. Osteosarcoma is a surgical cancer. Chemotherapy is used to keep the cancer at bay and hopefully "mop up" any metastasizing cells. It is not curative. If Jude was going to be cured, the present tumor would need to be excised.

The difficulty was the tumor resided in a delicate position. It originated near the proximal head of his tibia, just below the knee joint, and expanded explosively. His leg looked like it had a grapefruit squished irreverently into the side of his shin, grinning malevolently at any who chose to inspect it. When he donned shorts or cutoffs, the discrepancy between his legs was eerie. I could hardly bear to look. I knew what lurked beneath the surface, at the distress it caused and what it portended. Its presence in our lives sickened me. It had to go. The question was how? How could we excise this hideous monster while minimizing collateral damage?

Jude's surgeons at Seattle Children's Hospital were convinced the safest way was to remove his leg above the knee. This would guarantee eradication of all current tumor growth and potential future growth. Leaving any malignancy behind was obviously out of the question. Recurrence of the tumor at the primary tumor site was a death sentence.

We were desperate to find a way to guarantee a clean excision while salvaging Jude's knee. Thanks to many contacts within the medical community, we had access to some of the brightest minds and most accomplished surgeons in the country. I spent hours discussing options with osteosarcoma surgeons from Texas, Chicago, California, and Arizona. We had multiple chairs of various radiology departments review Jude's scans. We discussed cutting-edge techniques and innovative strategies designed to maximize efficacy and minimize resection. I agonized over Jude's predicament and became so emotionally tormented over Jude's decision it incapacitated me. I could not sleep; I could barely eat. All I could see was my beautiful, ebullient, able-bodied boy languishing on a single leg.

In an amazing act of focus, Jude abolished all thoughts of the future from his working emotional state and lived strictly in the present. As an endorsement of his father, he turned all research over to me and granted me the trust and faith to present him with salient information. Somehow, as the deadline for the decision approached, Jude maintained frivolity, enjoying video games, building Lego sets, and joking with his friends. He hated being sequestered due to his immune status, but the beauty and benefit of modern technology is that communication and social interaction are only just a click away. His relationships sustained him.

While he played, I wept. I was in awe of my own son, who could accept his fate, his altered future, with a complacent, almost gracious composure. As parents, we work with desperate integrity to protect our children. We assiduously mitigate perceived threats to their well-being. We cling tightly to the notion that what has worked favorably in our own lives will work to their benefit. We attempt to mold our children into better versions of ourselves. But our children are not us. Jude was not me. Culture, family, DNA, experience, and a host of other variables made him singularly unique. The temptation was to grieve Jude's potential loss of limb—to mourn for what would never be. As a parent, there is nothing more traumatic than watching your child suffer. I knew Jude could be irreparably altered in a fashion that placed him on an ineluctable trajectory, a trajectory far different from my own.

There is nothing I wouldn't do to remove his burden. I did not have that option, however, and it maddened me. Ultimately, the decision was his. How does an eighteen-year-old process a decision of that magnitude? How does a young man, who has spent his life running, jumping, dancing, cavorting—who has taken his ableness for granted—voluntarily become disabled? Jude was always a distractible and mercurial child. His early adolescence was riddled with emotional lability, recalcitrance, and a remarkable capacity to blurt shameful inanities at the least opportune moments. He discovered a circle of friends, a core group of brothers, through organized football. Part of his identity was tied to that sport. I coached football and one of my dearest privileges was coaching my son. For years, even during those times when Jude was least accessible, we could always go into the yard and play a simple game of catch. It was a rarity if a week passed without us tossing the football around. The day Jude chose to amputate his leg, he made a video labeled, "I found out I will never play football again." We watched it together and bawled.

As is the case with nearly all the choices Jude made, he did not look backwards. Once decided, he faced squarely into the headwind and marched forward. This amazed me. It was inspiring to witness him continue his journey void of any buyer's remorse. The entire affair emotionally eviscerated me. While Jude soared, I stumbled, digging my fists into the earth in a desperate bid to halt time. But the calendar inexorably marched towards the December 16 surgical date, gaining momentum like falling dominoes.

I could not talk to him about it, as I did not want to crumble his resolve, but I also did not know how to help shoulder his burden of choice. Finally, in a solemn act of celebration and departure, I ferried him to the park a few blocks from our condominium. It was cold and windy, yet crystal clear. The sun sparkled brilliantly off Lake Washington, highlighting the windsurfers, wetsuit-clad swimmers, and scores of geese. We stood side by side, marveling with unspoken solemnity as we watched children cavort freely on two legs, playing, laughing, skipping, jumping. My heart lurched in anticipation of the inevitable.

I deliberately removed a football from my backpack. It was one a friend had procured, personally signed for Jude by Hall of Fame quarterback Steve Young. The ball was meant for display, but I suspect Steve would both condone and encourage my intentions. I casually separated from Jude, walking a few steps away, and wrestled a smile into shape. Jude looked at me quizzically for a moment, saw the football, and nodded his head. He smiled as well. Maintaining balance was tricky for him. His leg was partially paralyzed, the tibia still fractured. It constantly throbbed, and if he pushed with any vigor, the response was staggeringly painful. But with his unplumbed resolve, motivated through the power of nostalgia and benevolence, he indulged his father. For a tiny instant, it felt casual, welcome, like donning an old shoe. Out of force of habit, we arranged ourselves in the equivalent of a first-down distance apart, and in the frigid wind and brilliant sunshine, Jude silently retrieved the last passes he would ever receive from me on his own two legs.

Normally, our ten-yard separation would stretch into twenty, and then possibly thirty. He would start to run around, and I would hurl passes to the limit of his reach, forcing him to stretch or dive in order to make the catch. Although his condition could not afford us the complete experience, time reversed, the anxiety of the moment evaporated, and we laughed and joked like we had for so many years—a dad simply playing with his son. No agenda, no pressure, no goals. It was as genuine a moment as the circumstances could conjure, and we basked in the purity of the experience.

I have never met a parent who did not, at some point in their parenting journey, wish for time to stand still. Jude's condition was too severe, and his misery too poignant, for me to pause time, but I wanted to freeze that feeling, to imprison it within an immutable capsule I could draw upon in the future. There is nothing more liberating than being fully invested in the present. Jude managed this with enviable regularity. It was rapturous to experience it together. Throwing that football drew me into my son's soul. However fleeting, it was a beautiful place to reside.

The wind blows hardest on the highest mountain tops. We were at the pinnacle, as father and son, but it did not take long for Jude to flag. He had no stamina. Any physical duress required herculean effort to sustain. As desperate as I was for him to persevere, this moment was not about me. None of this was about me. It was all for him, just as our game of catch was symbolic of our unity. I began walking a little closer, acknowledging his fading strength, but continued tossing the ball with as much gentleness as I could muster. I tried to aim for his chest, but my tears fractured this target into a glistening kaleidoscope. I tossed the last pass underhanded, intentionally off target, and he reflexively reached out with one large, strong hand and gripped the ball securely, tucking it into his chest with a sure, practiced motion. I gave him a powerful hug. It was an embrace which mourned that which would never be.

"It's okay, Dad," Jude spoke softly, almost tenderly. "It's going to be okay."

"It's not okay," I sobbed. "Nothing about this is okay." I gripped the front of his sweatshirt with both my fists, stridently exclaiming, "YOU…DON'T…DESERVE THIS," as if I could expel the cancer from his body by sheer force of will.

"This is what is going to happen," Jude replied. His succinct, necessary resolve unmanned me. "This is what is best. I don't want this, but it's the best choice. I can handle it."

"I don't want you to 'handle it,'" I growled. "No one should have to handle this. No one should have to make this choice, especially not an eighteen-year-old."

"This won't ruin me, Dad." He separated from our embrace and gazed sternly into my eye. The sun shone behind his head, creating a glowing penumbra that framed his shoulders. His frailty became regal, almost imposing.

"Don't think about what I won't be able to do. Think about what I will do. I'll still be me, just a different version, perhaps. But still me."

"I'm going to miss watching you run," I opined. "I loved watching you run."

"Just wait," Jude replied. "I'll still be able to beat you in a race." He laughed then, having no compunctions about teasing me in my sorrow.

"I will hold you to that promise." I smiled, but Jude recognized the desperate sincerity beneath my expression.

We walked for a bit in silence—he with a ginger, awkward drop-foot cadence that drew many stares. I leaned close, with the pretense of shielding him from the wind, but really just wanting to experience the shape of his whole self. I didn't want a different version of my son. I could feel the bitterness rising, a reflexive gall of disdain for the unfair circumstance precipitating this day.

"Dad, I mean it. I meant it. It's going to be okay." Jude had always been empathic. He possessed a keen sense of where he stood in the eyes of his parents. When he was younger, he used that preternatural skill to manipulate and dodge emotional tension, mostly created by his juvenile machinations. Age had cultivated a depth of insight he used to see directly into other's hearts. Now his grievous circumstance forced an artificial maturation, startling in its rapidity. I could not veil my remorse from him.

"I want to believe you, Jude. I really do. But I'm your dad. It's my job to protect you." I put my arm around his shoulder, forcing a tense laugh. He briefly leaned his head against my cheek with a rarely exercised tenderness. The world around us felt very heavy, but very clean. I sensed the unequivocal purity of his conviction. He raised his head and smiled.

"Dad, you've already done more than any person I know could have done. The reason I am able to go through with this is because if there was any other option, any better way, you would have found it. You and Mom have made the choice simple and easy for me." He spoke with such sincerity and certitude that I nearly believed it. "Besides, I know you'll get me the coolest new leg ever. Maybe it will even have a mobile my friends can connect to, or let me hop forward with the foot facing backward?!" He started laughing.

I found nothing funny about any of this. I forced a smile, but I suspect it looked more like a grimace. Jude started hopping about, trying to imitate a backwards foot. He was getting dragged through the bowels of hell, but possessed enough vitality to infect me with his contagious attitude. I started laughing, a genuine laugh. I'd almost forgotten how to do that. I imagined a new future with Jude showing off his prosthetic leg, performing party tricks, and manufacturing fun like he always had. We both laughed louder, drawing questionable looks from many bystanders. Jude was bald, with a hose hanging out of his nose. None of the passersby could look at him and envision humor on any level. Yet once again, Jude had reversed the script and managed to comfort me. His attitude transcended my vilest demeanor, cleansed my frustration, and proved how beautiful a life can become when it is lived without resentment.

A CLOSED DOOR

*"Of all the words of mice and men,
the saddest are, 'It might have been.'"*

KURT VONNEGUT

Being courageous in the face of adversity is a laudable character trait. Sometimes, circumstances foist courage upon us even when we prefer timidity. To this day, I still cannot comprehend the courage required for Jude to crawl into the car with Jody on a dark, dreary, emotionally oppressive morning and drive to the hospital with the express intent of having his leg removed. He had other options. We had explored everything. Up until hours before the scheduled surgery, I had either met with, or been on the phone with, a myriad of orthopedic surgeons, desperately grasping for alternative solutions. Some practitioners were rather confident they could save Jude's leg and free him from cancer. Their certainty was compelling, but when pressed, even the most confident among them agreed amputation was the safest route.

I do not know how he did it. Jody took a little video of him limping through the hospital doors. This was the last footage we have of him walking on the two legs God blessed him with. He walked with confidence and purpose. The beauty of Jude is that he lived life facing forward. He rarely, if ever, looked back with regret. He never wallowed or mourned what was past. I remember sitting with him in the hospital, asking him about this trait, which I found nearly inexplicable.

"Do you ever review, in your mind, things you've done or said in the past and wished you hadn't?"

Jude regarded me cautiously, not quite sure what I was driving towards. I have a bad habit of asking a lot of outlandish questions. He wasn't always in the mood to entertain them. "I suppose," he finally answered, "but I don't dwell on it."

"But you think about it?" I pressed.

"Sort of. If I've done something I regret, I remember to not do it again."

"How do you remember if you don't think about it? Don't you mull it over and figure out what a better solution would be?" I was genuinely curious. I had no conception of how a person could move through life without constantly reviewing their actions and being heavily influenced by past failures—or successes.

"No. What happened is over. I can't change it. The exact same situation will never happen again. I think I let my mistakes shape me, but I don't get obsessed with them or let them rule me. What a sucky way to live your life." He regarded me incredulously. It was as if my question had no context within his lived experience.

"So, are you saying you have no shame?" I really wanted to reveal the truth of his attitude. I did not believe him.

"I think there are times when I've been ashamed, certainly, but I don't keep looking back on those times and feel guilty or embarrassed. Well, maybe a little embarrassed." He laughed mischievously. "But only when I focus on it. And my focusing on it isn't going to change it. Why would you want to walk around hanging on to regret?"

"I would think to make yourself a better person," I answer quickly. "So you know how to avoid adding more mistakes to the growing pile. To limit the pile of mounting regret."

"I think you can improve yourself and even bless those around you without focusing on regret, or your past, or your history of mistakes. If you do that, all you'll do is become self-conscious and timid, living each day afraid.

That sounds horrible." He sank back into his pillows and peacefully closed his eyes. I contemplated those thoughts, unsure what to make of them. Suddenly Jude snapped his head from the pillow, like he'd been pinched, and regarded me rather seriously. I was paying very close attention now. It was not like him to vigorously analyze a thought.

He stared at me for what must have been the better part of a minute. I felt like an unenlightened pupil about to be chastised for my ignorance. "Part of forgiving others is the ability to forgive yourself," he declared rather sternly. Then he turned away and fiddled with his phone, instantly preoccupied with answering the thousands of Snapchats that had likely piled up while he was napping. I sat in the still darkness of his hospital room, wrestling with the deep wisdom lurking behind his words. I still wrestle with it.

．．．

The doctors and nurses created a painted stamp of his left foot, a memento by which he could remember his lost limb. He asked them if he could keep his severed appendage. This grisly request was met with grisly incredulity. I am not sure anyone had made such an entreaty, and they did not know how to respond. Jude was informed that the limb would need to be analyzed and taken apart for a proper pathological report and would need to be disposed of properly, as it was considered biohazardous material. Jude remonstrated by stating the very obvious yet unspoken fact that his limb was his, and although he was granting them permission to remove it, he was not giving them permission to take it. "What are you going to do with it?" they asked. "It's dead tissue. It's not attached."

"I understand that," Jude replied. "Maybe I'll just put it in my room. Or maybe I'll hang it from the ceiling or turn it into a cane. I don't know exactly. But it's my leg."

"Actually, it's not," came the definitive reply. "Once it's removed it becomes the property of the hospital."

"Isn't that like stealing?" Jude asked. "I grew it. It's me!"

"We understand that, but legally all biohazardous waste needs to be disposed of properly. This includes your leg."

"Alright," Jude replied, satisfied with their answer. "I thought it would be unique to have my leg as a room ornament." He laughed as if that would be a natural consequence of an amputation. The nonplussed staff attempted to laugh with him. They failed.

Modern-day amputations are not the hurried, haphazard affairs of the past. Because of rapidly changing technology and the potential for neural generation and cybernetics, Jude's surgeons wanted to preserve as much delicate tissue as possible. They dissected out the nerves which traveled to his lower limb, conserved the muscles in his upper leg, reshaped the severed end of his femur to round and soften the edges, and buried the ends of the salvaged nerves into the muscles of his upper leg in case they could be repurposed in the future. What used to take twenty minutes forty years ago, or ninety seconds during the Civil War, took nearly four hours for Jude.

When he emerged from the operatory, he was still Jude, but without twenty pounds of leg and one giant tumor. I was not there to bear witness to the big reveal. Covid restricted participation to one person, and I was virtually worthless at this point. I was so shaken by Jude's decision, I became a slave to my emotions. Jody was much more stalwart and realistic about Jude's choice. Additionally, she was a much more sensitive recovery room operative than me, with the patience and fortitude of an army of Florence Nightingales. They made a great team.

I fretted and mourned the entire day. I sat at home, alone, staring listlessly at the dark windows while I brooded over the imminent phone call. I anxiously anticipated Jude's response to his severed leg. I feared he would finally learn the meaning of regret and be emotionally terrorized when introduced to his abhorrent stump.

I was crying so deeply when the phone rang, I nearly missed it. The thought of his life being irrevocably altered was too potent to digest. It was impossible to discard my desire for what should be, instead of embracing what would be. My fear and anger reached the tipping point.

"Hey, honey, we're all set up in recovery." Jody's voice was pleasant, almost cheery. I could not get any words out because I was choking on my own tears. "Jude's doing really well," she assured me. "How are you doing, Jude?"

"Great!" Jude shouted. The energy in his voice startled me. "Everything feels good."

"Are you sure?" I muttered, stumbling over the words. I felt like I had a mouthful of crushed glass. "Does it feel weird?" I worked very hard to keep my voice from cracking.

"I don't feel much right now," Jude said. "When the blanket is on, I can't even tell my leg is gone."

"Do you freak out when you look down there?" I blurted. I wanted to snatch the words back, but I also wanted honesty—from all of us.

"No," he responded quickly. "I mean, I don't have a leg, and that's weird. But I knew that's what was going to happen. C'mon, it's not like I went in to get a tattoo removed or something and I came out without a leg." He started laughing again and Jody joined him.

"How's he really doing?" I whispered into the phone, so only Jody could hear me.

"Really, really well," she assured me once again. "It's all good. He's good."

After we disconnected, I slumped back into my chair, utterly exhausted. The last two months had exacted a ferocious toll. Our working mantra, since Jude's diagnosis, had been a call to arms from the broader community, soliciting prayer for Jude's faith, his life, and his leg. We weren't even three months into this battle and one of those requests had been emphatically denied. I buried my face in my hands, moaning in frustration. Parents have the pleasure of watching their children grow. Children evolve, accrete, and expand. With each passing day, these additions fold and coalesce, layering like an encaustic artwork. The physical, emotional, intellectual, and spiritual properties are additive. In a grisly reversal, Jude was diminishing. From my unenlightened perspective, it was as if the steadily evolving work of art that was my son had part of the canvas erased. His trajectory was unnatural. I shook my fist at the heavens, audibly groaning in anguish and abject frustration. It was becoming more and more tempting to hold God accountable. It would not be the last time I felt this way.

...

The day after surgery came with more laughter, jocularity, and playfulness. Jude charmed all the nurses while he attempted to pull various stunts with his stump. It also brought a great deal of pain. Immediately following the procedure, after Jude recovered from anesthesia, his stump was numb. His doctors had loaded it up with ample amounts of local anesthetic and then pumped him full of narcotics. The local anesthetic wore off during the night, just when the massive swelling ensued. This swelling, coupled with severed nerve endings, repositioned nerves, and a brain desperately trying to make sense of a limb that should still exist, invited exquisite agony. Agony may even be a gross misuse of the term. Incredibly, he remained enthusiastic and resilient. Had it been me in his predicament, I suspect I would have succumbed to intense depression. Instead, Jude charged forward. I wished to stay behind and remain comfortable in my sadness and doubt, but Jude pulled all of us forward into what would be a newly balanced life. He refused to let Jody and I embrace fear, because he would not be shaken.

This did not mean it was easy, however. The pain was intense, as anyone who has suffered an amputation of this magnitude can attest. The end of the stump swells, the nerve endings fire randomly, desperate to find something to plug into, gravity pools blood at the suture site, and phantom leg pain begins in earnest. Adding to the difficulties is the fact that your body is radically out of balance. Where there were once two posts, there is now only one—except it thinks it's paired. Your body wants to keep tipping over. Repositioning requires significant overcorrections, and the weight inequity elicits a proprioceptive dissonance that is difficult to shed. It's not like you or I just standing on one foot, because even when you balance on one foot, you have the other leg to serve as a counterweight. The first time Jude stood up to try and pee, he nearly shot across the room. Fortunately, his nurses and therapists were very familiar with this phenomenon, and they worked hard to guard against it. What potentially could have been a careening human pogo stick, pinballing off sensitive medical equipment, vases, and utilities, turned into a rather benign lurch before two helpers corralled him with a walker. Jude's support team was remarkably adept at smoothing his transition, employing any number of resources and aids to help him succeed.

Despite the help, the transition was very difficult. Cognitively, physically, emotionally—he had significant challenges to negotiate. It would be one thing if, after having the procedure, he could be fitted with a prosthetic and dive into aggressive physical therapy and a specific training regimen for prosthetic legs. Because of the healing process, it takes time for the stump to transform into something that can handle a prosthetic sleeve, and so he had to traverse a transitory period. This required crutches, wheelchairs, hopping, sliding, army crawling—nearly every mode of transportation except the most natural and readily accessible: walking.

We learned very quickly that our home did not remotely threaten to be wheelchair accessible. We had stairs everywhere. Every shower had a six-inch lip. Some of the hallways and doorways were too narrow, and of course, we had no grab bars or any mechanism to support oneself anywhere. I challenge anyone with two legs to take a shower balancing only on one leg—without cheating. On crutches, you can manage to get into the shower easily enough (try negotiating a shower lip without crutches—and no, hopping over the lip on one leg onto a damp and slippery shower pan is not a good idea). But then you need to store your crutches somewhere you can access them, either in the shower itself or just outside so you can reach them easily. So far, so good. Now adjust the water temperature and get settled into the stream while remaining in balance. If you properly negotiate that hurdle, then comes the real test. Shampoo your hair and rinse it all away with your eyes closed without the use of any grab bars. This is easier in a smaller shower, as you can lean against a wall or put out an elbow to maintain equilibrium. In a larger, modern shower, it is nearly impossible. Once you're comfortable with that skill, do it all again, but this time after ingesting a whopping dose of chemotherapy…

CHRISTMAS/ADVENT

"There are two ways to live your life. One is as though nothing is a miracle. The other is as though everything is a miracle."

ALBERT EINSTEIN

Covid allowed for only one parent to be present in the hospital. The only exception was on surgery days, when two parents were allowed to wait together during the procedure. This made little sense to me, as the one time your child was unaware of your proximity was when they were under general anesthesia. After the procedure was completed, the one-parent rule resumed.

From a scheduling standpoint, it made more sense for Jody to be with Jude during his procedure as well as the subsequent recovery period. I did not see the "new" Jude until they drove home together, five days later. I had been preparing for his arrival by creating wider walkways throughout the home and installing grab bars in multiple showers. His lifelong room and bathroom were in the basement, a full flight of stairs with a landing and 180-degree reversal near the bottom. I had no idea how he would be able to negotiate this challenge, so we prepared multiple contingencies.

I eagerly and anxiously tracked their progress home on my phone, emotionally steeling myself for Jude's arrival. I honestly had no idea what to expect. I did not know how he would respond with his new body once in a familiar setting. It is one thing to accept one's predicament when your entire frame of reference is novel. There are no comparisons, which enables the suppression of regret, frustration, and nostalgia. With the familiarity of home, I was deeply concerned his brave attitude would crumble, transmogrifying into remorse and unwarranted self-antipathy. As he crutched his way through our garage entryway, utilizing a somewhat stilted and ungainly one-legged technique, I forced myself to greet him with an approving smile and tender hug. This was, on the one hand, authentic. I was very excited to see him and incredibly proud of his capacity to fight through the trauma while embracing his new trajectory. On the other hand, my pleasant countenance may have been the most hypocritical expression I had ever produced. It is a terrible and torturous experience to witness the suffering and diminishment of your child. Internally, I battled a nearly irrepressible urge to fall to the floor, beat my fists into the ground, and berate the Almighty for the injustice in this world. Jude was maimed, and there was nothing to be done about it. I was unable to rescue him. I had failed my child, and he was the one to suffer because of it.

* * *

In our household, Christmas is unassailable, its presence magic. The anticipation served as a divine emollient, which somehow eradicated any strife, anxiety, or fracture which could be present in the Veltkamp home. Granted, we did not often suffer from any of those maladies, so the theurgy required rarely taxed the supernatural, but the ethos Christmas generated was very tangible. Even when Jude embraced his most irascible, incorrigible persona, Christmas blunted these manifestations and managed to draw our family close, like a complimentary, prepackaged bow. Everyone in our household enjoyed both giving and receiving gifts. Jody, who is a natural gift giver and one of the most generous people extant, worked doubly hard to cultivate this spirit of giving, and it made for a wonderful experience.

Advent means, "the coming." As Christians, we celebrated Advent, both the joy of knowing Christ has come and the enthusiastic anticipation of His return. Christmas is a time to celebrate what the Incarnation provided. Advent serves as a glorious reminder of what is yet in store. But this anticipation is not passive. Much like an expectant mother, waiting involves preparation, prayer, work, rebuilding healthy habits, and reorienting the self. Labor brings with it tears, joy, pain, blood, release, and an altered community. Jude experienced his own advent. Between the trauma of his diagnosis, chemotherapy, and agonizing choices, he had been simultaneously squeezed into the role of a mother in labor and a child reborn. Jody and I served as his midwives.

The timing of Christmas could not have been more glorious. Although Jude had a very long and arduous road of chemotherapy ahead of him, he had, for all intents and purposes, reached the nadir of his process. He had suffered through the worst of the poisons and learned he could handle them. He had worked through the anxiety of the unknown and fully grasped the enormity of his choices. He had experienced the indignity of losing his strength, his hair, a limb—and instead of jettisoning his identity, he had embraced the changes. He remade himself, freshly born, as the Jude who would emerge from this fiery trial. He blessed us that Christmas.

* * *

Despite his infirmity, weakness, and crushing malaise, Jude embraced freedom from therapy like a prisoner on parole. Adequate wound healing demanded a three-week respite from the rigors of chemo. The chemical harshness had obliterated the regenerative capacity of the cells in his body. His doctors did not want to wait too long—although three weeks was standard—as unabated carpet bombing served as the gold standard for remission of osteosarcoma. There was a fine line between allowing the right cells to regenerate and letting the wrong cells recover.

Jude came back to life. The week between Christmas and New Year's Day felt like a POW liberation party. Every day, Jude would either have friends over or be about town, enjoying the camaraderie of his old haunts. Never mind he was without most of a leg and had to negotiate a swollen stump with sixty ugly staples crimped into his flesh. He could be with people. His people. They served as the ultimate balm. Never discount the healing power of community or the regenerative capacity of friendship. Suffering alone is a cruelty that should be reserved for no one. Jude's three-week leave of absence from Children's Hospital and the sequestered confines of our condominium in Seattle was the ultimate Christmas salve.

It is difficult to recognize providence. It is harder still to discern miracles. The greatest miracle ever recorded was the birth of Christ—the Incarnation—and scant few witnessed or believed it. We were praying for a miracle. We desperately wanted Jude to be cured. We desired his faith to take shape and his life to be preserved. Obscured by those pleas, drowned out by cries for mercy, was the provision of providence. Jude's temporary surcease from chemotherapy fell on the exact dates all his friends were available. This happenstance was so unlikely it defied any other explanation. And while our feeble faith inexpertly grasped at the possibility of providence, we completely missed the true miracle occurring: friendship and family. We expect miracles to be a light show of radiance and power. I suspect most miracles are taken for granted. The miracle of Christmas is not just knowing Christ *was* and hoping He *will be*. Jude's resurgence reminded us Christ is also *now*.

TIME

"The two most powerful warriors are patience and time."
LEO TOLSTOY

The movies get a lot of things wrong. This statement will come as no surprise. The entertainment industry is so pervasive in our culture and exerts so much influence, however, that what is portrayed on screen possesses an insidious capacity to insinuate itself into our consciousness. Take relationships. Most movie relationships present as dynamic, irrepressible infatuations, which commandeer the sensibilities of a potential couple and inexorably drive them together, regardless of circumstance, responsibilities, or necessity. Eventually, they encounter a hurdle which presses against the irresistible, magnetic pull of their nascent love, forcing them to overcome an obviously contrived adversity. This hurdle is invariably surmounted. Not without some degree of angst, of course, but the resolution creates, in its wake, a future defined by tranquility and endless fulfillment. They live happily ever after.

No one has ever had a marriage like that. The answer is simple: People are complicated. Marriages change, mature, evolve, develop. Life pushes and pulls, strains and tugs. Infatuation is fleeting. What drew you close at your inception may serve to push you apart later. What was once endearing becomes aggravating. What was once exotic becomes banal. Those who have steadfast, enlivening, enduring, and fulfilling marriages recognize this.

They recognize that love, and the commitment which accompanies it, is not something that happens to you, but something you enact. Love is a choice. It is an accomplishment. It is not an event. For a relationship to truly "work," both partners recognize that they are faced with a daily choice—the decision to love for another day. Movies turn love into a passive experience. They depict love as an ephemeral spirit, independent and mercurial. This is quite the opposite of what love really is—and imminently devastating to any person believing this lie.

Another obvious example is the abuse of the laws of nature. It is a rarity in cinema to witness a screenplay consistent with how we understand physics, chemistry, and biology to operate. Often this is intentional, and agreeably so. There would be no Marvel superheroes, no Harry Potter, no Luke Skywalker without a deliberate bending or reimagining of physical reality. Imagining the supernatural and fantastical is compelling and endearing. This is the brilliance of cinema. However, most movies aren't designed to develop superheroes and transcendent, mystical superhumans. They are designed to portray a particular story in the world as we know it, in which all the laws of nature are intact and operating. Yet how many times have we witnessed a car fly through the air, flip over multiple times, come careening to a halt, only to have the driver, who is unscathed, push the vehicle back into gear and zoom away? How many explosions have we witnessed in the vacuum of space? How often does the protagonist recover, in minutes, from a grievous injury? Perhaps the two most pervasive violations of both biology and physics in the movies are the depictions of fights and self-arrests.

Have you ever been punched in the face? Even a mild blow to one's nose elicits a startling response. The pain is like an electric current through the skull. Cognition is dulled. Both eyes water uncontrollably, blurring vision, and the upper teeth go numb. Increase the power of the blow and the nose will break, causing almost immediate swelling and resounding pain. Consciousness is jeopardized. If you've ever watched a boxing match, you have some sense of what I'm describing. The *Rocky* movies are great drama, but the depiction of boxing is absurd. In a real boxing match, it usually takes one, possibly two undeflected punches to finish the contest. A street brawl is no different. A single full-force bare-knuckle strike to the face almost always finishes the fight. It is simple biology. And yet in the movies, fights between antagonists can last interminably, with multiple, unblocked blows landing with the staccato impact of a jackhammer. These blows rarely slow down or even stun the receiver, and the movies never depict the inevitable broken bones. The antagonists swing away, immune to the destruction their haymakers would really be causing, bouncing off each other like a pair of indestructible Weeble Wobbles.

Self-arrests are no different. Take a moment and hang from a chin-up bar. If you don't have one mounted in a doorway, imagine it, or try gripping a ledge (if you even can—it requires significant finger strength). Once you get the feel for that, now stand on a stool, allowing your outstretched arms to be positioned six inches higher than your grasping point. Step off the stool and try to catch yourself, arresting your fall. How did that feel? Was there a jolt through your finger joints, wrists, and shoulders? Now raise the stool to a slightly higher starting point, perhaps two feet. Doesn't seem like much, does it? Jump off the stool and catch yourself. Any luck? Now do what you see people do in nearly every action movie ever produced. Balance on the top of your chin-up bar, carefully, standing as tall as possible. Now leap off, free-falling until your chin passes the bar, and reach out with your hands to stop your descent. If you did not end up in the emergency room with multiple torn tendons in your hands and wrists, or a dislocated shoulder, then congratulations. You too could be in the movies!

Where movies really fail, as do books or any other storytelling medium, is the passage of time. It is very difficult to emote the weight of a transition period. You see characters change. They age, or gain a skill, or their surroundings mature, but as an observer, it is difficult to appreciate the personal investment required by that individual to navigate the depth of their persistence. We see this in the Bible as well. Abraham was granted a promise that he would be a father, and yet he waited twenty-five years for this covenant to be realized. David was anointed king when he was fifteen but would not don the mantle until he was thirty—a fifteen-year wait. Noah purportedly preached and worked on the ark for nearly one hundred years before the flood. To be able to maintain focus, faith, and persistence for those interminable lengths is remarkable.

After Jude's amputation, we all believed he had reached the nadir of his malady. The difficult decisions were behind him. He understood the vagaries of chemotherapy and the rhythms of living in Seattle, where he bounced between the hospital and his residence. Now he could focus on rehabilitating his leg and commence the challenging process of walking with a prosthetic. His hateful tumor had been eradicated. Jude just had to endure the torment of using poison to mop up any itinerant cancer cells that may be drifting through his ecosystem.

This was his attitude upon returning to Seattle. He was ready and willing to pull through this last stage. What neither he nor the rest of us anticipated was the wretched toll an uninterrupted barrage of caustic chemotherapy could exact. It ravaged him. To say he endured would be a kind euphemism. But this is where my rebirthed son emerged with new beauty. Despite the puking, weight loss, feeding tube catastrophes, mouth sores, headaches, wound contracture, and skin lesions, Jude never once, in any instance, desired pity. He never called attention to his discomfort. He never complained or bemoaned his circumstances. For five grueling, insufferable months, he endured a type of torture that would turn a stoic to compassion. He traversed his suffering with a smile on his lips and hope in his heart.

One evening, I was coaxing him to eat. Jude's weight was dropping again, and he detested his feeding tube. I tried to remain upbeat, but we both knew if he dropped any more pounds, the feeding tube would go back in. I kept asking him why he wasn't taking more food. Was he nauseous? Was the smell turning his gut? Did he have a fever? Instead of responding to my inquiries, he simply gazed at me with his brown, doe-like eyes, mockingly raised an eyebrow, and opened his mouth. Now, I've investigated thousands of mouths. I've seen nearly everything a mouth has to offer, healthy or diseased, and thought I was unshockable. What he displayed leveled me. His entire mouth—cheeks, tongue, gingiva—was an ulcerated, festering sore. It looked like he had crammed a cyclist's road rash directly into his orifice. Neither of us spoke. He slowly closed his mouth and delicately sipped on cold lemonade.

"How long has that been like that?" I asked timidly. He could tell from the look on my face it appeared as ugly as it felt.

"A couple of days," he replied. "It really burns." He couldn't help but grimace. The grimace elicited more discomfort—an infinite regress of pain.

"Burns!" I exclaimed. "Burns? It looks like someone attacked your cheeks with a cheese grater." He smiled amicably and took another sip. "Why didn't you tell me sooner?" I pushed. "We could have gotten you something?!"

"We knew this was coming," he reminded me. "You already got me some mouth medication. I just didn't want to bother with one more thing. It'll go away." He rose from his chair, moving like a ninety-year-old who'd just flipped off a scooter, and crutched over to the couch. After attempting another small sip of lemonade, he smacked his lips together, like a Michelin-star chef. "Hmmm ... I never knew lemonade could taste like metal. Interesting." He smiled, and then, as was his want, let out a hearty laugh, mocking his decrepit state. I cringed, fearing his mucosa would simply slough away from his mouth like a bloody placenta. "You know, this makes my toothpaste taste terrible too. I'm glad I don't have a girlfriend right now; I can't imagine how bad my breath is." He started laughing again. I was tempted to join his laughter, but the image of his revolting mouth suppressed my urge.

"You certainly could use the sympathy card to your advantage. Or the 'woe is me' card," I offered. "Chicks always go for that."

"Yeah," Jude agreed. "Look at this." He sat up on the couch and tossed his phone to me. On it were at least twenty recent Snaps from an assortment of women. Some of them I knew, others I'd never heard of. A few of the pictures were pushing the borders of propriety. I gave the phone back quickly, rather confident none of the pictures or messages were for me.

"Dude!" I exclaimed. "How thick have you been laying it on?"

"Not at all," he laughed, shaking his head vigorously. "I haven't even mentioned to anyone that I'm sick."

"Well, what are you sitting around here for?" I joked. We all knew why he was there, and leaving was out of the question.

"Dad." He looked at me with partially serious eyes, taking on the posture of a teacher instructing a dullard. "I'm bald. Not the best vibe for a date."

"True," I agreed in a comically super-serious tone. "But a bald eighteen-year-old makes for a good conversation piece."

"Do you really think I need to come up with stuff to talk about? That is not a struggle." He shook his head, once again an exasperated kid suffering through parental ignorance. I tried not to laugh at his response. Any sliver of fun was a blessed respite. I nurtured anything that could push beyond the boundaries of his tortured reality.

He did not say another word about his mouth. Not that evening, not ever. He had all sorts of options to choose from. He could have complained incessantly, or demanded medication, grumbled, whined, or made an excuse for not eating. Instead, he focused solely on discovering gratitude in each moment. I would never have guessed the insolent boy of fifteen, who was selfish, self-absorbed, lacking in wherewithal and void of determination, could transform into a magnanimous, empathetic, patient roommate—beguiled by joy. He humbled me.

* * *

If Jude's journey was a movie, we would have entered the stage where the protagonist, suffering from the ravages of cancer, would be rapidly highlighted in multiple states of duress, accompanied with a swelling musical score, artfully capturing time's passage. And this is where movies, books, and narratives fail. The reality was, each second of time piled on the former, making a heap too heavy to move. Any distraction, any change in scenery, was a blessed reprieve from the oppressive pall of time. Unfortunately, Covid stole many distractions, and Jude's misery amplified the burden. His health continued to decline, like a train wreck in slow motion. Cancer wrapped us all in a prison of time and space. Our world shriveled to the confines of our small apartment and smaller hospital room.

There was a blessing, however, for all that time. The two of us experienced something very few fathers and their eighteen-year-old sons undergo. We were forced to interact, incessantly, under trying conditions. Statistically, by the time your child graduates from high school, you will have spent over 90 percent of the total time you will ever spend with them for the remainder of their life. Although they are barely adults, your interaction is on the homestretch. Jude and I spent more intensive time together during his eight-month chemotherapy trial than most parents do in a lifetime. We were constantly forced to communicate, grapple, explore, and interact—with no reprieve. He was barely an adult, maturing faster than any eighteen-year-old should ever have to. I was at his side witnessing and guiding that transformation. It was my privilege, my joy, my benefit to be imprisoned with him. As weighty and oppressive as all that time was, the service it provided outstripped my imagination. Jude and I forged an ineffable bond, replete with an irreproducible, unique flavor. Joy, laughter, pain, sorrow, strife, patience, agony, faith, dialogue, and solitude fused into an amalgamation of unconditional love. It was stamped on our hearts. We were bound, in the purest sense, as father and son. Time served as the secret ingredient, and it was more precious than gold.

RECOVERY

"Out of all this struggle a good thing is going to grow. That makes it worthwhile."

JOHN STEINBECK

Jude was forced to navigate divergent tracks. One track was the rapidly descending spiral of chemotherapy. The other was the positive progression of recovery. He had lost his leg, and with it all the function a leg provides. He had lost a year of education and the corresponding college experience. He could never recapture what was lost. He could create something fulfilling. It requires a special attitude and unique commitment to ascertain present possibilities without letting the pervasive horrors of your everyday existence blind you to those options. Jude managed to be excited about learning to walk while dismissing the interruptions chemo imparted on his physical therapy. Chemotherapy just happened to be what he was doing. It did not define who he was becoming.

Learning to walk on an obstinate stump that both resisted healing and fluctuated in size and shape proved challenging. It also did not help that all his athletic, lean muscle had been scrubbed away by the chemotherapeutic agents. He hated what chemo did to his body. Fortunately, we were able to procure him the best artificial leg, knee, and socket money could buy. This required an insurance battle of epic proportions. And while the intricacies of that battle would be interesting to recount, the telling is also an unnecessary gratuity. Jude was oblivious to the fight occurring on his behalf, and we wanted it that way. Suffice it to say it is unwise to deny two hyper-dedicated parents an item they deem necessary for their child's well-being. Love is a powerful motivator.

Necessity breeds invention. The recent wars in the Middle East, with the ubiquitous, deplorable use of IEDs, created a rash of amputees. Advancements in prosthetic technology were the result of those tragedies. Jude's knee was a technological marvel. It also meant he had a steep learning curve and had to advance his training in an intentional, stepwise fashion to avoid incurable habits. Walking on an artificial leg is very difficult. Shortcuts are tempting. One can do this by manipulating the leg improperly with the hip, not learning how to adequately "break" the knee, or using the leg like a crutch or balancing rod. Unlike prosthetic legs of the past (starting with the classic wooden peg), the technology of Jude's knee was designed to mimic a healthy leg. This meant learning how to re-fire the muscles in your hip and butt as if they were still properly attached, maintaining balance and posture as if you were still symmetrical, and walking with an even gait. You must perform these maneuvers without feeling anything. This extends beyond numbness. There is no proprioception. Your brain lacks any awareness of where your artificial leg rests in space. You cannot tell if your foot is on an incline, the texture of the floor, how far forward your knee is bent, or if you need to recover from inadvertent movement.

It was much easier for Jude to get around the apartment by hopping or scooting lazily in an office chair. It was much more efficient to transport him in a wheelchair when we visited the hospital. Jude preferred a walker in the restroom. It was safer and cleaner. We tucked away enough vignettes about "when a prosthetic leg and toilet collide" to publish a novelette. But those shortcuts were not long-term solutions. If he was to fully recover (or at least recover to the maximum degree afforded by his infirmity), then incessant practice was paramount. When one is physically depressed, emotionally wasted, and keenly aware of impending travails, motivation to practice becomes problematic.

Jude did his best. To progress rapidly on a prosthetic contraption of that nature requires an intense willingness to ignore failure, embrace the hard work required to succeed, and employ a rare combination of brute strength and finesse.

Physical finesse was not an operative adjective in Jude's lexicon. He wasn't exactly the proverbial bull in a china shop, but he also wasn't genetically inclined toward ballet. It was more a lack of patience than physical giftedness. As a toddler, he once managed to wedge his big wheel between a box of toys and the door to the playroom. How he succeeded in doing this as he exited the room seemingly defied the laws of physics. I was jogging on the treadmill—which was also in the playroom—when he left, carefully watching this unfold. When Jude attempted to reenter the room, his big wheel thwarted him. He could only open the door six inches before it halted. He pushed for a moment, getting frustrated, and then tried to shove his large head through the gap. I could see from my angle all he had to do was reach through the opening and calmly turn the handle of his Big Wheel away from the box of toys. This would release the wedge. I recognized his view was somewhat obscured compared to mine, but even for a toddler, the predicament was hardly perplexing. Instead of fiddling through obvious options, he immediately became frustrated. He shoved harder, growing red-faced, only to be denied. Then he disappeared.

I was disappointed because I assumed he had given up rather quickly. I was hoping my son would demonstrate a little more ingenuity and gumption. About ten seconds later, the playroom door blew inward with a resounding crash, like someone ramming it with a Bobcat skid steer mini-tractor. The force of the impact launched the Big Wheel across the room and into the fireplace. I jumped off the treadmill just in time to see Jude ricochet off the door, a human wrecking ball, and caterwaul through two crates of toys, a mini train, and a box of Duplos before flipping sideways into a small bin of stuffed animals. The collateral damage was remarkable. A relatively organized room disintegrated in less than a second. Jude calmly extricated himself from the animals and casually tossed a small giraffe (with wings no less) over his shoulder, as if this mini disaster was all part of his well-laid plan.

He took to snow skiing in a similar fashion. I would characterize his technique as "safely aggressive, not accomplished." Skiing with him was an immense amount of fun because he would attempt nearly any slope, usually in an unconventional fashion. Occasionally, he would stumble into something brilliant, but more often than not, he was a test case for what not to do. He loved to ski moguls but never bothered learning any techniques to finesse his way through. He loved to "get air" but did not have the patience to acquire the bodily awareness while in flight to take advantage—or be safe—with his amplitude. And he loved speed. We once clocked him racing north of 60 mph as he skipped through a mogul field in blizzarding conditions. His unzipped coat flapped so violently it sounded like someone was operating a lawn mower. His wrecks were epic. I've had the privilege of observing all manner of skill levels on the mountain and have seen some fantastic wipeouts. Jude is the only person I've witnessed inadvertently perform a front flip, twice, in succession.

We were skiing down a rather steep mogul run in fresh, heavy snow. It took real effort to trudge through that snow—effort Jude had no interest in expending. As he careened down the run, pushing the limits of his control, both his ski tips jammed into the top of any unusually large mogul, flipping him forward. Normal skiers, even great skiers, would pull the rip cord at this juncture. Flipping forward over your skis while out of control is a great way to get hurt, so finding a creative way to cushion your fall and live to ski another day is the prudent choice. Somehow, Jude managed to absorb the shock of his skis coming to a near halt, and as he flipped through the air, face first, he kicked his legs over the top of his head in a gymnastic layout. Fortunately, his timing was perfect (I can assure you through no pre-planning on his part), and he landed directly on the center of his skis. Unfortunately, this unchecked momentum enabled his velocity to reach a degree beyond reckless. He skipped over the next mogul, but the following bump was steeper and more massive. He caught it on the upslope. The angle of attack launched him a solid distance through the air, directly into the face of another mogul a healthy distance down the hill. His skis bent into a U at impact. This is where the bindings should have ejected him, saving his knees from serious injury. I don't know if he had his bindings so tight as to be inoperable, but neither let loose. Jude's skis recoiled from the massive energy input, launching him like a trampoline. A normal person's legs would have buckled from the force of the thrust, but Jude was gifted with remarkably resilient thighs. He had tied the record for the standing broad jump at his high school, and he put that skill to good use in the moment. Once again, he found himself inadvertently flipping forward over his skis, high into the air and wildly out of control. This second time, he was not nearly so fortunate, for instead of adroitly sticking the landing, he performed the equivalent of a diver's one-and-a-half—except he did not have a welcoming pool of water to plunge into. He crashed directly on his head, whiplashing onto his back with a mouthful of snow and a modestly wounded ego. He also had two of the ugliest bruises I've ever seen appear immediately on his shins. I thought he'd shattered both his legs.

Those were the skills Jude brought to bear when learning how to use his prosthetic. He did not make it look easy. He was not always conventional. But somehow he managed to accomplish the task and provide laughter and surprises while he did it. Only Jude could make the loss of a limb comically endearing. Only Jude could make his physical therapists feel privileged to be working with him. Only Jude could stumble and weave his way into the semblance of a swagger. It was not a duplication of the familiar strut which made him so easily identifiable on the football field, but it was a Jude swagger, nonetheless. Jude made the loss of a limb fashionable.

EDUCATION

"A time is coming when men will go mad, and when they see someone who is not mad, they will attack him saying, 'You are mad, you are not like us.'"

DESERT FATHER ABBA ANTHONY

While enduring treatment, attending school remotely, or guided education of any stripe, was completely out of the question. I suppose a highly motivated and gifted student could have taken a stab at accomplishing some academics, but Jude had never been a motivated student. Jude balanced his life with two buckets: a negative bucket and a positive bucket. For Jude, the positive bucket was mostly filled by quality time with friends, sharing experiences, remaining in the moment, learning about cars, discussing topics of interest, and interacting with the opposite sex. His phone and capacity to play group video games served as a modest surrogate for those needs. He was also enlivened by the scores of get-well cards and associated paraphernalia which were delivered daily. His parents served as stand-ins, albeit poor ones, for discussion buddies. Cancer, and all the trappings surrounding it, easily filled his negative bucket to the brim, and beyond. Any attempt at formal education would have created a catastrophic breach in his negative reservoir, throwing his attitude dangerously out of balance.

We did not want his mind to be idle, however. He had virtually unlimited time to mentally explore and grow. It was simply a matter of finding the energy to invest in the effort. Fortunately, he did not lack intelligence, and surprisingly for someone his age, he appreciated a dialectical approach. Jude was not loquacious, but he enjoyed verbal sparring and was not afraid to form or express an opinion. So, I worked hard to take advantage of his captivity. He never realized he was in school while he convalesced. That was my secret.

Jude was raised in a small town. It was a wonderful community. It afforded him a host of friends, safety, and regulated social outlets. In addition, he attended a Christian school. This provided a wonderful education and a catered school curriculum which allowed him to explore and experience extracurricular opportunities oftentimes not accessible in a large, public high school setting. But it also meant he was surrounded by a relatively homogenous group of like-minded students, parents, and teachers, people who largely shared the same worldview and followed similar social narratives. This environment made for accessible connections and relational comfort. It also meant he matured in an echo chamber. This troubled me.

It was very important that Jude learned how to think for himself, to develop the art of critical discernment. In this age of instant information, our minds are overwhelmed by a continuous input of data. It arrives in such volumes that veridical processing for the uninitiated is impossible. People become receivers, not discerners. The requisite nuance for developing wisdom is bludgeoned away by the tsunami of boisterous, exercised opinions assaulting our senses. As a coping mechanism, most of us choose voices that seem agreeable. We choose ease over effort, comfort over discord. This smooths the incessant cacophony and opens space for us to hear our own voice. What we do not recognize is that our voice only tunes to the melody of those we let in. And if we only let those whose experience of life, and interpretation of that life, mimic our own, then our mutual music becomes prosaic, lacking vitality, depth, and richness of insight, void of the interlocking harmony which defines an exquisite composition.

I did not want Jude to sing a lifeless tune. I did not want him bound to an echo. I worked hard to invigorate that lonely, sterile hospital room with lively discourse as we tested each other, pressing the limits of our world views and social narratives. There is not a lot of joy to be discovered in a bustling chemotherapy ward. But we took pleasure in pushing our boundaries and exploring ideas, regardless of how radical or nonsensical they appeared.

One day, I might expose him to a Black Algerian lesbian's thoughts on the Christian virtue of socialism, and the next we might read material from a white Reformed pastor living in rural America and extolling the Christian virtue of capitalism. I developed libertarian arguments refined from a homosexual man living in England and contrasted them with the perspectives of a communist woman from China. When your world is small, it is easy to believe in self-evidence. The disparity in thought proved fascinating and provoking. Jude was amazed at how strongly different individuals could feel, think, and believe about ideas and subjects he heretofore had considered axiomatic. We both learned, after a great deal of reading and listening, that it is very possible for reasoned, sincere, intelligent, motivated, and empathetic people to possess radically different attitudes and perspectives on how the world works—and how it should work—than we do. And more importantly, their conclusions and desires were often just as valid—if not more so.

In addition, we learned the most aggravating, unattractive, and obnoxious advocates for a particular worldview were those who confined themselves to a personally constructed, sealed echo chamber designed to belch their opinion for all the world to hear, drowning out any response with their ceaseless, stentorian diatribes. This imprisonment squelched their capacity to apprehend the vast and variegated, interconnected social stratum compromising our world. They lacked charity, practiced selfishness, and worked overtime to dehumanize their neighbors. We called these types "pigheads"—signifying their close-minded stubbornness and constant squealing.

What was scary and revealing was the recognition that some of the voices Jude and I had at one time considered motivating and perspicacious fell into the pighead category. To be sure, just because someone presented in a pigheaded fashion did not necessarily mean what they were expounding was incorrect, but recognizing their lack of empathy and rigid myopy did motivate us to scrutinize their integrity.

I worked hard to present ideas and opinions with which I was unfamiliar, or downright disagreed, to Jude. To be clear, this was hardly a debate between David Hume and Thomas Hobbes. Jude was, after all, only eighteen, and his depth of thought was often a hole about an inch deep. But he was willing and able to exercise his thinking muscles, occasionally activating his mental shovel with enough vigor to dig a little deeper than customary. He demonstrated a degree of flexibility that was surprising, considering his environment and education. This made our discussions more didactic and worthwhile. I considered it fun. Jude humored me with his tolerance. Our conversation regarding abortion was emblematic of many such discourses:

"So … what is your attitude towards abortion?" I cautiously asked. Jude was three days past his last methotrexate infusion, which meant he was not incapacitated with nausea, and we were simply whittling away the hours until his overworked kidneys could clear the poison from his system. The silence in the room donned a sultry feel. It was time to liven it up. Jude put down his car magazine and glanced towards me, feigning opprobrium. He knew what was coming.

"I'm not planning on having one, if that's what you're asking," he sarcastically answered.

I laughed. "I'm pretty certain chemotherapy hasn't changed you that much."

"Nope," he agreed. "Although with my flabby body, I don't feel very manly."

"Hopefully that will change soon. In fact, I know it will." He knew it too, but a little reassurance was never discouraging. Neither of us expressed what we both knew. There was a possibility his heavy chemo regimen could sterilize him. Jude had trained me to focus on the positive. I was learning to lean into that training. Nothing good ever came from extrapolating to the worst-case scenario. "But what did you learn at school about abortion? Is it a horrible evil?"

"It's murder," he responded unequivocally. "Why would you even ask? Don't you believe in the sanctity of life?"

"Of course I believe in the sanctity of life. Life is good. God invented it, and He seems to be in the business of inventing good things." Jude remained silent, considering what I said. There was not a lot of good to be found in his circumstance. He was wrestling with the dissonance in my statement. "Let's be a little more specific. Do you think it is ever justified to get an abortion?"

"I'm not sure. Can you justify sin?" he answered. Now that was a great question, I thought. Can you justify sin? And is it considered a sin if it is justified? I tucked that away for another day.

"I think you need to be cautious about what you claim to be a sin," I responded.

"Are you telling me having an abortion, murdering a child, is not a sin? What is wrong with you? Is living in the hospital turning you into a Democrat?" Somehow, he managed to simultaneously giggle and look disgusted.

"Let's leave politics out of this," I suggested. "That's never helpful. What about rape?"

"I'm against it," he quipped.

"Thank you," I agreed. "This conversation would switch gears in a hurry if you weren't."

"I don't get rape," he continued. "Rape is horrible."

"Agreed ... but I'm not asking if rape is acceptable; even I have a limit to the zany questions I will ask." I shook my head and smiled. "I'm asking if someone gets raped, if it's acceptable to abort the child if the rape turns into a pregnancy?"

"You're still taking the life of another person. I don't think you redeem a crime by performing another one."

"That is true," I agreed. "But that's only if you think it's a crime."

"When would murder not be a crime?" he asked.

"What if it isn't murder?" I responded. "They have morning-after pills. They work by not letting the fertilized egg adhere. It just gets flushed away."

"Is that really any different than having a doctor go in and pull the egg away?" Jude's question startled me, and I felt a moment of pride. He was starting to think about some of these difficult questions with a little more nuance and depth than even a few months ago. I was tempted to congratulate him, but I knew that would be premature. Instead, I continued to press.

"It's just a packet of cells. You have packets of cells that break off all the time."

"But those cells can't become a person," he argued.

"No, but is there a difference between a potential person and a whole person?"

"Maybe."

"So, when does life begin? When do we become 'a person'?" I asked the question with air quotes to emphasize my point.

"If I remember correctly, when it is genetically distinct, it is a person," he answered.

"I think there are some really knowledgeable people, including Christians, who would disagree with you. Did you know that 50 percent of all embryos spontaneously abort? So, if what you say is true, that means we have a 50 percent infant mortality rate. Isn't that the worst health crisis in the history of mankind?"

"But there is nothing we can do about that," he replied incredulously. "How would that be an argument for abortion?"

"I'm not saying it's an argument for abortion. I'm just saying that to illustrate our lack of consistency in how we act on what we say we believe. If those are all legitimate persons dying, then one would think pastors would be a great deal busier performing funerals."

"True," Jude agreed. "But that's not how we think of them."

"So now you're telling me embryos aren't people?"

"No, that's not what I'm saying." Exasperation was setting in. "I just think it would be silly to have a funeral for an embryo."

"So, you're just making a logistical observation, but still claiming an embryo is a person?" I asserted.

"Yes," he confidently declared.

"So, what about in vitro fertilization?" I asked.

"What's that?" he inquired.

"That's the procedure used when a woman is having a hard time getting pregnant. They harvest her eggs and fertilize them outside the womb. Then they pick the best-looking embryo, or sometimes embryos, and reimplant them." I tried not to overwhelm him with too many details.

"Well that's pretty cool," he exclaimed. "But what's your point?"

"There are a lot of Christians who staunchly oppose abortion, much like you've been doing, but they are pro in vitro fertilization. Isn't that hypocritical?"

He was silent for a moment, mulling over the question. "Why would that be hypocritical? You're creating a life, not taking one away."

"You're only partway correct. Whenever they do IVF treatment, they always make extra embryos. Oftentimes, they take the extra embryos and put them in a freezer. This preserves them for a time, but eventually, even in a deep freeze, they degrade. And sometimes the parents decide they only want one child, or maybe two, and if the pregnancy takes, then they discard the other embryos. How is that any different from an abortion?"

Now he really started to think. It was a rarity when Jude had the patience to stay with a topic this long. I was also thankful we weren't being interrupted, something that happened with annoying frequency in the hospital.

"Yeah, I really don't know. They just want to have a kid. Is that a crime?"

"You tell me," I said. "If defending the sanctity of life is grounds for not having an abortion, doesn't it seem rather self-condemning to use the same argument to defend your right to have a kid?"

"Wait. I'm not sure what you just said?" He looked at me quizzically.

"What I'm saying is that in many cases of IVF, you create a life, but you also abort a life in the process. Many anti-abortionists promote IVF. That's hypocritical. If it is ethically allowable to commit an abortion while attempting to create a life—which is defended as being good—then is it possible that perhaps it is allowable to have an abortion to create another type of good—or even to curtail something bad?"

"I really don't know the answer to the question Dad," Jude admitted. "I haven't really thought it through."

"Exactly," I agreed. "Many people don't. Sometimes something that appears black and white becomes much, much more complicated depending on the circumstances. Let's think through a horrible scenario. Suppose Simone was raped and got pregnant—"

"Dad!" Jude interrupted. "Why would you even say that! There are so many things wrong with what you're saying."

"Yeah, that's not a pleasant thought, is it?" I agreed. "But just imagine with me, for a moment. These questions don't have meaning unless there is emotional investment. So, assume she was raped, is pregnant, and then discovers her child has a genetic mutation which will make it mentally challenged. The child is also deformed in such a way it will only experience a life of pain and has a life expectancy of six months to maybe three years, all the while requiring constant attention. Simone won't be able to go to college because she will be in a late-term pregnancy at the time of matriculation, and then she will be tied to this suffering child until such time the child perishes, and she will have to suffer through the emotional trauma of losing an infant. All this on top of the trauma of being raped." I caught my breath, appalled by my own grisly scenario. "Would not abortion be an ethical option to consider here? Would you want your beautiful little sister to go through all that?"

"Are you kidding me?!" Jude nearly got out of bed, he was so agitated. "I would pity the person who raped her, cause I'd kill him."

"You'd have to beat me to it," I replied, with a little more sincerity than I intended. Admittedly, my fabricated scenario was making me a little queasy, even though I was the one manipulating the details. "But killing him wouldn't solve her dilemma. Her entire life trajectory would be derailed, not to mention all the collateral damage."

"That's awful," Jude agreed, reclining back in his bed. "Why are we even talking about this?"

"I'm simply illustrating that sometimes issues we consider black and white, or open and shut, are a great deal more complicated than people would like to believe or let themselves consider. I'm also trying to point out that it's possible for people who claim to be Christians, who study their Bible, attend church, and have an authentic spirituality, to not always agree on ethical or moral conundrums. But it doesn't make them any more or less Christian."

"Yeah, I get that," he said, nodding in agreement. I remained silent, allowing our conversation to grow roots. I'd given him enough to think about for the day. I eased back in my chair and opened a book, trying to purge the horrific scenario I had just described from my mind's eye.

"You know what?" Jude asked. I lifted my head and watched him slowly close his eyes and sink deeper into the pillows.

"What?" I responded.

"I'm really glad I have two parents."

"Why is that?" I inquired, curiosity piqued.

"Because I get just the right amount."

"Right amount?" I prodded. "I'm not sure what you mean. Right amount of what?"

"Cause when I get sick of you wearing me out, then Mom comes and takes care of me. And then when she starts to wear me out, you come back... You see? Just the right amount." He gave me a big smile and rolled over on his side, deftly manipulating all the tubes and wadded IV lines draped across his chest.

He knew he was being a touch backhanded, and he relished his cleverness. But we both understood, in his uniquely "Jude" way, he had given his parents one of the greatest compliments they could ever receive. Some parents try to give their kids everything. Other parents do not provide enough. Jude thought we were giving him just the right amount. And that is every parent's hope.

THE MOUNTAIN

"The way up to the top of the mountain is always longer than you think. Don't fool yourself, the moment will arrive when what seemed so near is still very far."

PAULO COELHO

If you have ever been involved in a physical test of endurance, you are likely familiar with the danger of looking too far ahead. I enjoy climbing mountains, but I avoid spending too much time gazing at the summit while I am climbing. From a distance, it appears intimidating and insurmountable. No accomplished marathoner begins dreaming about the finish line when they are crossing mile eight, or a cyclist breaking the tape from the base of the first hill. They remain squarely focused on what is before them, setting small, achievable goals, which serve to propel them forward. The bigger picture is held at arm's length so as to not distract or threaten. I have guided groups of climbers where, invariably, an inexperienced participant will be progressing steadfastly upwards, only to surreptitiously steal a glance at the final destination and lose heart. Crestfallen, they will stop in their tracks, exhausted and defeated.

Jude was experiencing a significant test of endurance. At first, the intensity, novelty, and outright fear demanded his immediate attention. The next day, week, or month had no part in the conversation. This had its own drawbacks, as his daily suffering was so acute that there were times he was afraid existence would only persist in a continuous loop of misery. The thought of enduring another minute threatened to supersede his desire to stay alive. As the acute trauma receded, he established a rhythm and routine, doing a marvelous job maintaining focus on his blessings. He taught me a great deal during those ensuing months about finding joy in your present circumstances. He was able to be frivolous, express gratitude, and cultivate ongoing relationships. He rarely went to sleep dreading what the next day would bring.

Despite his frailty and physical decline, he managed to muster the energy to play online games with his friends, even though they were scattered across the county. These contests would sink deep into the night. Jude was invigorated by these games, and exceptionally vocal in his participation. We lived on the first floor with a second-floor neighbor who appreciated peace and quiet. Once, when I was staying with Jude in the hospital, I received a text from her indicating we had left our bathroom fan on, and the constant noise was a source of irritation. I tried to be generous and respect her concerns. But we certainly had more pressing issues than a bathroom fan. What this did mean, however, was that when Jude was in our condo I was constantly on alert for excessive noise. To mitigate his boisterous participation, we had his grandpa engineer a "sound chamber." This consisted of a PVC cage which supported several thick blankets and sleeping bags, hung in such a way as to absorb and baffle Jude's outbursts. The contraption demonstrated modest success, as we received few complaints after its construction. And it kept me from walking into his room every fifteen minutes, imploring him to "keep it down."

Distractions and immediate focus proved invaluable for Jude's progress. But just like the novice climber, he occasionally would "take a peek." That's when despondency would encroach. In these moments, I would sit next to him on his bed, often in silence, and be present. Occasionally, I would read Psalm 121, a psalm I prayed every day since the start of Jude's hospitalization, and talked about his plans once this nightmare was behind him. When he focused on the opportunity to return to college, or go skiing, or relax with friends in the summer, then his discouragement would fade.

Fortunately, these moments were few. Still, it's deeply discouraging to witness your child's dejection, especially when there's no immediate solution. The gloom possessed a weight that quickly became a burden. Jude abhorred pity from others. What he learned, in those crushing moments of despair, was not to pity himself. He recognized that no good ever comes from self-pity. It is only a recipe for self-loathing, hopelessness, and chronic depression. These were traits Jude shunned. I found his introspection inspiring.

As cautious as we were about looking to the future, it was impossible to not be aware of the calendar and the last few scheduled chemotherapy treatments. There comes a time when climbing a mountain where the summit is impossible to ignore. It is directly before you, demanding your attention, but intimidating in its proximity. It is in that moment, when you realize you will reach the summit, that you also become intensely aware of the degree of your exhaustion. That is the final hurdle—to push through the freshly realized onslaught of suffering—and attain the prize.

Jude's penultimate chemotherapy treatment was brutal. The anticipated joy of the finish line keenly reminded us how exhausted we all were. Jude's body was shutting down. For a time, he had been clearing his methotrexate so efficiently that the hospital would discharge us early, allowing us to finish the last of his rescue medication at home. It was a welcome gift—one we deeply appreciated. The problem with repeated bonuses, however, is that they become expectations. When Jude did not clear his methotrexate during his penultimate treatment, and the nurse broke the news he had to remain for another twenty-four hours—if not longer—you would have thought he had just received a terminal diagnosis. What was one more day? He had essentially been living in the hospital for eight months. He should have been able to do another day standing on his head. But that is the crushing power of unmet expectations.

After the nurse left, we silently sat dejected in his dim hospital room.

There was nothing to be done. We were out of distractions, bereft of hope, and woefully discouraged. I did not want to drag Jude into my own frustrations. His robust emotional cloak was becoming threadbare and weathered. It was proving insufficient insulation against the storm of despair. My job was to drag him to the finish line, not erect more barriers. I was out of energy.

We both silently cried to God for mercy. This was not a new prayer. We implored the Almighty for mercy regularly. This took on a new tone, however. We were singing to the tune of despair. We hoped this was the discordant incantation that would startle God into action. Somehow, this time, our irreconcilable harmony would be so jarring that only a passionless tyrant could ignore it.

God did not appear in a flash of lightning. We were not bowled over by His thunderous rescue. We did not even hear His still, small voice of assurance granting us a quiet peace in His presence. We remained in that room, isolated and rejected. The oppressive quiet blanketed us like an irresistible nightmare—the eerie calm before the monster leaps out. But in our hopelessness, God provided the same merciful miracle He had been so generous with from the outset. We were not alone. Jody called to check in, we delivered the bad news, and in her positive and realistic enthusiasm, quickly put our dejection into perspective. She reminded Jude how far he had come and illustrated how little he had to go. She both encouraged and admonished, and somehow, despite her own exhaustion, invigorated the two of us to face another day. Soon, the texts and notes of encouragement came flooding in. Jude was refreshed. I was relieved. Loneliness only exacerbates despair. The presence of my wife and love of God's people was His miracle of mercy. Be mindful of what you pray for, or you may not recognize it when it appears. There is no miracle like the love of friends and family.

THE LIGHT

"You are strong only as long as you don't deprive people of everything. For a person you've taken everything from is no longer in your power. He's free all over again."

ALEKSANDR SOLZHENITSYN

Jude's final chemo treatment could not have been more underwhelming. We were exhausted, staggering to the finish line, desperate for the entire ordeal to be over. May had arrived, spring was in full bloom, and nobody wanted any part of a hospital room. It was torture for Jude to lay in his bed, immobilized from nausea, with the sun pouring into the room. He yearned to be anywhere but there.

For months, we had eagerly anticipated this moment. The last treatment. The sounding of the bell. The declaration from the staff and the doctors that the hard work was over. Instead, the entire affair was no different from the seventeen that had occurred before. Jude was admitted, got injected, got sick, wallowed in misery, made his nurses laugh, was a shining light of encouragement and positivity to those he encountered, and was released. In some ways, this was a blessing. I don't think Jude had the energy to celebrate. He was out of patience. His robust physicality, a hallmark of his persona, had been stripped bare. He was bald, soft, pasty white, enfeebled, and crippled. It pained him to smile. Not only because his lips and mouth were brittle and cracked, but because the very essence of his personality had been scrubbed to the core. He timed his battle well. He had given his best, and his best was fully depleted.

Like so much of his hospital experience, his departure from the chemo ward at Children's Hospital was simply the two of us working together, swimming upstream in desperate hope of respite. The discharge nurse was new and had no experience with Jude. It was on the first sunny weekend of the year, so the chemo ward was understaffed and distracted. She presented us with his discharge papers, gave us instructions for follow-up, and surreptitiously excused herself. When we walked by the front desk, the lady working there had known Jude from the outset. She was the only person on the floor that day who recognized the momentous nature of his departure. She gave Jude a great big "whoop" accompanied by a demonstrative thumbs-up, but that was the sum total fanfare for his accomplishment. Unbeknownst to us, the classic "ringing of the bell" and formal congratulations were not in order until the following week, when Jude was scheduled for his final scans and subsequent debrief consult with the oncologist.

Jude struggled to make it from the seventh floor and down the long, torturous hallway to the hospital atrium. We stopped to rest multiple times. Even though the day was cool, he doffed his sweatshirt to abate vigorous perspiration. I knew he was tempted to have me run and grab a wheelchair, our customary mode of transport. But this time he was determined to do it on his own, on his new leg, entering his new life. I patiently supported him. And as we slowly trudged our way towards the exit doors, we felt the oppressive pall of depression fragment and scatter. Everything felt lighter. Jude's gait increased. He stood more upright. I ran ahead, through the doors, and filmed him walking out of the hospital for what we desperately prayed and hoped would be the final time.

I am not sure it is possible to put a bounce in your step on a prosthetic leg, but Jude managed to do it. Our car was located up a flight of twenty stairs. We both decided it would be foolish to navigate that hurdle, so I ran ahead and pulled the car into the loading roundabout, where he patiently stood absorbing the glorious sunshine. From a distance, he looked like an oversized infant, hairless, white, and blinking from the brightness. In some ways, he was an infant, newly born from the crucible of chemo. I got out and opened the door for him, and he tossed his crutch into the backseat. Instead of impatiently diving into the seat as was typical, he slowly turned and looked back at the hospital, gazing directly into the sun, and firmly nodded his head. As beaten and depleted as he was, that nod was the gesture of a victor. The trial was over. His battle waged. Only Jude knew the toll it exacted. Only he could bask in the glory of a campaign brought to fruition.

Keeping in character with the son I was familiar with, Jude quickly levered himself into my car and said, "Let's get out of here." There was no reflective dialogue. No summation of the last eight months. He was possessed with a determined need to move forward. We zoomed through the roundabout and onto the arterial with a quick burst of acceleration. I felt like we were making a jailbreak. Jude instantly reminded me that he was still incredibly nauseous, and every swerve and pothole was one small jolt closer to him barfing in my car. As desperate as we both were to escape prison, vomit in the car was irrefutable grounds for caution. Jude and I experienced nearly every contingency possible on his journey. Puking in the car was the one box we had yet to check. When we safely arrived at our destination, we took pride in noting we hadn't experienced everything.

GOLDEN

"In the depths of winter, I finally learned that within me there lay an invincible summer."

ALBERT CAMUS

When we moved Jude home after his last infusion, it was as if we had driven backwards in time nineteen years and were returning from the hospital just like we had after his birth. We helped him limp into the house, get arranged, and then Jody and I looked at each other and asked, "Now what?"

For the last eight months, our singular focus was to save our son and carry him through this trial. We were never face to face, our councils of war always via phone or text. I woke up every day, alone in bed, with an anxious knot in the pit of my stomach. Jody did the same. The stress had taken a toll. Weight loss, fatigue, irritated bowels, gray hair—the weight of anxiety hanging menacingly above us like old canvas drapes, with the power to suffocate if you let them ensnare you. Suddenly, we were free. Granted, we both recognized we had a long way to go, and Jude was far from officially cancer-free. But we let a little sunshine filter into our hearts, however tentatively, and relished its comfort.

Six days after his last treatment, Jody took Jude back to Children's, where they performed Jude's final scans, and he experienced the pleasure of ringing the bell. Jude was rarely conventional. His first ring was a little lackluster, so before anyone could stop him, he coiled his torso and proclaimed his victory with an aggressive swipe. The blow threatened to knock the bell off the wall, and the resulting clang reverberated down the hallway with vengeance. It was a ribbon cutting of sorts, signifying Jude's first step into his new life.

Parenting grows more challenging as your children age. I recognize that sounds counterintuitive. It takes more energy (generally) to parent young children. The constant attention, organization, cooking, cleaning, ferrying to events, volunteering etc., is all a whirlwind. In the middle of that, the parent is primarily in charge, driving with both hands on the wheel. You are the one making most of the decisions. You are the one providing direction. You are the one determining where and how time is spent. Your child's trajectory falls squarely within your guardrails.

At some point, a transition occurs when the hands on the wheel are no longer yours. Many times, this transition turns into a wrestling match. The child wants to start driving way too soon, and the parent is unwilling to relinquish their control, or the parent is afraid to hand over autonomy and retains a death grip on the wheel. The smoother the transition, the better. The best transitions are the ones you don't notice. There is one outcome that is absolutely certain, however. Once the parent lets the wheel go, they cannot ever get it back.

Jody and I were in the awkward position of being handed a new steering wheel. Jude was through chemo, but his future was uncertain. It was difficult to know how to help him make plans. As helpful as his "live in the moment" attitude had been for navigating chemo, it was not a useful character trait for planning his future. There were so many unknowns laid before him that the thought of executing any plan was paralyzing. Jude survived in day-to-day mode. We somehow needed to reactivate his life and help him make arrangements despite all the uncertainties.

He thought he wanted to return to college but wasn't sure if the challenges his leg presented would prove insurmountable. Dorm life was erratic enough when operating at full capacity. Managing group bathrooms, stairs, bunk beds, and all the rest seemed very intimidating for someone just learning to limp about, and still horribly weak and sickly. We recognized it was only May. He would not matriculate until late August. There was a lot of physical repair that could happen in the duration. It was difficult to guess how much he would improve, however.

What I did learn, during that post-chemo period, was what it meant to have freedom to parent. Many parents live in fear. Fear that their child will get poor grades, not make friends, make awful choices with irreversible consequences, be exposed to subversive or degenerate material, or even accept a life trajectory out of step with what the parent considers to be in the best interest of their child. Jude had experienced the worst. The two of us had placed our feet squarely on the threshold of the abyss. We knew what the end could look like. Suddenly, the worst possible outcome was defanged. This liberated our relationship. He was free to be a son, and I was free to adopt an ecology of parenting strategies unburdened by the weight of anxiety that characterizes so many relationships.

One of the worst mistakes a parent can make is tying your identity and self-worth to the accomplishments of your child. It is imperative to guard against this possibility. The moment you fall prey to this temptation, your values, your desires, your wishes are projected onto your child, and you attempt to fabricate them into the ideal image you have of yourself—an image untainted by mistakes or unaccounted circumstances. These ideals were unrealistic and unattainable for you, and doubly so for your child. Fear and selfishness drive this tendency. They create the narcissistic impression that who your child is becoming is a direct reflection of your capacities and qualities as a parent. This notion is simply untrue.

There are many numbers of fantastic parents who have awful children. There are even awful parents who have wonderful children. This does not mean we should adopt a fatalistic approach to parenting, jettison all responsibility, and selfishly indulge, allowing our children to fend for themselves. Parents have the ultimate responsibility. But what allows you to freely parent—to care, nurture, guide, and instruct—is unmooring your identity from theirs. Our children do not steal our identities. They must have the freedom to mature as individuals. It is the parent's job to shape that process. You are the one who helps them discover and pursue the car they will eventually drive. They are the ones who are responsible for what they do behind that wheel.

The summer post-chemo was a golden summer for our family. Jude started working in a limited capacity at Lynden Door. Every night, we would engage in a family dinner, often stretching well beyond an hour rife with laughter, chatting, teasing, joking, and finally ending with devotions. Jude held court, guiding the festivities, his robust personality drawing us into a mutual repartee of respect and amusement. His sister and brother were old enough now to challenge him, and it was utter joy for Jody and me to observe our children interact independent of our machinations. They were forming a generational identity, which was exciting and beautiful. I had hoped and prayed for this development since Jude was born. It materialized before our very eyes.

We were blessed to vacation in Mexico, with four-wheeling, kayaking, and general merriment. Jude started to recognize that much of what he had enjoyed before his amputation was still available. Despite his perennially upbeat attitude, the toll of the winter threatened his effervescence. Memories of his old life were vivid reminders of what was lost, and the hard work required to recapture his capabilities intimidated him. As we four-wheeled through the Baja desert, however, racing each other past gnarly scrub and into dry wadis, Jude embraced a newly minted movement, a freedom of pace and rashness which had seemingly abandoned him. In the middle of our tour, the guide tore around a blind corner, screeching to a dusty halt. Jude half stood up on his machine, sliding alongside the leader, breathless and smiling. I nearly upended myself stopping next in line. Simone halted abruptly behind me, with Johann clinging tightly to the second seat, face full of dust and grime. Jody came last, throttle fully engaged, not wanting to be left behind. We could all hear her careening around the last tall shrubs, hidden from view. She emerged with determination, completely caught by surprise at our phalanx of halted vehicles, and unavoidably rear-ended Simone. Her machine popped vertically onto its front wheels and nearly flipped Jody onto Johann's lap.

Jude guffawed with a deep belly laugh. It was as natural and effusive as the laugh he was born with. On that dusty, hot, sunny Mexican afternoon, he recaptured the joy of life which epitomized his character, shredding the pall of his travails with the powerful bellows of a man reborn. I could have basked for eternity in that laugh. It was a spontaneous hug, a sweet caress, a carefree incantation. That four-wheeling extravaganza captured the heart of our family, and Jude's laugh framed it like precious art. He created our golden summer.

THE GLOAMING

"Let us then with confidence draw near to the throne of grace, that we may receive mercy and find grace to help in time of need."

HEBREWS 4:16

One summer, before I had children, I climbed Glacier Peak with my brother-in-law and father. Glacier Peak is one of the volcanoes in Washington State, and a tremendous climb. It does not receive many accolades, unlike Mt. Rainier or Mt. Baker. There are several reasons for this, not the least of which is its inaccessibility. There are limited points of ingress to the mountain, and it is not observable from many populated vantages. It is something of a hidden gem.

The summer we climbed, there had been some spring flooding which washed out the primary access road and obliterated the shortest trail to base camp. This did not deter us, even though we knew it would require more lugging about with heavy packs than we desired. We were, after all, climbing a mountain. A few extra miles only added to the adventure.

The hike was smooth and straightforward. We managed to navigate our way through washed-out terrain, deadfall, and rising creeks without many difficulties or delays. We arrived at base camp as scheduled, settled in, and prepared for our summit day. The following day brought beautiful sunshine without a breath of wind. It made for hot trekking at the lower elevations, but as we climbed, the conditions could not have been more pristine. Unlimited visibility and moderate temperatures greeted us at the summit. We reveled in our accomplishment, letting the unfiltered UV rays burn our skin as we contentedly nourished our tired bodies.

The descent was rapid and uneventful. Though fatigued, we were pleased with our progress when we arrived at camp a few hours ahead of schedule. As we thankfully rested our weary legs, it soon became apparent the early afternoon heat would grow oppressive, so we elected to break everything down and hike back out through the shady forest instead of resting and trying for home the next day.

Upon attaining the much cooler forest, we applauded our decision. The packs were heavy, our legs worn out, but the tradeoff seemed a great deal better than baking in our tents. The idea of making it to the car, jettisoning our rucksacks, and diving into a refreshing shower spurred us on. We knew we would be racing daylight, so we pressed hard, stolidly fighting the post-summit fatigue which plagued our aching legs. At the higher elevations, where the trails had been ravaged by the spring storms, picking our way out was a little dodgy, but manageable. Navigation would be untenable in the dark.

As evening fell, we managed to reclaim the main trail—part of the Pacific Crest Trail system—and redoubled our pace. Our way out was a small turnoff from the main Pacific trail. Once we started down the turnoff, there were only six miles remaining. Those six miles would be on a well-maintained downhill. Even significantly fatigued, we knew we could finish the hike from that point. Unfortunately, we could not locate our turnoff. We hiked and hiked, vigilantly spying for any break in the brush, trail signs, or boot tracks that would take us on our last leg. Nothing.

By this time, darkness became a legitimate concern. We knew we would never locate our egress point in the dark. Between the summit distance and the hike out, we had trekked for over twenty miles, much of it with heavy packs. We were hungry, tired, and ready to be done. The worry over being lost, or at least displaced, augmented our deprivations. Emotional and physical misery gained a significant toehold.

As we hiked around a narrow bend in the trail, eyes straining for any sign of a break-off point, we stumbled across a hiking couple who were resting on a felled tree.

"Hello," I greeted them somewhat breathlessly but relieved to see other people. We had been alone for forty-eight hours.

"How are you?" the man responded. "I did not know we had people catching up to us."

"We've been moving pretty quickly," I replied. "We are trying to hike out of here before nightfall. Where are you two headed?"

The man raised his eyebrow and shot a quick glance at his partner. I don't know why my question would make him nervous, but the two of them seemed jumpy. "We spent the afternoon at the hot springs, and now we are trying to get a little further south before we make camp. Beautiful day, isn't it?"

"It sure is," I agreed. "That's great you were at the hot springs. We are looking for the turnoff trail that heads down to them. They are on our way out. But I thought you said you were heading south from the springs? Aren't you north of the turnoff?"

"North?" the man replied. "No, we've been moving south from there. The turnoff trail is at least four miles back that way." He pointed towards the way we had come.

"Four miles!" I gasped. "What are you talking about? We came off the summit of Glacier Peak and took the base camp trail down. According to the map, the turnoff trail should only be two miles from the base camp trail."

"I don't know where the base camp trail feeds onto the Pacific Crest Trail," he replied. "But I do know we hiked up the hot springs trail this afternoon, and it is definitely north of here."

I carelessly dropped my pack onto the trail and slumped down onto the dirt. For the briefest moment, I was seized with complete despair. Somehow, in our fatigue and unfamiliarity with the terrain, we must have taken a second, unrecorded trail from base camp, which deposited us further south than we knew—far past the turnoff trail. To make our way home we would have to backtrack, mostly uphill, the way we had just traversed and beyond—some four extra miles. This would only get us to the trail that would put us another six miles from our car. I wanted to scream at my own incompetence but was too tired. The three of us sat there dumbfounded. We were too fatigued to make a good decision. The feeling of abject despair weighed heavier than our packs. I felt crushed.

...

In August, as our golden summer wound down, Jude had to go back to Children's Hospital for his first follow-up scans. A couple of days before his scans, Jude and I talked about the anxiety cancer survivors could have about "scan day" and the emotional difficulties leading up to it. Jude had no such anxiety. He thought it was a waste of time and bemoaned the fact he had to take an entire day to bother with more testing. He was through with hospitals. Life was getting good. The summer had been restorative. He had regained much vitality, was exercising regularly, and went out nearly every evening to fraternize with his buddies. He was finally starting to get excited about returning to college. We had even spoken with his former football coach and arranged for Jude to participate as a student-coach for the team. Jude's football coaches had been incredible during his chemotherapy, continuing to check in on him, inviting him to Zoom chapels, and lifting him up in prayer. Even though Jude had only officially been on the team for less than a month, he was included in their brotherhood, and it was marvelous.

I went to the office the morning Jude and Jody drove to Seattle. In the early afternoon my receptionist interrupted and told me Jody was on the line. The moment those words came out of her mouth I knew something was very wrong. In twenty years of practice, Jody had probably interrupted me less than five times.

"Hello," I spoke blandly, trying to mask any trepidation. I didn't get a response. "Hello?" I repeated with a little more force. "What's up?" I heard a faint sob on the other end of the line. Then nothing. "What is it?" I heard a gulp, and then the distinct tone of my wife clearing her throat.

"It's in his lungs," she sobbed.

"What's in his lungs?" I stupidly responded.

"His cancer," she wailed. "It's in both lungs. All over them."

"Okay, okay, take a deep breath," I replied as calmly as possible. My hands started shaking, and it felt like someone uncorked a steam kettle within my intestines. I thought my guts were simply going to fall out of my body. "What have they told you?"

"Just that there are some spots on his lungs, and we will need to address them." Jody sounded like she was hyperventilating.

"Okay, this is a cruel twist." My mind was reeling. There were many questions. This new development was a brutal blow. We were aware of this possibility, but had naively felt the three-month mark was too soon for it to manifest. I could feel the nightmare enveloping me. "Nothing is going to be solved today," I continued as soothingly as possible. "We will have to figure this out together. Just come up with an initial plan with his care team and then get our son home."

We briefly chatted through a few more details, and then Jody hung up. I finished my workday in stunned silence, wracked with absolute despair. The despair I felt years ago on my hiking trip seemed so paltry compared to this, it was laughable. Jude's battle was so unjust. He had already suffered terribly. How could this be happening now? He had paid his dues. He had jumped through all the necessary hoops. He had *wrung the bell!*

I wracked my brain for the best way to handle this horrible revelation with my son. I could not imagine the despair he must be feeling. My heart also ached for Jody. This trial had only magnified our love for Jude. She was a mother with a full heart. Now it ruptured with grief.

When they got home, I greeted their somber faces with a smile. It was a gloriously warm August afternoon. Jude was nineteen. His hair was growing back, the crown of curls beginning their nascent re-emergence. He smiled back, looking none the worse for the bomb that had been delivered. That was my incredible son. Pity and despair had no power over him.

"Why don't you take a load off and grab a seat on the deck," I offered.

He looked at me a little funny, then nodded his head and ambled through the living room and out the back. I gave Jody the tightest hug I could muster. I tried to squeeze the despair out of her soul. I hoped she could squeeze it out of mine. "I'll take over for a bit," I said. She nodded in acquiescence, as one large tear slowly tumbled down her cheek. Neither of us had any words.

I fetched a couple of cold beers and joined Jude on the deck. We clicked the bottles together and both took a long gulp.

Parents eagerly anticipate milestones in their child's maturation. The first word, first step, first day of school—all mark progress and confirm expectations. These milestones are weighed with varying degrees of excitement. Jody will forever cherish Jude's first violin recital. I wept tears of joy when I tossed out the diaper genie and lit the changing table on fire.

Many of these milestones are not fixed or expected, just appreciated. A first tackle or basket, a first girlfriend, a first haircut, a profession of faith, falling in love… Others we highlight on our parenting calendar years in advance. What parent, who has spent years of their life driving their child from event to event, doesn't desperately yearn for the day their child receives a driver's license?

Birthdays are obvious milestones. Each is significant and accords a point of reflection on our child's trajectory. I had always looked forward to Jude's twenty-first birthday. Not because alcohol plays any role of significance in the life of my family, but because the advent of the twenty-first year represents the erosion of the last barrier to adulthood. There is something symbolic about a father having a drink with his son. A declaration resounds: "I have arrived!"

When Jude's cancer returned, we were keenly aware of the possibilities. On that fateful afternoon, in silent recognition of the potential dissolution of his twenty-first milestone, we resolutely basked in glorious sunshine and enjoyed our beers in relative silence. In that moment, we were not so much father and son but fellow sojourners, colleagues, "celebrating" Jude's introduction to adulthood—a milestone achieved both prematurely and unjustly.

Not surprisingly, Jude finished his beer quicker than I. I declined to comment, but I could tell he was somewhat proud and rather amused by this accomplishment. It was his not-so-subtle way of demonstrating he was his own person and had chosen to experience life in a manner after his own choosing. Before his cancer, this would have irked me. I would have been frustrated if he did not follow the rules or accede to my wishes. Instead, I could savor his independence and appreciate his participation. It was a blessing indeed to just *be* with my son. Every father should be so privileged.

I shared the story of my experience coming down from Glacier Peak. When I got to the point where we slumped to the earth in despair, I could see his interest was piqued.

"What did you do?" he asked.

"We did what we had to," I responded, with as much resolution and clarity as I could muster.

Jude leaned forward in his seat and slowly set his empty beer bottle down on the deck. He looked up at me and then stared off into the distance. I waited calmly. The silence grew uncomfortable, but I could tell he had not let the story go. He was thinking with some degree of intensity, not a common exercise for my son.

"And what was that?" he finally inquired.

"We got off our asses, shouldered our packs—which felt like they were lined with mercury—and started the arduous hike back to our car." I chuckled and leaned forward, grabbing his empty beer bottle and setting it next to mine on the deck table. I stood up and patted his knee. "It sucked, but we did it. There is nothing sweeter than climbing out of the pit of despair."

Jude could have been insulted by my story. I was not attempting to insinuate on any level that what I experienced on my climb was even remotely equitable with his situation. Although tired, worn out, and frustrated, I was never in any sort of mortal danger. Sure, these variables added up to a certain level of palpable misery I would not want to regularly experience, but that was merely a trifle compared to Jude's journey. My entire point, and one I hoped he readily grasped, was that sometimes, even when you think you are done and desperately want the entire affair to be finished, there is more left to do. It really isn't a true test of resolve until you honestly believe you're fully depleted.

Jude looked up at me and smiled. "Do you think it was tougher than me hiking down from Copper Ridge with a broken leg?"

"No," I quickly responded. "That's one of the toughest things I've ever seen."

Jude nodded his head and let a little smile turn up at the corners of his mouth. I could see his heart swell with a touch of pride. He still possessed a large measure of confidence. This was reassuring.

I looked him directly in the eyes and squeezed his leg reassuringly. "Jude, what do you think is going to happen now?"

"I think they are going to have to cut this shit out of my lungs, and if it comes back, they will cut it out again. They told me this happens, and they can just go in and pluck the little hunks of cancer out like picking up stones on the beach." His words were steadfast and calm, with a touch of disdain. I did not detect even an ounce of fear. I marveled at his resolve. All our plans for the fall were shredded. He would not be going back to college. His friends, home for summer, who had brought so much joy, would be leaving again. Once more he would be alone, battling, suffering, fighting a relentless enemy that disrespected all the hopes and dreams of any possible future. I wanted to scream in protest and shake my fist at God. Where was the justice in this? Where was the mercy? I felt abused and deserted. But not Jude. He just whimsically smiled and shrugged his shoulders. Despite his lack of years, he demonstrated all the attributes of a hero.

ANGEL'S WINGS

> *"The ultimate measure of a man is not where he stands in moments of comfort and convenience, but where he stands at times of challenge and controversy."*
>
> MARTIN LUTHER KING JR.

I am easily awed by acts of bravery. Not that I fancy myself a coward, but when the heat is on, I often ask how I would respond in a similar situation. Every brave act is situational in nature. I would not think twice about sprinting into a burning building to save one of my family members. Would I be so recklessly inclined for a colleague? What about a stranger?

I think about the heroes who stormed the beaches of Normandy. Those were valorous acts demanding unparalleled bravery. Would I have possessed the fortitude to huddle uncomfortably in those amphibious vehicles and thrust myself headlong into enemy gunfire, all for a cause that was not immediately tangible or personal? Many of the soldiers who participated knew it was going to be dangerous. They knew their lives were likely forfeit. They knew the day would reek of danger, violence, and tragedy. Those men were exposed to horrors inconceivable to most of us today.

Can you imagine the bravery required to do it a second time? How many of those surviving soldiers, with working knowledge of the carnage and terror irrevocably burned into their psyche, would have the fortitude to muster enough courage to strap into another boat and see if they could survive another day? Thankfully, we don't have any data to answer that question. There was only one D-Day.

When Jude discovered his cancer had returned, he also learned it was in multiple places. Osteosarcoma loves lung tissue. It acts like a great big catcher's mitt for those rapidly multiplying cells which are displaced from their original home. Once they achieve a foothold in the lung, they rapidly requisition blood vessels, which provide the tumors with an exorbitant nutrient supply, enabling exponential multiplication. Osteosarcoma is a hard tissue tumor. It is repurposed bone. The lungs must remain pliant and flexible to function. The two tissues are radically incompatible.

Jude had multiple tumors in both lungs. The only way to remove the invading horde was to perform a full thoracotomy. This meant creating a fourteen-inch incision between his ribs, spreading them apart, and delicately extricating each lung from its compartment to attain complete access. It was necessary for the surgeon to run his fingers over every millimeter of lung tissue. Comprehensive excision required tactile discovery. It was the only way to uncover every nidus of growth. Imaging was not precise enough, and this was not the sort of surgery one performed multiple times, if possible. More importantly, if anything was missed, it would continue metastasizing. There were even worse places the tumor could travel than the lungs.

Each lung required a five-to-seven-day hospital stay followed by a solid three-week recovery. The rehab was difficult. Jude toyed with the idea of doing both lungs at the same time, but the surgeon and his oncology team talked him out of it. The recovery would have been unbearable, and the risks—collapsed lung, infection, or other unpredictable complications—would have increased significantly. Jude was forewarned, as were all of us, that a major thoracotomy was considered the single most painful surgery possible. It's impossible to know if this is true, but when multiple surgeons independently express this truth, it lends validity to the assertion. Unfortunately, that meant while he plied his way through the misery of recovery, he had to look forward to enduring the exact same procedure all over again. There was no justice with Jude's disease, and this event only highlighted that fact.

The first surgery and subsequent convalescence were textbook. There was suffering, but Jude was buttressed by a positive pathology report (clean margins and no indication of extra, non-visible nodes). The second surgery less so. When he woke up in the recovery room, he was in intense pain. He had a difficult time describing it, other than a deep, compressive ache originating near his neck and radiating down his arm and into his chest cavity. He squirmed in discomfort and kept recoiling away from his left shoulder. This created all sorts of other difficulties, as he had a wickedly long incision extending from spine to arm.

The nurse attempted to keep him steady. She needed to protect his incision. All Jude wanted to do was curl up in a ball, and fresh out of anesthesia, he was having a difficult time understanding what was going on. I grabbed his hand, attempting to soothe his discomfort. Like so many times before, I was disgusted with my ineptitude. I only desired to shoulder his burden. It was a desire impossible to realize. Since his infancy, I had promised Jude I would protect him. After his diagnosis, I awoke every day mocked by the knowledge that I was living a lie.

As I leaned over my son, squeezing his hand and gently holding him steady, he opened his eyes, took a very painful, deep breath, squeezed my hand in return, and shed the largest tear I've ever seen. This broke me. My impotence was maddening, his need overwhelming. With as much calm as I could muster, I sternly implored the nurse to garner the attention of someone who could ascertain Jude's difficulty. Between the orderly, myself, and the nurse, it seemed we were helpless bystanders in a Danse Macabre.

Thankfully, she responded with alacrity. Within minutes, a couple of residents, along with an attending physician, rushed in. They rolled through various differentials, finally ascertaining a large gas bubble was pressing between Jude's lung and his pleural lining. To say it was unpleasant may be the baldest understatement of the year.

Having the correct diagnosis was reassuring. It was not particularly helpful. There really was nothing to be done for it, other than let the bubble slowly resorb. Jude could comprehend this, and with an inspiring force of will, managed to quell his overt displays of agony and retreat into a pain-suppressing trance. I could do nothing other than stand by his side.

Eventually, his sharp pain subsided. This took many hours, and despite Jude's stolid reserve, a few more tears were shed. We both knew it was only a matter of time before the pain would diminish. When one is in physical agony, however, time never seems to cooperate. The minutes felt like days. The evening took an eon. By midnight, however, he was able to eat and hold a conversation. The first thing I said to him when he was ready to talk was, "Boy, let's hope and pray you never have to do this ever again."

I wish prayer worked the way most people think it does. But that is a conversation for another chapter.

A few days later, when we received the pathology report, we discovered that one of the lesions examined lacked clean margins. There was a strong possibility that some tumor remained firmly ensconced in his lung, most assuredly serving as an ugly breeding ground for additional osteosarcoma cells to continue their inexorable march.

Now Jude had a very difficult decision. He had just suffered through two thoracotomies—two more than anyone would ever wish. He had to decide if he wanted to be subjected to a third procedure—where they would reopen his partially healed incision and do it all over again—or continue with his rehabilitation, knowing a ticking time bomb was sewn into his chest. He deferred to my wisdom, which was an unnerving burden. I appreciated the assurance and confidence he placed in his parents. What parent doesn't sincerely hope their child will grow to appreciate parental love and wisdom? To have this appreciation manifest in such an impossible situation, however, was imminently frustrating. We were all tired of his misery. The suffering seemed endless. The alternative untenable.

I spoke with the surgeon at length. He was a kind, sincere, and realistic gentleman. It was one of those delicate and diplomatic conversations where what is officially stated, and what is implied, are not coincident. Statistically, there was very little difference in outcomes between a "soft" margin and a clean margin. Unsurprisingly, some of the tumors present in Jude's lungs were not the typical firm nodule, but were more of a perfuse, cottage cheese-like consistency. Those types were less predictable, and sometimes partial resection was adequate. He would not say it, but it was easy to interpret: Regardless of what we chose to do, Jude's potential outcome was bleak.

I asked him the question most doctors do not like to answer but was necessary to drill through the uncertainty of the matter: "What would you do if this was your son?"

After a significantly pregnant pause, he very quietly answered, "I don't know."

Leaving life or death decisions up to a coin flip is rather unnerving. We discussed all the new information with Jude, collating the facts and conjectures into neat little mental piles. Those piles of information provided very little clarity. After discussion, prayer, worry, and study, our best advice to Jude was to excise the rest of the tumor. We all knew what that advice entailed. He would have to abide another thoracotomy.

To subject oneself to a third thoracotomy, let alone in a five-week stretch, merits rarified status in the pantheon of bravery. It requires a very deliberate and intentional fortitude to willingly undergo such a painful procedure—and subsequent recovery—for an ill-defined and intangible benefit. He was treading uncharted territory. The only guarantee was his own misery. When we helped pack his bags and situate him in the car—readying him for the long trek back to the hospital and the even longer stay in surgical recovery—all I could do was salute him. He never once complained, even though it was impossible for him not to wince in pain just buckling his seatbelt. He was inviting someone to cut through his bruised, torn, and scarred muscles. He was willingly exposing his lungs to another air bubble episode. In doing so, he proved that his depth of character was, by any practical measure, unmeasurable.

My heart ached.

I've never been prouder.

A FINAL REPRIEVE

"To me, there is no picture so beautiful as smiling, bright-eyed, happy children; no music so sweet as their clear and ringing laughter."

P. T. BARNUM

The week of his third thoracotomy was also the anniversary of his first procedure. Through every poke, prod, stab, and cut, Jude smiled, laughed, and thanked the nurses for their attentiveness. His grateful perseverance, however inspiring, was waning. Not because he was any less thankful for those trying to help him. Alas, as heroic as he had been, no man is unlimited. He was not demonstrating any overt signs of withering, but as his father and hospital companion, I knew the symptoms were simmering under the surface. One more bump, one more piece of bad news, would likely crack his façade.

Remarkably, within two weeks after the third procedure, he was back on the exercise bike. His resiliency bordered on the preternatural. I knew we had an army of people praying for him. This was one explanation for his astonishing capacity. He was also extremely motivated by the opportunity to be social. The idea of convalescing in solitude was an absolute nonstarter. He also abhorred the notion of friends and family visiting him as if he was a decrepit sick person confined to a bed. He was determined to enjoy the company of others on his terms. Thankfully, his companions were excited to oblige him. Never underestimate the health benefits of friendship.

Parents are overjoyed when they witness their children thriving. I pray for my children daily, and part of those prayers is a supplication for motivation, desire, and inspiration. I want my children to pursue a calling with bold ambition. To recognize an area in their life where they can apply their talents and gifts that both glorifies God and is energizing. Few problems are more disturbing to a parent than observing their child foundering, without purpose or meaning.

Cancer radically transmogrified Jude's purpose. Before he fell sick, Jude's trajectory was ambiguous. He was unsure about his faith, sometimes openly hostile, and not motivated to explore or examine his own hostility. His actions were primarily selfish in nature. The idea of serving others, although nascent, had not taken root. He loved others but was not purposeful in his intent. Life was something that happened. His participation within that life was ill-defined and mostly meaningless, from his perspective.

Rehabilitation was transformative. Every day he spent in the hospital, Jody encouraged him to actively be a blessing to others. She prayed for him, and with him, working to instill this attitude into his very persona. Before they would check in for each chemo treatment, Jody would sit with him in the car and encourage him to be gracious and thoughtful towards everyone who was treating him. He took this challenge seriously, incorporating it daily. Unbeknownst to him, his practice of being a blessing ultimately worked from the inside out. The more labor and energy he put into consciously blessing others, the more he was transformed. The more he transformed, the more influence he imparted. Jude's hostility towards Christianity had mostly circled around selfishness. He "wanted to do what he wanted to do." He viewed Christianity as an oppressive, legalistic, anachronistic, suffocating contrivance, ill-formed for his style and desires. What he did not know is that the heart of Christianity is easily distilled into two accessible maxims: Love the Lord with all your heart, and love your neighbor as yourself.

Jude did not realize he was embodying a Christian posture. Had someone been foolish enough to point this out to him, he likely would have pushed against it. We are what we do, however, and like it or not, Jude's heart was actively aligning with Christ's.

Jody and I were privileged to bear witness to this transformation. His potential, always obvious but never tapped, began to manifest in ways we had only hoped and prayed for. He was battered and bent, but we were as excited for his future as two parents could be. When my relationship with Jude was at its absolute nadir, and Jody and I would crawl into bed frustrated and exhausted with our stubborn, wayward, and recalcitrant son, we both agreed it would take something radical to reshape his heart. Our insight proved prescient. Unfortunately, it was Jude who suffered the radical assault, not either of us. Would that it was otherwise. Regardless, the effect was astonishing.

* * *

Autumn proved a welcome blessing. Jude forged new friendships and rekindled old ones. He continued rehab with his leg, and slowly regained strength and function in his upper body. He started lifting weights, pushed his cardio limits, and embraced a new strut with his prosthetic. His confidence grew, his smile broadened, and his lust for life rippled into ever-expanding boundaries. We re-enrolled him for classes in the New Year. He was ready to embrace a collegiate lifestyle and take advantage of the opportunities it afforded him. We could not wait to see him flourish.

AN INCONVENIENT TRIAL

"There is no experiment like experience."
LAILAH GIFTY AKITA

The odds of surviving refractory osteosarcoma with lung metastases are roughly 20 percent. Those odds drop further with age and the number of metastases present. Jude had three major strikes working against him. There was no way to ascertain what was silently happening in his body as he rehabilitated. We could only study the odds and react accordingly. Knowing the odds were long, we elected to become proactive and enroll him in an experimental trial. Surgery is always the number one line of defense. We needed to go on offense.

Cancer is such a difficult disease because your own cells are working against you. They fool your immune system and run amok throughout your body, disrupting organ systems, co-opting function, and invading sensitive areas. The Holy Grail of any cancer treatment is to instruct and retrain your immune system on how to recognize your cancer cells, categorize them as "other," and then eradicate them. In the last twenty years, cancer immunotherapy has made significant strides. This will likely be the cure for cancer we have all been praying for. It is only in an embryonic stage, however.

Immunotherapy is most effective when the cancer cells have something distinct about them that your immune system can be trained to exploit. Naturally, some types of cancer lend themselves more readily to this therapy. Osteosarcoma is not one of these. It is an extremely indistinct cancer. Essentially, it is bone progenitor cells that do not have a shut-off mechanism. On the surface, there is nothing indistinguishable about them—apart from possibly one small protein marker. Jude's trial attempted to take advantage of that marker.

The most efficient way to introduce that marker into Jude's body was to flood him with the listeria bacteria, engineered to manifest this exploitable surface protein. Listeria works well, as it induces a potent immune response. Unfortunately, that immune response can also be deadly. Jude's bacteria were attenuated so as to not provoke an active listeria infection. We just wanted to hyper-stimulate his immune system. Once induced through the listeria assault, the hope was that it would also attack any potential osteosarcoma cells that may be setting up camp throughout his system.

Flooding oneself with listeria is not fun. The invading bacteria cause an immediate and acute response, which results in fever spikes, chills, shakes, and sweats. The testing team was so worried about septic shock (even though the bacteria was not technically infectious) that they had an emergency team on the ready outside the door to Jude's room. If his body overreacted, the subsequent cytokine storm could cause multi-system organ failure. The team had every available piece of life-support equipment at their disposal if resuscitation became necessary. Consistent with Jude's demeanor, he expressed very little concern for this noteworthy possibility. The rest of us were sweating bullets.

What Jude did exhibit was a very acute Pavlovian response. For over a year, every time he entered the doors of Seattle Children's Hospital, he was subjected to abuse. Granted, it was agreeably intentional, but abuse, nonetheless. Whenever he entered the HEMOC clinic (hematology/oncology), it was for bloodwork—drawn only when he was already miserably nauseous from chemotherapy. The listeria trial also took place in the HEMOC ward, cementing the association.

No sooner did they stick the needle in his arm than Jude immediately got sick. His reaction was remarkable. We had been warned that when the bacteria hit his system, he may react quickly. Jude reacted to the saline. There was nothing pumping into his system. His mental association between that ward and nausea was so inextricably intertwined that his psyche hijacked all pretense of stoicism and reacted violently. We did everything to distract him, to no avail. HEMOC clinic, needle, puke. It was Psychology 101.

Remarkably, Jude forged ahead with the treatment despite his psychological idiosyncrasies. This required astounding fortitude on his part and forced Jody and I to overcome burgeoning barriers of emotional dissonance. A parent's initial instinct is to protect their child. Here we were encouraging our child to let himself be injected with an experimental and potentially lethal concoction. It strained our sensibilities. It also made us reevaluate—like we had so many times on this journey—and analyze the cost versus benefit of Jude's purported therapy. We were fully cognizant of the extreme measures sometimes inflicted on cancer patients. We did not want our son to be turned into a punching bag. We were also desperate for his survival.

Jude's first injection proceeded as planned (aside from the Pavlovian setback), although to say anything was planned is a bit of a misnomer. Jude was the very first osteosarcoma patient at Seattle Children's to have this procedure. There was little data to draw from. Presumably, the first hour would reveal nothing. Then he should exhibit the physical manifestations of a small blood infection—fever, chills, sweats—which should subside within thirty to sixty minutes. Jude followed this pattern until his fever suddenly spiked, he was wracked with intense lower back pain and abdominal nausea, and he began shaking uncontrollably. We thought he was having a seizure. As his condition worsened, he began writhing in pain and had to curl into a ball to prevent rolling onto the floor. Some members of the crash team entered, and all the staff associated with the experiment went on high alert. As his fever threatened to crest 105, they started to inject him with all sorts of anti-febrile medication, along with anti-inflammatories. The room next to his, intentionally, was an emergency crash facility. It had a retractable wall that could be shoved aside for immediate transport. Two orderlies stood on the ready, expecting to take the wall down. Just as the ER doctor was about to give the signal, Jude stopped shaking, emerged from his semi-catatonic state, and took a deep, peaceful breath. Within minutes, his fever reduced, the chills relented, and he lay back on his bed a sweaty, achy mess.

Everyone exhaled simultaneously. The palpable tension in the room evaporated. Jude, of course, found all the fuss somewhat amusing. Of course, he had no idea how close to the edge he had come. What he did not find amusing, however, was his headache. He had been pumped with so many different sorts of medications in such a short period of time, I had no idea how he could function. His constitution defied explanation. Even now, I get nauseous just thinking about all the vials opened and introduced into his IV. It's a wonder his liver didn't explode.

Thankfully, his next two injections, serviced at three-week intervals, were not as dramatic. He still suffered through the same sequence of events. They were not nearly so malevolent or threatening. The Pavlovian problem persisted, however, and even grew worse, which I did not think possible. The last time I took him for his treatment, he started retching before they even put the needle in his arm. As a scientist, I found this fascinating. As a father, mortifying. Jude took it all in stride. After he finished puking into a bucket, I pointed out to him that his IV wasn't even hooked up to anything yet. He looked at the unattached plastic tube coiled on his bed and started to laugh, while he wiped the puke from his lips. "I don't care," he said, between snorts. "It doesn't matter what it's hooked to. It just makes me sick." I tried to laugh with him. Forced mirth is an acquired skill. I did not find any of this amusing.

SILENT NIGHT

"My God, my God, why have you forsaken me? Why are you so far from saving me, so far from my cries of anguish? My God, I cry out by day, but you do not answer, by night, but I find no rest."

PSALM 22:1–2

Experiments aside, Jude continued his road to recovery with marvelous aplomb. Family life had almost recaptured a feeling of normalcy, even if it looked quite a bit different than any of us imagined. It was odd to have our oldest son, who should have been a sophomore at college, join us every night for dinner. It was also a blessing and a boon. Modern families rarely have the opportunity to consistently interact as their children enter adulthood. We relished this unique opportunity. It was pure joy to watch three separate strands wind their way into a braid.

Because Jude had to receive injections every three weeks, it was unreasonable to ship him back to college. He would live at home for the spring semester and take classes at a local institution. We were fine with this arrangement. Jude was a little relieved by this development, for as much as he wanted to catch up with his college experience, it meant one less stressor in his tumultuous life. I think all of us were ready for an extreme bout of ennui.

From the comfort of home, Jude started pushing the limits of his prosthetic. He wanted to run. He did not quite have the strength or balance to manage this yet, but it was on the horizon. He tried to hide his progress from me. His plan was to surprise us all one day, by hopping up and jogging across the yard.

One evening, the second week in December, after a moderate workout, Jude was relaxing after dinner and started complaining about his sore back. "It hurts when I lean forward or twist. Riding the stationary bike seems to aggravate it."

"What about sit-ups?" I asked.

"No, that doesn't seem to bother it. It just aches at odd times."

"Were you lifting? Did you feel it strain or pop?" It seemed like an exercise-induced injury to me. He was not very fit yet, and any overuse could be problematic.

"Not that I can remember. But everything feels weird back there. I did get my torso sliced open." He gave a little cynical chuckle. "Maybe the twenty-eight inches of scar tissue are barking at me." We all nodded in agreement, and the conversation moved on.

. . .

A few days later, Jude complained again. He indicated it hurt on both sides, across his mid-back, and radiated in a broad semicircle which stretched across his oblique muscles. "It feels like I have a side stitch from running," he described.

"What happens when you take a deep breath?" I inquired. He took two very long, deep breaths.

"Nothing," he replied. "Feels totally normal."

"What about when you twist?"

"Yeah, that hurts. But it isn't sharp pain. It almost makes me feel nauseous."

"Well, the last thing you need is more nausea in your life," I said jokingly. "I'm voting we let nausea remain in the rearview mirror."

"Yeah," Jude agreed. "I will take it easy working out and see if it just goes away."

. . .

The next couple of days, the pain ebbed and flowed. It did not seem restrictive, and Jude was not too uncomfortable. Christmas was rapidly approaching. Members of the extended family were scheduled to arrive in town. We were planning on a large gathering on Christmas Day, including the unfortunate pleasure of taking family pictures. More importantly, our immediate family was eagerly anticipating a return to our Christmas Eve traditions. The previous Christmas Eve had been extraordinary as a rehabilitative vehicle, but the anomaly did not demand a reprise. One amputation was one too many for a lifetime. We didn't need another Christmas soiled with post-surgical pain. The last advent season mostly served as a backstop to our shock, more than a celebration of Christ's birth and return. This was the year we would recapture the true joy of the season.

We were not obtuse in our anticipation. We recognized the future is not guaranteed. Each day is a gift. This Christmas, however, celebration was the operative attitude. We were fully functional as a family, morale was high, Jude was recovered, and the spirit of Christmas pervaded the atmosphere of our home. Jude took special care anticipating what his siblings might enjoy as gifts. This is no mean feat for a nineteen-year-old male. Exceptions aside, it is hardly controversial to assert that most young men are not empathic or charitable. This was a positive step for Jude and exciting to observe. He had worked so hard to be a blessing to those serving him in the hospital. As those roots deepened, his circle broadened. The cultivation of gratitude, once only reactive, became proactive. He was uncloaking the spiritual gift of selflessness. We caught his fever.

Unfortunately, the week of Christmas saw an increase in Jude's discomfort. His symptoms were so nebulous, and inconsistent, that it was difficult to pursue a course of action. It also did not help that he had no interest in pressing the matter. He kept reassuring us it was not a big deal and would eventually pass. His assurances held no water for Jody and me. The anxiety meter pegged to maximum as our hypervigilance over his health continued to burn.

After multiple inquiries to his oncology team, no answers were forthcoming.

Everything about his presentation was baffling. We tossed out all sorts of differentials, ranging from pulled muscles, to referred pain from his incisions, to possible abdominal inflammation from his listeria treatments. The latter was a bit concerning to the research team, so Jude was referred for an ultrasound. This would reveal if any of his large organs were inflamed or insulted.

From a positive perspective, his caretakers secretly hoped it was his immune system hyper-reacting and aggressively attacking newly emerging growth sites of osteosarcoma, neutralizing and destroying their capacity to gain a toehold in his system. Perhaps the ultrasound would reveal pockets of pseudo-infection illuminating this very process?

The ultrasound was maddeningly inconclusive. They noted some spots on his liver and kidneys but informed us that was typical in an ultrasound and likely only clusters of blood vessels. There certainly was not any excessive swelling, gas pressure, or abnormalities indicative of Jude's symptoms. What Jude did note was that it was rather difficult to lie flat on his back while they performed the procedure. He could barely lie still while they monitored him, noting this was the most discomfort he had experienced since the inception of his novel symptoms.

On the morning of Christmas Eve, Jody and I went down to his bedroom to check on him, as had been our practice since the very beginning of chemotherapy. All our children are precious and deserving of our absolute attention. Jude's ordeal had created a different parenting dynamic than for Simone and Johann, however. The last thing they wanted every morning was for me to barge into their room and bother them with a health checklist. Jude welcomed the care. We all functioned better knowing he was doing just fine.

Christmas Eve found him half-propped in his bed, with pillows strategically piled to support him in a half-crescent shape.

"That's sort of a weird way to sleep," Jody exclaimed. "What are you trying to do?"

"I can't lay down," Jude replied. "This is the only way to get comfortable. If I try to lie flat, either on my back or stomach, it just hurts."

"Have you taken any Advil?" I asked. "Does that seem to help?"

"Yeah... I took some. I don't know how many. They don't seem to make a difference." Jude winced as he tried to sit up further. "It only feels normal when my back is curled."

We had an entire day planned. Food, festivities, a special church service, and our family's Christmas package-opening extravaganza, which typically lasted into the late hours. Jude had no interest in siphoning joy away from the moment or erecting any speed bumps along the road to our brilliantly planned day. He dismissed his discomfort as an insignificant anomaly which was sure to "sort itself out eventually."

I took one glance at Jody. No words were necessary.

"I hate to say it, son, but you and I need to take a ride down to Children's and get to the bottom of this. Nothing is adding up, and your parents are much too gun-shy to take any chances." I patted him gently, reassuringly. "Let's get dressed and get going. If we are efficient, we should be able to make it home in time for dinner and presents. It will all work out splendidly."

* * *

The drive down to Children's was a drag. Jude was frustrated and despondent. He had no desire to go to the ER, especially not on Christmas Eve. The weather turned cold, and snow began falling. Those were ideal conditions for celebrating Christmas. They made navigation miserable.

We both attempted lighthearted and festive conversation. Jude was never one to let any circumstance disable his enjoyment of the moment, so he rightfully focused on how his siblings would respond to the gifts he had chosen. I had never seen him so excited to give something away. I did everything within my power to mask my growing anxiety. I knew something was not right. This instinct pressed against me like a weighted blanket, pushing the potential joy of Christmas into the hidden crevices, and replacing it with despair. I lost my appetite. My heart would not stop thumping. I had to grip the steering wheel with two hands to keep them from shaking uncontrollably. While Jude napped, I prayed. I prayed prayers with no words. I simply sat in the presence of God, a supplicant sinner begging for his son. It was a prayer propelled by the power of unconditional love. I would not be ignored.

The ER was a madhouse. On the afternoon of Christmas Eve, no one wanted to be there, and yet it appeared the entire Pacific Northwest was sick. By this time, Jude and I had navigated the ER on multiple occasions, and he was something of a celebrity to boot. Jody, thankfully, had called ahead, so Jude's entire oncology team was in the loop, having ordered labs and imaging in advance.

They whisked us through the triage center into a private and quiet room. Nothing could completely shield us from the mayhem, but this was a positive start. Within minutes, they drew blood. Two doctors came in and did a full exam, prodding, poking, and contorting Jude in every way imaginable. They were at a loss. His bloodwork revealed nothing. I asked them to take an image of his back, as that was the original source of his discomfort. They balked at first, mostly because they were short-staffed, and the MRI machine was reserved for significant emergencies on holidays. I begged them to see what they could do.

Eventually, the MRI was cleared. The only problem was Jude could not lie flat. The pain was too intense. This forced us to wait for an anesthesiologist to sedate him enough so he could remain still during imaging. Jude and I both watched the clock closely. Despite the scheduling nightmares, our Christmas Eve festivities were still possible. Jude stared wistfully at the exit. He had lost patience with hospitals months ago. Neither one of us was leaving without answers, however.

When they rolled a pleasantly sedated Jude out of the ER, I was left to the mercy of my imagination. My only recourse was to pray, which I did with a fervency that defies description. This was not a new strategy. Prayer had been my accomplice from day one. I was not about to desert it. Could God ignore the prayers of a desperate father?

When Jude returned, he was feeling well. The drugs had diminished his back pain, and this lightened his mood significantly. It also indicated how much pain he had likely been in for the last few weeks. Much like the proverbial frog in the slowly heating pot of water, Jude's pain must have incrementally ratcheted into the insufferable category. Eschewing pity, Jude purposefully hid it well.

"What do you think?" I asked him. "Do you think the pictures will show anything?"

"I have no idea," he replied. "None of the techs said anything. They just wheeled me back out—business as usual."

"Hopefully that's a good sign." My mouth was so dry I could hardly form the words. "And hopefully they expedite the results so we can go open presents!"

Jude smiled in return. "Man, that would be really cool," he exclaimed. "A lame day, but a fun evening. I can't wait to see what Simone thinks of my gift."

"Don't tell me what you got her," I said, holding up my hand. "I want to be surprised too."

. . .

The wait was interminable. Time was a glacier descending and retreating in tantalizing steps. We knew it was moving, we just could not see it. Every minute that passed, my anxiety worsened. Jude kicked me out of the room because he could not handle my pacing. How he could remain so calm, almost peacefully serene, was baffling. I thought they were going to have to peel me off the ceiling.

Thirty minutes stretched to sixty and then expanded into ninety. I returned to Jude's room and adopted a meditative posture of prayer. Jude Snapchatted his friends and fiddled with his phone, pleasantly unconcerned by the delay. As the minutes stretched to two hours, my pleading with the Almighty reached a zenith. Briefly, I imagined what Jesus must have felt when his sweat became mixed with blood. I oozed anxiety and desperation. I knew nothing, saw nothing, felt nothing. I was supplication personified.

Finally, the door retracted, and Jude's initiating doctors entered, followed by a new female doctor. She appeared to be in her early sixties, fully attired in anti-Covid gear. I had never met her, even though she seemed familiar. There was an energetic bounce to her step which commanded attention. The other doctors deferred to her.

"Jude," she said, smiling briefly, "I've been observing your case from a distance." She looked us both squarely in the eye, then smiled again. "I'm an oncologist and have been treating osteosarcoma for over thirty years. It's a nasty cancer. I hate it."

"We do too," I blurted.

"Yes, it's just so difficult to treat. We're really in the dark ages when it comes to that one." She shook her head wistfully, briefly lost in thought. Then she took a couple of steps forward and sat down on the corner of Jude's bed. "Jude, I've been poring over your MRI results with the radiologist. We've had multiple doctors look at it, just to make sure we aren't missing anything and have a really clean handle on what the pictures are telling us."

"Okay," Jude replied, cocking his head. "I've never really done anything normally you know," he joked.

"You're right," the doctor agreed. "I've looked at your case file, and nothing you've experienced these past sixteen months conforms to textbook progress. And that's what I want to talk to you about right now."

My heart was seizing. I was not sure what to expect or what she was going to say. For some reason, she was approaching the diagnosis obliquely. In a fit of desperate hope, I fantasized they had discovered Jude's immune system had mobilized and was chewing up itinerant osteosarcoma cells in an epic, one-sided battle.

She leaned forward and put a hand on Jude's knee. "We discovered your cancer has returned. It has metastasized to three places in your spine. One of the growths is so large it's pressing dangerously against your spinal cord. This is what is causing so much pain. In addition, it has somehow managed to adhere to your liver and kidneys and is starting to displace your bowels." Her eyes never left Jude's.

The shock of her revelation was an emotional tsunami. I had known for days this was a potential reality but was never willing to openly express it. I had tried, during the previous weeks, to buttress my psyche against this possibility, but the wave of knowledge effortlessly flung aside my feeble defenses. I was a helpless rag doll in the face of this onslaught. All I could do was look at my son in abject desperation while my heart bled uncontrollably. What would this do to him? How would he respond? How could a nineteen-year-old who had suffered miserably, yet managed to beat back despair with a smile and a laugh, absorb this horrific explanation? Why my son? Why us? What could I possibly do for him now?

Jude looked at the other two doctors in the room, briefly nodding at them both. When he regarded the oncologist, he was as serious as I had ever seen him. He slowly sat up in bed and pulled his single leg over the side, as if he needed the floor for solid bracing. The oncologist stood up, her eyes locked with Jude's in somber approval.

Jude cleared his throat, and the noise echoed through the tension in the room like a rifle's retort. "I want to thank all of you for taking time away from your family on Christmas Eve to be here with me. I know that isn't easy, and it's not something you want to do. I know I don't want to be here." He smiled wryly and sat up even straighter. "I appreciate your willingness to be honest. This isn't great Christmas Eve news."

I turned to the oncologist, who stared at Jude in stunned silence. She was a veteran of thirty years. She had delivered all manner of bad news during that time. She was as realistic and battle-hardened as they come, wielding professional stoicism like a shield. But as Jude regarded her and expressed his appreciation for her care and diagnosis, despite the devastating news, I witnessed a small tear emerge from the corner of her eye and trickle slowly down the side of her cheek. She did not wipe it away. Instead, she surprisingly turned to me, and with all the solemnity the gravity of the moment demanded, stated, "You have an amazing son."

Yes. Yes I do.

The other two doctors informed us they would have some instructions and strategies after another consultation with the oncology team. I sat down on Jude's bed, shoulders slumped in abject defeat. This was news no one ever prepares to hear. Even if you think you know, you really do not. It is against the core of human nature to fully apprehend our mortality. If we were constantly conscious of it, we would petrify, so we guard against this realization until the very end. I was deeply concerned about Jude's mental state, how he would process this horrible revelation. I was not sure where to begin. I finally reached over and grabbed his hand, like a loving father aiding a child during his first steps. We sat there quietly for a bit, both understanding words would only be distractions.

"I love you, buddy," I finally blurted. I could not keep the tears at bay any longer.

"I love you too, Dad," he answered. And there were tears there, too. We both knew what his diagnosis meant. We did not have to discuss it. Jude had managed to thwart the terror of his journey by adopting an air of blissful ignorance. That time was now past. He was fully cognizant of his path. He had, against his very will, purchased an accelerated ticket to a destination we will all eventually face. "I think I need to be alone for a bit."

I did not want to leave his side. The thought of abandoning him in this desperate moment was inconceivable. And yet I understood his request. Some burdens are too personal to share. As much as others want to bear them for you, they are destined for you, and you alone. Jude recognized no one could take this from him. Nor would he ever consider giving it to someone else. He was much too selfless for that. When he had first received his diagnosis, he had expressed thankfulness that none of his friends had gotten this disease. Now he was trying to shield me from his forlorn despair, recognizing my helplessness would be my undoing. Jude's magnanimity, when he had nothing to give, was the personification of Christ. I was not worthy to be his father.

The burden I had to bear, that even Jude could not protect me from, was the obligation of calling his mother. It was Christmas Eve. Jody, Simone, and Johann had been patiently waiting at home, desperate for news, wanting to celebrate and see us all together. The ER did not have any cell coverage. They were in the basement of the hospital, and reception was impossible. The Wi-Fi was down. So, when Jude requested solitude, I wound my way through the maze of triage desks and treatment bays until I finally discovered a little pocket of cellphone reception. I have never dreaded a phone call more.

Jody knew. Like me, she did not want to accept it and had fantasized a miracle, but back in August, when the cancer revealed its tenacity, we knew this day was likely. That knowledge did nothing to dull the sting, however. I could barely get the words out. They were words she didn't need to hear to understand. It was the knowledge every parent fears more than any other. I was happy she could be there for our other children. I was sorry she could not be here for Jude. I was utterly helpless. My son's fate was inevitable. My wife was inconsolable. I sat by myself in a hospital on Christmas Eve, a heart torn in two, desperate for a miracle. I prayed to God for mercy. I prayed for a miracle. I prayed for my son, and I prayed for my wife. I slumped against a drab, sanitized wall in the corner of a boisterous, frenzied ER, and prayed that the gift of His son, whom we were set to celebrate, would provide us with peace. All I received was silence.

• • •

Eventually, I made my way back to Jude's room. He had Snapped some of his close friends and divulged his diagnosis. The reality was very present, but he was already gripping his fate. We chatted casually for a bit, and then started to gripe and moan about how slowly hospitals worked and how badly we just wanted to be home. As my demeanor evolved from sorrow to impatience to outright frustration, Jude interrupted my complaining and said, "You know, Dad, since I don't have much time left to live, I ought to work on my one-legged dancing."

He hopped out of bed and began twirling around the room, hopping, bending, gesticulating, and laughing. His prosthetic was still in the corner, removed for his MRI. He bounced around the room, keeping time to a song in his head, until he finally fell over attempting a one-legged limbo. We both laughed so hard we started to cry. Just as Jude picked himself off the ground, an attending physician arrived, oblivious to Jude's antics and obviously shocked that two men—one of whom had just received a death sentence—would be laughing uproariously. We both looked at him like he was the one out of order.

In an effort of composure, he expressed his condolences and provided us with all the discharge information. I'm not sure either of us heard a word. We just wanted to go and be with the rest of our family. Desperate times will always reveal what fills your heart.

* * *

We drove the first thirty miles without speaking. We were exhausted. It was ten at night. All we wanted was to be home by midnight. As we departed the greater Seattle metro area, I gingerly reached my arm across the seat and clasped Jude's hand. He clung to it desperately, like a drowning man. Love was our buoy. It is remarkable what can be conveyed through silence.

Snow began to fall. It rapidly transformed into a full-on blizzard. The road was treacherous. Visibility was fleeting, and the wind began to dangerously buffet our truck. I had no desire to slow down or exercise any caution. It was a stupid and immature way for me to mock God, to dismiss the Almighty for His lack of intervention. I was so forlorn, so aggrieved, nothing made any sense. And through this maelstrom of emotion, we stubbornly refused to let go of each other. Then Jude started to cry. His present reality welled forth from the center of his heart. The truth of his predicament, his unfortunate demise, the knowledge that his coming journey would be fraught with pain—both physical and mental—erupted in an uncontrollable emotional surge. The dam burst. He was awash with pure emotion.

"My family," he cried. "What is going to happen to my family?"

I started to answer, and then realized I wasn't sure I understood the nature of his question. "We will miss you with all our hearts," I finally responded.

He looked at me sideways, and I noted frustration in his eyes. I hadn't fully understood him. "I know you'll miss me," he scoffed. I laughed briefly at his hubris. He was still Jude. "That's not what I'm worried about. I don't care about me." His statement cut me to the quick. Oh, for a heart like his. "What is going to happen to you guys?"

An outsider, who had not been privy to Jude's transformation, might have interpreted the question as originating from a selfish, narcissistic nineteen-year-old boy. *How can the rest of you possibly go on living without me?* But that's not what he was asking at all. Jude was already seeing what I was unwilling to face or even consider acknowledging. He knew he was the lightning rod. He knew he acted as the nuclear force which bound us tightly together. He recognized the crucial role he played in our family dynamic. He was genuinely concerned about what his absence would mean for how the rest of us would continue to operate.

Fear, pain, and desperation mercilessly strip away all veneers and force us to confront ourselves with naked honesty. Jude squeezed my hand, revealing his desperation while also conveying the truth of his heart—a truth startling in its bravery and benevolence. "Dad ... I'm not afraid to die," he admitted. "But I'm afraid to leave you guys."

"I'm afraid too," I cried. "I don't ... I can't ... I love you, son, more than you can ever know, and more than my heart can bear."

And we drove on, piercing through the snow, two grown men clinging desperately to each other.

* * *

The phone rang when we were halfway home. It was the ER.

"Hello?"

"Yes, hello. Is this Jude?"

"No, this is his dad. What can I do for you?"

"Is Jude there?"

"Yes, he's right here and he can hear you. We're battling a snowstorm. What's up? Did we forget something?"

"No, nothing like that. Look, we've been looking at Jude's scans and we think you should come back."

"What?" I cried, looking over at Jude. He appeared ready to unbuckle his seatbelt and fling himself out of the car. The last thing we wanted was to turn around on Christmas Eve. "What could possibly have changed in the last ninety minutes that would demand such a maneuver?"

"Well," the doctor stammered, "we showed your results to another neurologist and to the attending neurosurgeon. They think if you don't have surgery tonight, you could be paralyzed."

Jude and I glanced at each other, eyes wide. This was certainly a turn of events. Our discharge orders had prescribed opiates for the pain and steroids to reduce swelling. We were to reconvene with Jude's oncologist after Christmas to outline a palliative plan. No one had mentioned paralysis.

"Okay, okay. Hold on just a minute," I argued. "You're making a pretty bold claim there, which is frightening both of us. It's almost Christmas. How important are the next thirty-six hours?"

"I can't answer that," the doctor replied. "I'm just conveying what was said to me."

"Spinal surgery is a big deal," I responded. "Are you telling me you have the team in place to do this tonight? This isn't our first rodeo. It is likely we will turn around, be admitted, and then Jude will sit in a bed for forty-eight hours until the team comes back from holiday."

"Not in circumstances like this," declared the doctor.

My mind spun precariously. I had not looked at the images myself. I couldn't bear to do it. Just the knowledge of what was growing inside my son was difficult to swallow. Pictures made it worse. "Why don't you ask the team, if Jude hammers his steroids and limits his mobility, what his thirty-six-hour outlook would look like, and then call me back?"

"Okay," the doctor agreed.

We battled the snowstorm for ten more miles. Not only were we emotionally and physically spent, we now had this new development accosting our sensibilities. Jude wanted no part in returning. I think even if paralysis was imminent, he still would have refused. He was done being subjected to the whims of doctors. I didn't blame him, but I also didn't think he was realistically considering his quality of life. When the phone rang again, we were very anxious.

"Is this Dr. Veltkamp?"

"Yes, hello. What did you find out?"

"Okay, here's the situation. We're going to let you go home, as long as you double the steroid dose and promise not to be too active. We will set up a meeting with his team on the 26th to outline a game plan."

"What about surgery?" I asked. "I thought this was critical."

"They are going to see how he responds to the steroids and take it from there."

"Okay. Great. Merry Christmas. Thank you," I replied wearily.

"Yes. Merry Christmas." *Click.*

Jude looked at me and smiled. "We dodged a bullet," he happily exclaimed. "Thanks for talking me out of that one."

I smiled back, amazed how he could be happy about "dodging a bullet" when his present reality was the equivalent of being manacled to ground zero for an atomic bomb test. But that was Jude. Gratitude in the moment.

We arrived home just before midnight on Christmas Eve. Jude's back was killing him. Remaining in any position for an extended period increased his pain, but moving was also tenuous. We gingerly pried him out of the pickup and took him down to bed. He had plenty of pain meds, and we pushed the steroids. Our hope was for some relief in the next twenty-four hours.

After the bustle of getting him situated died down, Jody and I retired to our room and tried to decompress. That is when the real tears began. Together, we sat in stunned silence, incapable of fully processing the fate of our beautiful boy.

Tragedies occur every day. Fatal accidents are part of our existence. And yet there is something grossly unjust and unnatural about a parent outliving their child. We had been exposed to all sorts of scenarios we never fully anticipated as Jude's parents. But we were not naïve. We knew parenting required flexibility and compromise at times. This was altogether different. Everything felt wrong. The emotional dissonance tore the fabric of our very souls.

As we sat holding each other in silence, I charged my wife, and myself, with a mission no parent should ever have to accept.

"Jody," I quietly whispered.

"Yes?" she replied through muted sobs.

"It is our final task, as Jude's parents, to help him die well."

We collapsed into each other. Hopeless. Helpless. We accepted the truth of our grievous circumstance and braced ourselves for this final assignment.

JOY TO THE WORLD

"It is Christmas every time you let God love others through you."
MOTHER TERESA

How does one die well? Is this something that can be taught, or even expressed? The personal experience of death is absolutely unique and completely isolating. The journey towards death may be observed and even commented on, but that is prospective in nature. No one has ever experienced death and returned to provide an analysis. Death is never retrospective.

Jody and I were at a loss. Every parenting hurdle we had faced, until this juncture, had afforded some level of experience, training, or intuition to draw upon. This was altogether different. Was it our job to enable Jude to fulfill his bucket list? Should we cram as much into his remaining days as possible? Should we pull out all the stops and throw one great party? Should we focus on eliminating pain? Should we take extreme action and enlist specious methodologies to save him? Should we jealously hijack all his time and keep him completely to ourselves, selfishly absorbing his last months to assuage the pain of our impending loss?

The questions were endless. Many we discarded immediately. Like we had done from the outset, we turned to the Lord and prayed for wisdom. We did not receive any writing on the wall. There was no "still, small voice" that spoke directly into our hearts. The epiphany we did receive, on that fateful Christmas morning, was a son who made his way up to the living room and sat down next to the Christmas tree. The metaphor was obvious. He was a gift to us, and to others. Very soon, that gift would not be present, and the grief associated with that knowledge pervaded the very fabric of our existence. How would it be possible to honestly celebrate the birth of one son, even if he was the son of God, knowing our own son would be unjustly taken?

Jude solved the problem for us. As he had done many times in the past year, it was his attitude and perspective that provided both answers and direction. With a welcoming smile and gracious embrace, he exclaimed with utmost sincerity, "Let's celebrate Christmas."

Jude's posture drilled to the very heart of Christmas and Christianity in his charitable declaration. "Let's" and "celebrate" epitomize the new dimension Christ's incarnation brought to humanity. Christianity is not, first and foremost, a doctrine or a proposition (the very things Jude had pushed against); rather, Christianity is a new social order—a community. The declaration of Good News, the coming of Christ, frees us from the bondage of unsatisfiable legalities and incorporates us into an elevated kinship. The pinnacle of those outmoded legalities is loving God and loving neighbor. Christ's social order, a distinct and peculiar process of growth and formation into which we all are recruited, is *koinonia* (fellowship). "Christ in us" is the summum bonum of Christian existence: Loving God, loving neighbor.

Jude's attitude on Christmas morning revealed to his parents how you help a child die well. The same way you help them live well: Enabling them to love their neighbor and love the Lord.

So, we celebrated Christmas. There will never be another Christmas like that one. No one considered, for an instant, what they were receiving—they only cared about what they could give. An uninformed observer would have never guessed the pending tragedy. They would only have seen smiles, hugs, laughter, and charity. The pictures we took characterized our family's story: Jude's levity sustaining the moment. I never knew what it meant to be joyful during a grave trial until that morning. Jude's future eradicated any possibility of happiness, but his attitude ushered in undiminished joy. As we finished our morning gift exchange, Jude and Johann ushered us into the library and played a beautiful duet of "Joy to the World." When I close my eyes and visualize a tapestry that epitomizes the heart of our home, all I see is Christmas morning—the last Christmas morning we ever had.

* * *

Jude's Christmas attitude enabled us to function. I have never awakened with more trepidation than I did on that day, but the path forward was revealed rather clearly. Jody and I continued doing what we had been attempting to do for nineteen years—unconditionally loving our son.

There is a radical shift in perspective when every event you participate in is recognized as a potential *last*, instead of a *first*. That afternoon we joined the rest of our extended family to take pictures. I hate taking family pictures. I am not alone in this sentiment. And it was only magnified knowing this was the last family picture Jude would ever be in. It was agonizing watching my son joke with his siblings, cousins, and uncles and aunts. His capacity to engage the immediate, appreciate the company of others, and bring joy to those around him astounded me. I sat there trying to smile, and it was impossible. Every couple of minutes either Jody or I would have to run to the restroom, wipe our tears, and splash cold water on our faces just to remain functional. Remarkably, we were able to capture some beautiful family photos. A picture may be worth a thousand words, but that day they were a thousand lies. No one wanted to smile that day.

We learned a lesson through that torture, however. The act of living, the process of functioning in community, cannot be superseded by the act of dying. Jude recognized this. His situation was tragically unique, but he had no intention of usurping the beauty or joy to be found in daily interaction. He would never be able to live with himself if he thought his presence, or his trajectory, was derailing another's flourishing. He did nothing in his comportment to evoke pity. His fortitude and selflessness may be his most profound message. I still hear it every day.

Alas, every Christmas must come to a close. When we turned out the lights that evening, we were emotionally exhausted, yet somehow content. Our prayers for wisdom, our desire for guidance, had not been delivered in a thunderclap of revelation or deposited in our laps on tablets of stone. Instead, our epiphany was realized through the attitude of our dying son, who taught us more about loving and living than we could ever teach him. In an ironic twist, Jude was becoming an evangelist.

MIDNIGHT EXPRESS

"We can ignore even pleasure.
But pain insists upon being attended to."

C. S. LEWIS

Our oasis of joy did not eradicate the gravity or urgency of Jude's situation. The primary tumor had infiltrated four vertebrae and pressed dangerously against his spinal cord. Instead of a straight tube of neurons that should run vertically from the base of his skull to his tailbone, he had a sharp u-bend halfway down his spine. By all rights he should be paralyzed. If your spinal cord was assaulted in such a manner, the results would be immediate. The growth of Jude's tumor had been slow enough that the deformation accommodated necessary functions. Unfortunately those accommodations did not keep it from hurting—badly. Eventually the synapses would be cut and everything would cease functioning. The neurosurgeons felt he was fortunate he had lasted as long as he had. They gave him a window of function defined in hours. We knew Jude's fate was inevitable, but one of our goals was to provide a positive quality of life while it was still available to him. Excruciating pain and paralysis did not fit in that algorithm.

The problem defied an obvious solution. Chemotherapy would not help. There was some discussion about starting palliative chemo if we could resolve the spinal cord issue, but it would not be effective for Jude's current predicament. Surgery was a consideration, but it was potentially dangerous and might accelerate or even cause paralysis. Eventually we settled on a plan to shrink the tumor with radiation, evaluate how it responded, and decide on potential surgical interventions after that. We had no time to ponder, for obvious reasons. It was surreal having these conversations, because ultimately they all centered around how we hoped Jude would die. Our goal was for him suffocate to death from the growing lesions in his lungs. We did not want him to suffer through obstructed bowels and catastrophic organ failure from the tumors on his pancreas, kidneys, and liver, and we really didn't want him to waste away in exquisite torment from the multiple tumors lodged in his spine. All the options were terrible. Suffocation, paralysis, organ failure, sepsis—if only it was a macabre joke. Contemplating possible scenarios sickened us.

Our attempt at radiation turned into an absurd fiasco. We transported Jude to Seattle, at the University of Washington, for this procedure. The first day it took forever to manage the imaging and devise a radiation strategy. The worst part was Jude could not lie down. For him to stand straight or lie flat caused intractable pain. It was pain you could not fight through, or momentarily ignore, to accomplish a procedure. It was pain manifesting in the purest sense—sharp bone pressing directly on neurons.

He had to lie perfectly flat and remain still for the radiation to be effective. This proved impossible. Jude attempted, with all his courage, to make it work, but he couldn't come close. We brought in an anesthesiologist to sedate him for his five-minute procedure. After rather extensive rigamarole, red tape cutting, and pleading, we managed to achieve his first two doses in one day. We were going to do another dose the following day, before New Year's weekend, hopefully suppressing more growth and potentially creating relief. At this point Jude was tied to a bottle of opiates for daily function. He was desperate to cut back.

That evening we stayed at my sister's house in Seattle, which was a wonderful blessing. This minimized travel time and eliminated another intolerable car ride. Sleeping arrangements required engineering an intricate assortment of pillows and blankets to keep Jude propped in a half-sitting, half-curled position. Any time he moved beyond his narrow window of tolerance he would awake in agony, crying out in pain. I slept on the floor just outside his room, on high alert. We were sixteen months into his treatment, and we had managed to come full circle. Just like the first night I brought him home from his initial chemotherapy, I reclaimed my position outside his door. I would do anything within my power for my son. I yearned to do more. Not sleeping was hardly a burden.

The next morning brought snow and freezing rain. They threatened to cancel his appointment, but after significant remonstration eventually relented. The inclement weather allowed for only a skeleton crew at the radiation center. Jude's atypical situation overwhelmed them. Logistically, he was a treatment nightmare.

We finally managed to procure an anesthetist amidst the chaos, and just as he began administering the sedative, a large clang rocked the facility. It reverberated through the foundation, killing the power. The entire hospital was thrown into disorder. The anesthetist literally pulled the needle out of the IV and set it back on the tray with a heartbreaking clink. We had already waited four hours. We were hungry, tired, and very frustrated. Then we learned, as we sat in the dark, that the power surge had thrown off the calibration for the radiation machine, which would delay the process even more. No one knew when the power would come back on. In addition, Jude's anesthetist had other obligations, and presumably the hospital would officially close due to weather by midafternoon.

Uncovering facts and receiving sound advice was impossible. No one knew what was going on. We were desperate for treatment. Jude's situation was dire, and urgent. We had never felt more let down, and considering all that had preceded this circumstance, that was a powerful sentiment. I shook my fist at God, completely devastated by this turn of events. How could a loving Savior be so callous? He was already going to deprive me of my son, at the very least He could have the courtesy to allow it to happen with some modicum of painless grace. Jude was being tortured.

We were finally able to track down the chief of radiation therapy. He advised us to go home. It was impossible to recalibrate the machines before the entire operation was suspended. He assured us that the two doses the previous day would be effective in suppressing tumor growth, and as long as Jude stayed consistent with the steroids, his discomfort should improve.

After twenty-four hours of hard-fought misery, we made the arduous trek back home. It was becoming an unpleasant theme: Jude and I driving away from the hospital, devastated by a horrible turn of events and unsure what we would face next. We really wanted a change in tune. This melancholy dirge had exceeded its usefulness.

...

Fortunately, Jude's pain appeared to stabilize. It had been escalating at a logarithmic rate, which was terrifying. After the two doses and continuous steroids, it was far from better, but it was manageable with pain medication. Because of hospital issues and the holiday, he could not receive another treatment until the new year. We were all fine with this, as it meant a long weekend of recovery and an opportunity for Jude to re-engage with friends who were home from school. As long as we could manage the pain, he could take advantage of his respite.

Our house was busy with people, and we all loved it. Jude was in his glory. He revealed to his closest companions that the current prognosis was not positive, but he did not dwell on it. I suspect the majority of the people in his orbit were somewhat oblivious to his reality. Jude would not lie. He also wanted no pity. The only way for him to maintain his integrity was to deflect any concern for his condition onto other more palatable subjects. When his friends were over, all we heard was a lot of yelling and laughter. Jude was still holding court. The atmosphere was glorious. His friends served as the ideal anesthetic.

On New Year's Eve, Jody and I went out to a party. Jude planned to go out also, and he assured us he would be fine. I even let him use my car. This was something I assiduously avoided, as Jude was notorious for his lust for speed and impulsivity—not a great combination for safety. As the evening wore on, I kept checking the tracker on my phone to see where he landed, but his marker kept registering his presence at home. Finally, I called him.

"Hey, buddy. What's going on? It looks like you're still home. Are there no parties tonight?"

"Yeah," he sighed. "There are some parties. I'm just not going. No big deal—" I could tell from his tone he was not being forthright.

"Why wouldn't you go?" I interrupted. "You've been looking forward to this." My stomach started to turn. Jude refusing a social gathering was extraordinary.

"Yeah, I want to go. I just can't make it." He sighed. His voice lacked energy.

"Is something wrong with the car?" I asked. It was a new electric vehicle and not intuitive to drive.

"No," he responded. "The car is fine. I just can't sit in it."

"Does your leg get in the way? I know the seat is low. Why don't you take the pickup? You've driven that no problem with your prosthetic." I tried to be as encouraging as possible. He seemed overly depressed, which was very concerning.

"It's my back," he finally admitted. "I can't sit. I tried to drive your car but had to get back out again. I'm really uncomfortable."

"Oh, man," I sympathized. "That's no good. What's your meds status? Have you taken any Percocet?"

"I did," he admitted. "And then I took some more. I hate that stuff. But it's not touching it this time. I'm just going to hang out in my bedroom."

Knowing my son, and knowing he knew this was likely the last New Year's Eve party he would ever attend, I recognized just how serious his condition was and how intense his discomfort must be. Jody and I took our leave and raced home.

Jude was lying in the fetal position on his bed, wincing in pain. We tried to unfold him, and I got him a medley of medications. After thirty minutes of intentionally distracting conversation, the meds seemed to kick in, relaxing him. My level of concern deepened dramatically, however. We were out of options this holiday weekend. His pain plateau appeared to be disintegrating, and it was evident his condition was not about to magically improve. It was moving in the other direction. Other than more painkillers, we were stuck.

A different sort of magic did happen, though, when a pile of friends came to our house and brought the party to Jude. Twenty-year-old men are not typically known for their selflessness. However, Jude's companions recognized his need and came to his rescue. For every person who arrived, Jude's discomfort abated a notch. It was an incredible testament to the power of friendship. I cannot thank those boys enough for attending to my son.

Jody and I went to bed, mildly relieved, knowing Jude was in good hands. Deep into the night we listened to a steady stream of boisterous guffaws, accompanied by the cacophony of energetic men all working overtime to speak past the next person. It was an appreciated balm.

Eventually the noise abated, and we drifted off to sleep. I was rudely awakened at 2:30 in the morning by my ringing phone. It caught me completely off guard.

"Hello," I croaked. There was no sound on the other end. I thought it was a random solicitor or a butt dial. I started to turn it off then noticed, through my blurry vision, the call was from Jude. "Hello," I replied with a little more intensity.

"Dad," came a faint whisper.

"Yes, yes, it's me," I responded. "What's up?"

"I can't—" He choked quietly, the last words cut off by a sob.

I leapt out of bed and sprinted downstairs. When I pushed open Jude's bedroom door, the look of terror on his face stopped me short. He stood at the edge of his bed, partially hunched over, with one leg raised on a makeshift pile of clothes. His prosthetic leg was unattached, but his "sock," the undergarment he put on his stump to fit into his prosthetic, remained. He was using one arm to brace himself upright, with the other arm clenched around his midsection. His entire body was sweaty and shaking.

"What's happening?" I asked quickly. "Let's get you in your bed. I'll adjust it to make you comfortable."

"NO!" he rasped. His breathing was shallow and labored. "I've tried everything. I can't make it stop!" His voice sounded like used sandpaper, scratchy and uneven. "I can't hold myself up any longer."

"How long have you been like this?"

"Almost an hour," he answered. "I tried to get into bed, but I'm just stuck." His sweaty hand slipped from its tenuous grip on the nightstand. That little twinge sent a jolt of pain searing through his entire body. Sweat was beading on his brow, and then I saw a little tear emerge from the corner of his eye. We were well beyond serious now.

"When were your last meds?" I asked.

"About an hour ago. I took two more Percocet."

"And before that?"

"I took one around midnight, along with a Vicodin and Advil."

"Okay. I'm going to get you some more." I quickly ran to the bathroom and grabbed all his pain meds. He was able to raise his head enough to swallow, thankfully. He continued to quiver from the pain and the strain. I put an arm around his chest and another against the small of his back and held him partially upright so he could relax the core muscles which were beginning to seize. The minute I applied pressure, I could feel his entire torso relax.

"Oh, thank you, Dad," he sighed. "That's a little better." I didn't want *a little* better. I wanted *a lot* better. I sat there and held him that way for five minutes, but the awkward position and twisted posture was difficult to maintain.

"Let's try and get you on the bed," I suggested.

"I'd love to," he gasped. "Not sure I can do it."

"Let's just try," I encouraged. With a gentle nudge, I attempted to ease him forward and roll him sideways onto the bed, all the while maintaining the soft curl to his spine. He started to groan as I applied pressure. I changed his position about an inch every ten seconds, but even that was too abrupt.

"Ahhhhh," he cried, moving back into his original position. "The pain … Dad.

It hurts so much. I'm frozen in this position." His good leg was wobbling. The movement sent spasms through his torso, causing him to contort further. His whole body was rigid, like it had been electrified. "If I move at all, it's like someone is shoving molten sabers into my back. DON'T...LET...ME...MOVE." That was a command I would die trying to obey.

So, there we stood, father and son. I held him upright while he shivered in agony. Any twist, torque, or easement away from his chosen position sent him into paroxysms of anguish. Soon my legs and arms began to shake as well. I could not maintain this posture indefinitely, and then what were we going to do? For thirty minutes I held fast, whispering prayers of healing and comfort. Those eventually turned into prayers for mercy, which finally devolved into desperate groans. No words could suffice.

"Dad, it's getting worse," Jude cried. "I would rather die than be like this any longer."

And there it was. That acknowledgment was what I had dreaded more than anything. I knew it was coming, I just didn't expect it to be so soon. For the first time since this ordeal began, I recognized Jude's strength and resiliency might be a liability. He was fighting tooth and nail in a battle he could not win. He would never give up. I was so very proud of him. This pain was unendurable, however. Something was going to give, and in our current straits, it looked like it would either be his sanity or assisted suicide.

"Let me call Mom," I said softly. "Hang on a bit longer." Thanks to voice controls, I could hold Jude while calling. She raced down immediately. The look on her face spoke volumes. Two grown men, sweaty in their undergarments, grappling in a contorted posture of agonizing discomfort.

"What's going on?" she asked, not hiding any shock.

"We've been like this for an hour," I rasped. "Jude's beside himself with pain. We don't know what to do."

"Let me call 911," she said quickly.

"What are they going to do?" I asked. "He's stuck."

"We've got nothing else," Jody replied.

A blizzard was raging outside. Fortunately, it only took five minutes for the ambulance to arrive. When the responders made their way downstairs, they were rather taken aback by the scene. Paramedics are trained to handle any number of predicaments. Jude's situation was a bizarre amalgamation of the acute and the chronic. No immediate solution was forthcoming. We went through Jude's medical history and current situation and brainstormed together. We all knew he had to be transported to the hospital, the question was *how*. Short of bringing in a team of anesthetists—the logistics of which would have taken multiple hours—we were at a loss. After more discussion, we determined they had some nitrous oxide available. With minor finagling, we mobilized their unit and primed it for maximum flow. The governor would not let us knock him out completely, but at 70 percent, it was enough to dull the edge.

There was no way Jude could lie down. Even with an overabundance of pain meds and nitrous oxide blowing wide open, he was at his limit. Adding to the difficulties, paramedic regulations stipulated Jude must be transported on a gurney. We bypassed the regulations and I half-carried, half-dragged him up the stairs and out of the house as gingerly as possible. When I finally heaved him into the ambulance, he still could not sit, and the gurney was completely out of the question. So, I wrapped my arms around his torso and looped my wrists through two plastic straps that hung from the ceiling. This suspended him upright, effectively tying him against my chest.

The ride required an agonizing forty minutes. The horrid weather and previous snowfall kept our pace to a crawl. Snowdrifts, frozen into massive speed bumps, jostled and jolted us for fifteen hellish miles. I was in horrible agony from holding Jude so awkwardly. The straps had cut off the circulation to my wrists and hands, my back was burning with fatigue, and my legs were shaking from the effort of keeping us both balanced. Keeping him upright and trying to absorb the jolts and bumps had taxed me to the limit. My discomfort was nothing, however, compared to what Jude was going through. With eyes clenched, he had turned white as a sheet and dug for any remaining vestige of inner strength. Any alteration in his position broke through his trance, eliciting yelps of anguish. And yet, in an effort of goodwill beyond my ken, Jude managed to thank the two responders for coming to our house in the middle of the night and apologized for interrupting their evening. It was the only thing he said for forty minutes between gulps of nitrous. Despite his pain and obvious despair, Jude's first and only response was one of gratitude. By this time his evolution should not have astounded me. I was shocked nonetheless. In that moment, I couldn't spare a thought for another human other than my son. And yet, semiconscious from drugs and absurd discomfort, he still considered others.

Jody had alerted Children's Hospital and the local ER of our impending arrival. Thankfully they were prepped for Jude's arrival, and an ambulance was also on its way from Seattle. With a herculean effort, I lifted Jude down from the ambulance, and while he sucked the last lungful of nitrous from the canister, I carefully dragged him into a treatment bay. In minutes they had an IV in his arm, pumping delicious morphine into his vein. After a substantial bolus, the tension slowly eased from his torso, the sweat stopped beading on his brow, and I was able to lay him gently onto a semi-reclined bed. I crashed into the cheap plastic folding chair sitting in the corner, closing my eyes with exhaustion. The relief of seeing Jude resting, the rictus of pain finally controlled, coddled my emotional frailty like a gentle caress. That broken, ill-formed plastic chair felt like the most comfortable piece of furniture I've ever had the pleasure of sitting on.

OPERATION CLANDESTINE COUPLE

"The best and most beautiful things in the world cannot be seen or even touched—they must be felt with the heart."

HELEN KELLER

Early during Jude's diagnosis, in a fit of madness, Jody and I had pulled his treatment coordinators aside and boldly asked them what it looked like to perish from osteosarcoma. Worst-case scenario, what will happen to our son? It's fairly straightforward, they assured us. His lungs will slowly occlude from growing tumors, which will undoubtedly metastasize there, and as his air volume decreases, he will peacefully drift away from limited oxygen.

What they did not speak about was the hellish road Jude would have to walk before his lungs *peacefully* stopped working.

Recently I was driving home from work listening to a podcast. The topic was "The Big Questions," and they had a roundtable discussion of philosophers and scientists engaging in metaphysical discourse. The conversation turned to the question of the existence of God. The group was divided into theists (there is a God) and atheists (there is no God), each presenting arguments for their belief. Finally, an atheist interrupted the conversation and stated that he could "unequivocally assert God did not exist."

"On what grounds?" the others asked. "What is your proof?"

"Childhood bone cancer," he forcefully stated.

I wrestled my car to the side of the road, weeping uncontrollably. His accusation resonated into the core of my very being. What he was really asking was, "What sort of loving God would allow for such a heinous disease? That is not a God I could love... It is better He just didn't exist."

Jude was living the wretched, inescapable terror of childhood bone cancer. It gripped him like an iron vise, squeezing his vitality with ineluctable hatred. The more this parasite devoured, the hungrier it became. It cultivated pain, feeding voraciously, provoking more growth. With exponential pleasure it fed, and fed, and fed, its fangs sinking ever deeper like a malevolent evil charged with scouring Jude of any remaining vigor. Its grip was indomitable.

There were several factors we needed to deal with on Jude's behalf, the central concern being pain. He was miserable. After long discussions, consultations, and educated guesses, it was determined the best course of action was to continue the emergency radiation to shrink the tumor enough for pain relief. Hard-tissue tumors do not necessarily shrink, per se, but in their initial, rapidly growing phase they push a swelling bubble ahead of their main locus. Theoretically, the tissue response to radiation should compress that bubble, thereby alleviating discomfort. Jude's first couple bouts of radiation had caused an acute swelling of that bubble, exponentially exacerbating his condition. Between more steroids and radiation, the hope was to reverse this process.

He was kept in a state of opioid euphoria for multiple days. Whenever his dosing was curtailed, the pain violated him. Morphine had a grim grip on Jude's sanity, acting like a switch. You could watch the clock, anticipating the next bout of torture. He tried to brush it off as just another step on his journey, but you could see the latent fear he harbored. Every person has a breaking point. Unadulterated pain is an equal opportunity enemy. Jude was its current adversary.

Every day Jude was transported via ambulance to the radiation center at the University of Washington, dosed, and then returned to Children's Hospital for pain management. We all eagerly anticipated the moment when relief would come. Although Covid protocols were still active, we managed to acquire a pass for Simone so she could come visit her brother. They still only allowed one person at a time. It was a little unnerving leaving Jude in the care of his sister. However, those two had grown close the previous year, and his parents had been monopolizing his time. We did not know how long he had left. They needed to be together; she needed to experience her brother in his suffering. The strongest bonds are forged in times of trial. Those two became like iron.

Relief never came. Jude's pain only grew, if that were possible. Despair set in. No person should ever suffer so. As helpless bystanders, we were tortured by our ineffectuality. Our only recourse was to be present. Our limitations were maddening. As parents, we felt like hypocrites. We would have done anything, without hesitation, to alleviate Jude's pain. Unfortunately, *anything* was not at our disposal. Watching his merciless suffering was a heinous cruelty. We shouted prayers for mercy, dousing the heavens with unmitigated pleas. Our shouts echoed back, empty and broken. Was God deaf, uncaring, or even worse, malevolent? We had no recourse other than to vent our frustration with the Almighty. He absorbed our blows in silence.

The radiation therapist suggested we shut down Jude's treatment plan. He was worried the continued swelling was doing more harm than good and was concerned there was no relief or positive outcome on the horizon. The team reconvened. The only other option was surgery. The orthopedic neurosurgeon was very skeptical and attempted to rightfully scare Jude away from back surgery.

"It will be very painful. There is no guarantee it will work—in fact, it may make everything worse, and it won't stop this cancer," he averred.

His presentation scared Jude. As a second option we also discussed heavy, emergency chemotherapy—uncharted territory with no guarantee. This had even less appeal. Being in pain was bad enough; coupling it with extreme nausea was wholly unacceptable. Jude wanted to push through with more radiation, giving the initial plan more time to bear fruit. That morning everyone agreed.

When Jody arrived to relieve Simone, a new development emerged. The initial fear, paralysis, now materialized. Jude also started to experience issues with urination and defecation. The tumor had reached the stage where all the motor functions downstream from its position were suffering deleterious effects. Within hours Jude went from normal muscular function in his right leg to marked tingling, numbness, and weakness. He could not support himself. The effect was unnerving. Jude's capacity to absorb pain was unrivaled. His capacity to tolerate loss of function was minimal. It petrified him.

He prayed. Together with Jody and Simone, the three of them joined together, seeking wisdom. This was new for Jude. It was not a wholesale conversion experience or blessed epiphany. It was Jude recognizing his circumstance was fully beyond him. He had no control. He was looking towards God, not in desperation, demanding healing, but rather in acknowledgement. "I know you've always seen me, God," he was saying. "Now I also see you."

Sometimes there is beauty in the ashes.

Jody alerted me to Jude's pending disaster. I called the neurosurgeon, and we had a long chat. He was quick to state, and rightly so, that surgery in a lost cause was excessive and extreme. I fully understood and agreed with his point. However, in Jude's case surgery would not be a quest for a cure or even a means to prolong life. This would be palliative surgery. Any surgical sequelae that may arise—discomfort, loss of function, infection, delayed healing, morbidity—would not be any worse than his current state but could make his quality of life better. The surgeon grudgingly acquiesced.

I raced to Seattle while they prepped Jude for surgery. I arrived in time for him and me to crack a few jokes while pensively anticipating the future. Jody and I had essentially been living at Children's Hospital for sixteen months, and yet we were always separated. It felt odd for the three of us to be together. Loneliness is a catalyst for anxiety and fear. Together, we felt reassured.

Jude's surgery proved uneventful. The surgeon removed a length of tumor which stretched across four vertebrae, tunneling a larger opening for Jude's nerves and alleviating the pervasive pressure on his spinal cord. He was not able to scrape the dura (the protective sheath around the nerve bundle) clean, although he was rather pleased with how much he was able to accomplish. Time and strict rehabilitation protocols would determine the procedure's value.

Although Jude had his spinal column exposed and bone scraped away from various vertebrae, he was ecstatic. The colossal agony of spinal cord compression was relieved. Surgical pain he could manage. He'd already had a major amputation, numerous small procedures, and three thoracotomies. For the average patient, mid-back surgery is a very tender and delicate recovery. Jude may be the first person to awaken, after having been knifed in the back, sporting a smile.

He spent the night in the ICU. Jody and I stayed with him. He had one nurse dedicated solely to his room, and she was amazing. Because of the swelling, the position of the tumor, and the damage already done, his recovery was sensitive. In addition, he had been pumped full of opioids and was struggling to urinate and defecate. These were the dangerous and potential side effects of nerve damage. What made his recovery even more difficult was the fact that he could not use his torso, or any core muscles, to move his body. He had to learn to roll a certain way, using his legs for primary propulsion and his hands for stability. Except he was missing a leg and the other one was working at about 20 percent capacity. This meant we (the nurse and I) had to move him.

Between the local anesthesia, lingering opioids, and a ketamine drip, Jude thought the ICU was a wonderful experience. He chirped with his nurse all night long, discussing everything from football, to dating, to the plight of the harbor seals in Puget Sound. Any other night, laying on the much too-short couch with sensors squawking and chiming, I would have growled with irritability. That night, Jude's deafening dialogue and the accompanying bells and whistles was a peaceful harmony. The relief from pain settled on all of us like a cozy blanket.

* * *

Jude was going to need time in the hospital to recover. The last two weeks of his life had been hijacked with pain, and when you do not know how much time you have left, two weeks is excessive. We all wanted him home. Social engagements were his lifeblood. As morbid as it seemed, he was planning a farewell tour of sorts. Now that the very dangerous tumor was removed, his care team assumed his cancer would resume a more traditional course—lung consumption. They wanted to start him on "chemo lite," a maintenance drug that would retard tumor growth without many adverse effects. They assured Jude he would not even feel sick, maybe just a little tired, and the tips of his hair would turn silver. That sold him. Leave it to Jude to include his hair as a decision-making variable. Four to twelve months was their realistic timetable.

While I sat with him in the hospital, we discussed various options for those months. He was excited about the possibilities. His capacity to engage with the present and only think positively about the future continued to amaze me. He did not dwell, for a moment, on his trajectory. He was much more worried about not being able to take a shower than he was about his future.

While he convalesced, I received a phone call from a dear friend who lived across the country. Her daughter wanted to come and visit Jude. Now, she was not the first young lady who had made this request. Most of these requests were brushed off by Jude. He recognized there would not be a future with any of them, and so he wanted to guard his time and their emotions. However, when I mentioned this particular request to Jude, his response surprised me.

"Yes. I really want to see her."

"Why? What's the difference? Besides, you're stuck in this hospital. She can't get in here." I did not understand the importance of this engagement.

"I want to see her, Dad. Please."

When your dying son makes a request, you move heaven and earth to support him. Thus began Operation Clandestine Couple. Taryn (my friend's daughter) flew from Michigan to Washington. She had made this arrangement with her mother before we knew Jude would be having significant back surgery. She was waiting on standby for Jude to be released, but his care team thought it would be at least five days before discharge. Our only recourse was to sneak Taryn inside. Thankfully we had managed to procure a security badge for Simone the week prior. Taryn became Simone. Now, those two look nothing alike, but you would be amazed what a hoodie, a sense of purpose, and good manners can accomplish.

I managed to smuggle Taryn into the chemo ward, which provided three hours of desperate intimacy. When I reluctantly returned, I was greeted with an emotional intensity fueled by laughter, surprise, relief, and joy all simultaneously flourishing—not a combination one often discovers emanating throughout a chemo ward. Pressing down on that delightful mixture, however, was a profound yet unspoken knowledge of imminent loss. Language proves inadequate to fully capture the texture of that tableau. When I stood in the doorway, witnessing their goodbyes, a scene of what-may-have-been emerged. This fractured my soul. It provided the first bitter taste of what it means to lose a child. Not only do you mourn what is lost—the deep hurt of losing what you have—you also mourn all that could have been.

Jody had prayed, from the day our children were born, for their future spouses—the ideal blend of God-glorifying personalities. Jude, always flamboyant and mercurial with relationships, often tempted by women not likely the best fit, worked hard to thwart Jody's prayers. Now, in an about-face of maturation and wisdom, he had managed to open his heart, inviting an incredible gem into his life. Taryn was Jody's answer to prayer. I was gifted a preview of their potential synergy. It is a grievous travesty that Taryn and Jude will never have a life to share.

THE MARK WE MAKE

*"What is hell? I maintain that it is
the suffering of being unable to love."*
FYODOR DOSTOEVSKY

"Well, how did it go with Taryn?" I casually asked after escorting her outside. "You were together a long time."

"I'm really tired, Dad," Jude sighed, "and my back is really sore."

"Yeah, no offense, buddy, but you look tired. Do you think she was happy she came all the way out here?"

"It was good. I'm happy she came out. I can't speak for her. I hope she was happy." Jude lay his head back against the pillow, letting his eyes droop. He looked uncomfortable, yet content.

"I wasn't sure what I would find when I came back to the room. That's a long time to leave two people together when they haven't spent any time together. I'm just glad I didn't interrupt something… ummm… delicate," I said with a smirk.

Jude's eyes flew open while he groaned in disbelief at my insinuation. "Dad!" he all but yelled. "I haven't showered in three days. I'm wearing a hospital gown, and it feels like someone twisted a lightsaber in my back. What a ridiculous thing to say."

"Hey, I didn't *say* anything. I'm just letting you know I'm grateful I wasn't subjected to something untoward."

"Untoward? Who talks like that? Anyway, you do realize I have a catheter?" He shook his head in disgust. I'm not sure if it was at me or because of his catheter. Probably both.

"Yeah, I know you do," I laughed again. "I suspect that's a nonstarter for almost anything."

"You are welcome to quit speaking anytime," Jude admonished.

The following morning Jude revealed he and Taryn had been communicating since the previous summer. He even admitted the two of them had decided, if they had not met someone else, to marry when they were thirty. These are the sort of fanciful promises silly twenty-year-olds make, a covenant "writ with water." When I pressed, however, his sincerity was evident. "Dad," he said, speaking to me like I was seven, "Taryn isn't the sort of girl you date. She's the one you marry."

• • •

Jude's diminished pain enlivened his spirit. He was anxious to leave the hospital. Unfortunately, the after-effects of the surgery, as well as the initial tumor damage, produced significant side effects. His remaining leg had no strength. He would try to stand on it, only to wobble and fall over. He attempted to push its capacity with a frustrated fervor, to the point his leg would shake uncontrollably, like it was having a localized seizure. Jude clenched his fists in anger. Cancer continued to steal from him, and it was merciless.

His anger had limited options for outlets. The healing wound in the center of his back did not lend itself to any degree of exertion. Jude pushed the limit, daily, between leg remediation and wound healing. Surprisingly, he was more stable on his prosthetic. His hip strength, although depleted, was not as paralyzed as his lower leg. With the prosthetic, he was accustomed to impoverished neural feedback and only accessed hip and core strength for balance. The major problem with relying on his prosthetic as his functionally dominant leg is that, between the surgeries and erratic exercise, his stump kept changing in size. These vacillations made it impossible to create a snug socket, which is imperative for any degree of stability. He possessed two legs working at 25 percent capacity, both dysfunctional in different ways. Every time he took a step, he had to remember the functional idiosyncrasies in each leg, hope those impairments hadn't changed, and pray he had the strength and patience to make them function enough to move without crashing or falling. These hurdles were depressing, especially because a solution did not appear forthcoming.

His deprivations in movement paled in comparison to the ever-growing recognition that the nerve damage also affected his bowels and bladder. His large intestine had lost some of its motility and coordination. Defecating was arduous, if not impossible. The pain meds also hampered that process, and his distress over his GI troubles grew by the hour. He was incredibly uncomfortable. There was no position in which he could fully relax, and postures which had once been bearable options continued to decrease.

Every few hours we worked through the formidable process of wrangling him out of bed onto a commode. Privacy is a privilege in the hospital, and one he was not afforded in his condition. He had no energy or conviction to make it all the way to his private restroom. His back was too tender for him to be carried, and his legs were too weak and unbalanced to travel more than a few steps. Fortunately, Jude was never particularly modest. He did possess a streak of vanity, however, and not being able to stand under a shower, scrub clean, and then groom himself irritated him to no end. Eventually we would cross that bridge.

Jude's efforts on the commode proved maddeningly unfruitful. One evening, while he dutifully made another attempt, a woman let herself in, interrupting Jude's private business. We did not recognize her, and I was a bit put out by her aggressive insertion into our delicate affair. She was dressed in civilian clothes, but instead of gasping and apologizing for her rude interruption, she smiled pleasantly and projected a warm hello—totally unflummoxed by the drama (or lack thereof) unfolding before her.

Jude gave me a wry look, then said, "Uhhh, hello. How are you?" He arched an eyebrow and curled up one side of his mouth into a questioning smile.

"Oh, thank you," she replied quickly. "I'm just fine. I came to check on you."

"You did? Well, that is so kind," Jude responded. He caught my eye a second time. Neither one of us had a clue who this person was.

"I can see I found you a little busy." She smiled again. "That's great. I'm so impressed you're totally out of bed."

"Thanks. Yes. As you can see, I have work to do here. Besides, I needed a change of scenery. The view from the bed was getting a little old. It's way better five feet away." Jude elicited a pleasant little chuckle. The awkwardness, already intense, continued to mount.

"Yes. You're focusing on the important aspects of life." She took a step closer, continuing to smile. "I thought I would have a few more days to find you, but I talked to the doctor, and he said you were healing so quickly they may discharge you tomorrow."

"Now that would be awesome," Jude exclaimed.

"That would be amazing," she agreed. "That's why I came tonight."

"I wasn't really hiding, you know," Jude teased. "I'm pretty much stuck in one spot—and I think my name's on the door."

"Yeah, I didn't have to search too hard. But you guys are a long way away." She nodded her head as if that revelation should mean something. A long way away from where? Her home? Where she works? Kansas? The moon? "You know," she started laughing, "I really should have reintroduced myself. I just realized I'm not wearing scrubs. You guys probably don't even recognize me!"

Jude and I shook our heads simultaneously. "Nope," Jude thankfully answered.

"I'm your ICU nurse," she answered. "I spent the night with you four nights ago. Remember?"

"*Ohh!*" Jude exclaimed. "That explains it. Thank you so much for coming up. You didn't have to do that."

"I know I didn't," she agreed. "I usually never do. In fact, I don't know if

I've been up here on the seventh floor." She looked around curiously, as if she'd stepped into a fairy tale. "I just wanted to check in. I was so impressed by how you handled yourself the other night and how you treated me. I've never been with any patient who was as thoughtful and kind as you."

"Thank you," Jude replied soberly. "It wasn't my best night. You made it possible."

"I had nothing to do with it," she argued. "Your success was all you." She smiled briefly, regarding Jude silently for a long moment. "I hope the best for all my patients," she finally admitted. "But I usually never go visit them. I'm really hoping for you. You might be the best patient I've ever had. Certainly the bravest." She backed up a couple of steps and continued to smile. "I hope you come visit me when you get out of here and get healthy. No one deserves it more." She briefly stood at the doorway, holding the curtain away from the entrance. I could see the moisture form in the corners of her eyes.

Sometimes words don't have to be truthful to be honest.

Jude sat on his throne, smiling back at her, unfazed by his presentation. "Thanks for visiting," he said, smiling. "You made my day."

. . .

As predicted, Jude was discharged the next day. It was not without bother, however. His rehab team wanted to leave his catheter in, afraid his neural trauma would leave him unable to void. Jude was beyond annoyed with the idea of going home with a catheter. We begged them to remove it. They resisted, and finally said they would not let him leave the hospital without the catheter. I thought Jude was going to rip it out without permission.

I called a private meeting together with the team principles outside of Jude's room. I very forcefully instructed them to remove the catheter, give Jude an opportunity to try and pee, and if he could, then send us on our merry way. They balked at this, primarily because if he couldn't pee, then he would need to be re-catheterized. For some reason, they were vehemently opposed to this procedure.

I was tired of Jude suffering. It was more than that, however. I was tired of being helpless. No matter how hard I researched, pushed, schemed, and prayed, the worse it went for my son. This was something I could do for him. The conversation grew heated. I was careful not to become belligerent, rude, or disrespectful. Impugning their expertise or the value of their care would be both inappropriate and incorrect. They were trying to treat Jude as they saw fit. They just did not have sixteen months of misery to frame their decision making. I did not budge. Eventually, one of the nurses on the outskirts of the discussion peacefully stepped over to my side and gently told the rest of the resistors he would be happy to re-catheterize Jude if peeing proved impossible.

The two of us marched into Jude's room and the nurse removed Jude's catheter. This is not a sexy procedure. But we could now add it to the list of insulting experiences Jude underwent through his ordeal. In classic Jude fashion—it only took moments for him to recover from the abrupt shock of having a plastic tube pulled from his penis—he defiantly stood up on one leg, wobbling like a drunken soldier, and proceeded to pee at will into the provided catch basin. We both may have cried tears of joy. He punched his ticket home.

• • •

Jude knew he was terminal, but he was not ready to admit defeat. His body was wrecked, racked with pain, and dysfunctional. Yet he did not feel sick. Mentally, he thought he would heal. Emotionally, he conducted his affairs with that mindset.

He started physical therapy for his paralyzed leg. He commenced stretching his back, working his arms, and tightening his core to aid in mobility. He refused to sleep on the main floor, battling the stairs every morning and night, just to experience the joy of remaining in his bedroom. He continued to hold court at dinnertime, and even throughout the day, as disappearing into his bedroom required too much effort. We were blessed to receive a full dose of Jude from morning to evening.

Jody and I were exposed to the extreme length and breadth of his friendships. There is a theoretical limit to the number of people with whom an individual can maintain meaningful social relationships, usually estimated around 150. Jude's capacity proved the exception to this rule. People came out of the woodwork. Undoubtedly, the presence of many was spurred by his diagnosis. Nevertheless, Jude dismissed any talk of his condition, as he found his predicament much less interesting than the personalities who came to visit him. He treated all his visitors like they were the most important person in the room. I marveled at his social art. There were very few to whom he could not relate.

Jude had spent less than a month at Whitworth. Seventeen months after his matriculation, having not set foot on campus since he left, ten of his friends drove across the state to spend the afternoon with him at our house. I know a lot of people who spend four years at college and don't make ten friends, let alone ones willing to repurpose an entire weekend for your sake. Having those young men over was an unimaginable delight. They came from all different walks of life, brilliantly illustrating Jude's talent as a collector of people. Sitting on our deck underneath a row of heat lamps (some of them were Covid-positive, but they could not bear the thought of missing out), they joked, laughed, told tall tales, and reminisced.

A couple of the men were avowed atheists. Jude's faith was nascent, dodgy at best, undoubtedly reflecting the tenor of the group. Most of the men, even the religious stalwarts, had never been pushed in their faith. But on that afternoon, blanketed by a dank, foggy, depressing winter day, those men spontaneously opened their hearts to God and prayed with a fervent zeal that could only be inspired through kindred blood. Quietly watching from a silent vantage, chills rippled through my soul. They surrounded Jude, and with a conviction only reserved for the uninitiated, praised and pleaded with the Almighty. The authenticity was irresistible. I would not have been the least bit shocked if a fiery chariot descended and, in a dramatic conflagration, swept them all away to paradise.

After the Whitworth weekend, our home was a revolving door. Normally, Jude liked to go out and meet his friends. That could not happen anymore, so they came to him. It was a fascinating, encouraging, and sobering experience managing a home filled with so much merriment when a dying man was the center of attention. From a distance, the daily fanfare had all the trappings of a fairy tale. Even in death, Jude was living his best life.

All dreams end. What we did not know, and were not prepared for, was how aggressive, ugly, and irrepressible Jude's disease really was. It had been a merciless monstrosity, but now it transformed into the true definition of evil incarnate. Like all living creatures, we knew Jude was terminal, we just didn't know when. While his due date was more apparent and tangible than those who are healthy, the predictions regarding his longevity were varied, but even the most pessimistic ranged from three to six months. Some of the experts concluded with some luck and strategic medications, he could stretch to a year. It is the vilest type of evil, however, which ascertains our deepest desires and deftly twists those wishes, like the huntsman's knife, into the places where it hurts the most. We hoped for time. It was the last hope afforded us.

Jude cherished experiences with friends. They were the fuel that ran his engine. His friendships gave him purpose and fulfillment. He rigorously worked to deflect any attention directed towards his affliction and abhorred attempts at pity, regardless of sincerity. What he slyly concealed to all who visited, even the perspicacious, was the unrelenting, rabid intensity of his misery.

Just days after his return from the hospital, Jude's pain returned. It was not the same acute, neuralgic pain that had initially emanated from his back. This time it took the form of a deep, welling, abdominal ache which he described as something akin to "being stuffed with an overripe sausage then having an elephant step on you." I cannot attest to the veracity of his description. I can attest to his misery.

Hospice came on board to help with his pain management. They were a wonderful godsend. They could not abate the insidious torture, but they could attenuate it, enabling Jude to function with modest success. Even their aid was not bulletproof, however, and occasionally his agony spiked to such a sinister degree that Jude's world would shrink into a capsule of mere existence. I never imagined, as a parent, that I would beg the Lord to take my son, but during those moments of exquisite agony, I pleaded for Jude's release. There was no other solution.

The cancer in his abdomen squeezed his intestines and displaced his internal organs. He would try to pass the constrained gas from his bowels, but sometimes it would not move. One morning, I helped him to the toilet, where he strained bitterly, finally breaking down into tears. He was too bloated to move, but sitting upright remained untenable. When I tried to move him from the bathroom, he collapsed on the floor, incapacitated. I called hospice for emergency relief. As was the case from the outset, I remained at his side, eager to help, yet utterly helpless. Being present was the only medicine in my arsenal. So, I laid down next to him on that unforgiving tile and held his hand. We lay together for over an hour, counting the seconds for a rescue from hospice, both of us desperate to trade places with the other.

It was in this moment I understood the Catholic sacrament of Extreme Unction and realized how impoverished my own modern, Protestant, Reformed Christian tradition had become. Lying there with my suffering son was sacred. We were both being baptized by fire, aware of our frailty, insignificance, and resounding need of God's grace. Our modern world has attempted to sanitize death, to cover it up, to make us forget until it is too late. But death is the final punishment and the very reason for the Incarnation. It serves as the final revelation. If one is unable to recognize one's need for grace while the curtain descends, then apprehension is unattainable.

Death should not be celebrated. It should be reviled. There is nothing glamorous about it. It is anathema to God and man. But it cannot be ignored. The journey to death is an outward sign of an inward grace, and I was walking with Jude along his sacred, inexorable, and undesired path. Part of dying well is to recognize the sanctity of life. It also requires recognizing the sacramental nature of death.

* * *

Jude had no interest in dying. He was not afraid of it, he just loved living. Even after the initial shock of his terminal diagnosis abated, he got on with the serious business of living. This meant daily radiation treatments to forestall the growing cancer in his spine, routine visits from hospice to manage the cancer in his gut, physical therapy for his paralyzed leg, and continuous external oxygen support for the cancer growing in his lungs.

These inconveniences were all a simple trade for his opportunity to spend each day with his family and friends. Simone and Johann participated in the routine, growing closer to their brother through his care. One day, we let the two of them drive Jude to his radiation appointment, which occurred nearly an hour away at the Mt. Vernon radiation clinic. It was during that appointment I received a call while at work from Simone. Jude needed to go to the ER (I should have learned, by this point, that going to work was foolish. Every time I received a call while I was there, the outcome proved ominous). His breathing had taken a turn for the worse, and the oncology nurses were deeply concerned for him. They gave him a Covid test and discovered he was positive.

Compared to osteosarcoma, Covid seems rather trite. However, his lung capacity was so compromised that any extra burden could prove fatal. Much to Jude's chagrin and frustration, Simone and Johann took him to the Bellingham emergency clinic. My father was gracious enough to meet them there until I could pull away from work and take over.

From a Covid standpoint, the trip to the ER was a waste of time. We already knew he had Covid, he was on supplemental oxygen, and he had multiple vaccinations. Nothing more could be done for his Covid situation. We went purely to assuage the concerns of the radiation nurses, who loved Jude and were very flexible and accommodating for his care. Our stay was interminable.

They insisted we take a CT image of his chest, get bloodwork, and engage in all types of testing, which would reveal that he was in fact having breathing problems and he had Covid, a diagnosis we were keenly aware of. My cynicism and Jude's impatience with hospitals was working to full effect that evening.

We were thankfully dismissed, after six hours, and were able to sleep in our own beds. The next morning Jude felt a little better, so we went to his subsequent radiation appointment. When the nurse wheeled him outside, I could see Jude laughing and chatting with the nurse, brightening her day in his wonderfully unique way. After the two of us got Jude situated back in the car, the nurse looked at me and said, "We love your son. But I'm surprised we got to see him today."

"Oh," I responded, raising an eyebrow, "why's that?"

"Well, because of his bloodwork."

"His bloodwork? What about his bloodwork?" I asked.

"Didn't they go over it with you in the ER?" she replied with a look of astonishment.

"No. They just confirmed he had Covid. What should they have told us?" My anxiety spiked.

"His hematocrit is 22 percent," she said seriously.

"Oh boy," I gasped. "That's like standing on top of Mt. Everest. No wonder he feels so short of breath."

"I'm surprised he's even conscious," she agreed. "You really want to get that checked out."

I drove Jude home, and he deteriorated rapidly. His typical swarthy complexion transformed in less than an hour. First, his skin paled, and then it acquired a translucent hue, which only accentuated the bluish tinge to his lips. Every breath was labored. I put our handy pulse oximeter on his finger and choked when the metrics were revealed. His oxygen levels were acceptable, but his heart rate was nearly 170. He did not have enough blood in his body to distribute the oxygen required. His heart was racing like an Olympian trying to keep up with demand.

We monitored him closely that afternoon, and he slowly stabilized. By the evening, he was in full form, discussing plans for the AFC and NFC football championship games the next day. He even made menu demands and started putting together a list of people he wanted to come over to watch the games.

The next morning, his heart rate was pushing 180 beats per minute, his clothes were soaked in sweat, and he was gasping for breath. I did not even ask him any questions, just loaded him into the back of the minivan, grabbed all our oxygen bottles, and raced to Seattle. It was a harrowing ride. Whenever I looked in the rearview mirror, all I saw was his head lolling from side to side as he struggled to remain conscious. He slumped over multiple times, panting and sputtering. I had to squeeze his leg to keep him awake, careening down the highway with one eye on the road and one eye on him.

Seattle Children's welcomed us with open arms and whisked him back to a treatment room. While we anxiously waited for the cavalry to assess his situation, Jude looked at me with bloodshot, exhausted eyes and whispered, "I'm sorry, Dad."

"Sorry?!" I cried. "Sorry for what?"

"I'm sorry I ruined our day of football. I was so looking forward to watching the games with you today."

"Nonsense," I chided. "We can watch the games here." There was a small TV in the corner of the room. The first game was set to start in an hour. "Besides, as long as we're together, it doesn't matter where we are." He gave me a big smile and let out a relaxed sigh. Here he was, struggling to live, gasping for air, wracked with pain, and his primary concern was ruining my day. I did not deserve to be his father.

In less than an hour, they hooked Jude to an IV, which pumped whole blood into his arm. It is a slow process to receive whole blood, unlike plasma, but it was the elixir of life. I watched his skin grow pinker by the minute. By the time he was through the second bag, he looked like he was ready to go for a jog. I don't know how long he had suffered through red cell deprivation—likely weeks. His body soaked up the transfusion like the nectar of the gods.

We sat together all afternoon, watching football, reminiscing, and relishing his newfound constitution. Our relief was transparent. The nurses thought we were a couple of crazed lunatics as we yelled at the TV, giggled like teenage girls at our own jokes, and played armchair quarterback after every play call. Even though Jude was Covid-positive, they opened the door to his treatment room just to let his laughter filter down the hall. He was a dying man bringing joy to others.

* * *

Jody relieved me that evening, once again running the all-too-familiar relay that epitomized our existence. She stayed with Jude for the next two days as he received even more blood. For some reason, his cancer was chewing through his red blood cells. Not satisfied with ruining his internal organs, this voracious parasite now turned to cannibalism. Additionally, the tumors in his lungs had expanded to the point that they were breaking blood vessels, letting blood leak into his lung tissue. Jude could not produce enough blood to keep his physical machine operating effectively.

Before he was discharged, Jude's entire oncology team, as well as some of his surgeons and various nurses, stopped in to thoughtfully say both hello and goodbye. These interactions were much more poignant and permanent than when he had received his terminal diagnosis on Christmas Eve. After that horrible news, much discussion centered around strategies for quality of life, extension of life, and even radical lifesaving considerations. All such talk was exhausted. Now it was simply "farewell." Jude handled all the conversations with admirable aplomb, spending more time consoling than being consoled. It is not the average nineteen-year-old who can simultaneously thank someone for acknowledging his own imminent demise and wish them well on their future endeavors. Remarkably, he was being more than polite. He was being authentic and honest. His treatment team recognized this and appreciated him even more because of it. Honestly hoping the best for someone and genuinely encouraging their success—while your travails prove insurmountable—is a uniquely endearing character trait. Jude relished the achievements of anyone who encountered him.

His two treatment coordinating nurses pulled Jody aside and officially put the final stamp on our endeavors at Children's Hospital. "There is nothing more we can do." Although we had known Jude was terminal for some time, to hear those words spoken aloud, with complete conviction, was still an arrow through the heart. Those words did not mean, "Yes, he's terminal, and we will continue to make him comfortable and treat him for as long he wishes," like they had on Christmas Eve. Instead, although uttered with the deepest respect and sympathy, they meant, "There is no reason to ever bring him back here. His time has come. Godspeed."

* * *

Jude's homecoming was all smiles. He hated the hospital. The hospital was isolated. Jude could not abide being cut off. From home, he began his version of a farewell tour. Friends and relatives came and went. He mustered the energy to see them all. The new blood had provided him with so much strength and vitality that his pending demise seemed unrealistic. He was tempted to leave the house, to simply hang out, but he was tied to oxygen, and his leg had weakened. The post-surgical swelling in his back never decreased to the point that his nerves could recover. It was this, more than anything, that enervated him. Until the assault on his leg, Jude hungered to continue living. He had discarded his terminal diagnosis, and although he wasn't unrealistic about it, he embraced the life he had, attempting to enjoy the fruits it provided. There was so much yet to appreciate. Why focus on the end?

After his leg became useless, his attitude flipped. He never admitted it, and likely could not have precisely articulated it had anyone probed, but the demise of his remaining leg was the proverbial last straw. His outward demeanor did not change. His lack of mobility did not leave him bitter, resentful, or angry. Nobody but his parents could recognize the subtle switch. Instead of beating his infirmities back, holding them at bay with sheer force of will, the leg burst his dam of fortitude. The day Jude could no longer move without aid was the day cancer won.

Jude's body was ravaged and betrayed. He was exhausted, uncomfortable, and resigned to his fate. We had prayed, from the very outset, for Jude's life, for his leg, and for his faith. We would never be so conceited as to limit God's power. A true miracle cannot occur unless all hope has expired. However, our first two petitions appeared to be failed exercises. His faith, though embryonic and only budding, had been pummeled, questioned, and nearly jettisoned, but also refined and matured in ways that were impossible to imagine. This was the truth to which we clung. This was a hope realized. This was our final prayer.

* * *

On Friday evening, Simone was to be celebrated and honored as a senior cheerleader. As her parents, we had the privilege of joining her at center court, to take pictures with the other seniors. Jude was excited for her, as he had fond memories of his own senior day. That entire week, Jude had been sleeping in our bed. Navigating the stairs was too much to handle. Jody and I took turns spending the night with him. Friday morning, I checked his pulse and blood saturation. His pulse was pushing 170. He had no energy, unsurprisingly, and he was sucking hard at his oxygen. I gave him some breathing treatments to help relax his lungs, but that did little to soften the strain. Jude desperately wanted to honor his sister that evening. He knew in his current state that desire was unattainable.

We contacted the local hospital, and with the help of Children's Hospital, managed to set up an appointment to receive more whole blood. Everyone recognized this was not a sustainable long-term solution, neither was it an extreme measure, but it was a way to ease Jude's strain and discomfort—our only remaining objective.

Jude and I sat together in that hospital the entire day. His caretakers were extremely cautious with Jude's infusion rate. We watched the clock tick together. Simone's celebration was to begin at 7 p.m. Each bag of blood required a four-hour infusion minimum, and they did not start the second bag until 3 p.m. Knowing what we did about hospitals and their inefficient discharge routines, we assumed our opportunity to see Simone was ruined. Jude was despondent. Not only was he not going to honor his sister, he was also stuck in a hospital. It was the first time during his entire trial that I saw him openly frustrated and unruly. He was still polite and gracious with his nurses, but he did not hide his impatience. There were multiple times I had to restrain him from ripping the needle out of his arm.

Unlike earlier in the week, this infusion proved ineffectual. I had fully expected Jude to perk up and attack the evening with renewed vigor. Even with the new blood on board, his vitals barely changed. He was still sucking oxygen, his heart rate never dipping below 150. It was as if his body was in an all-out sprint to the finish line. Internally, he was a mess. Nothing was working right, physical betrayals at every turn. The only positive outcome was the nurse agreeing to speed up the process for the remaining portion of the last bag. At 6:30 p.m. we received our discharge orders. Simone's gymnasium was thirty minutes away.

I pulled the van around to the hospital's back exit while Jude expectantly waited in a wheelchair. "I just don't feel good, Dad," he said. "Getting that blood kind of took it out of me."

"Yeah, I was hoping it would give you a kick in the pants. It's okay, though, we can go home and get you settled. It's just nice being out of the hospital, isn't it?" I tried to simultaneously console him and help him recognize seeing his sister was not in the cards. He would have to congratulate her later in the evening.

"Do you think we can make it to the game?" He looked up at me expectantly, his soft brown eyes moist with tears.

"If we race, we can," I said. "Is that something you really want to try to do?"

"I just want to see my sister," he replied. He was convicted, but his statement possessed no energy. He had nothing left to give. All that sustained him was love for Simone.

"Let's go for it then," I agreed. I nestled his wheelchair alongside the front door and started to lift him up. He tried to help me, but he was incredibly weak. I managed to prop his left leg over the front seat, but as I attempted to push him completely onto the chair, he let out a strained gasp.

"Dad!" he wheezed. "Dad...I can't breathe. I can't get any air." He panicked. His sides heaved, straining with urgent intensity. Tendons strained in his neck, pulling his mouth wide open, trying to suck up life-giving oxygen. "Nothing's...coming...in," he rasped with staccato gasps, gripping my arm like a drowning man grips his rescuer. Except there was no suffocating water to retrieve him from.

"The more you strain, the more your lungs will tighten up, son. I know it's hard, but you have to relax, and it will start to flow."

"Nothing's...coming...in," he panted. He leaned forward and started clawing at his chest.

I gripped him as confidently and tenderly as I was able. Was this it? Was I going to lose him, alone, in a dark parking lot? Scenarios flashed through my mind. I knew he was on the edge, but he'd just received blood. He should be able to draw sustenance from it. "Jude, I can drive around to the ER entrance, and we can admit you right away. They can give you a breathing treatment." He looked at me with wide eyes, knowing that going to the ER meant not going home, and certainly not seeing his sister. He strained harder, reinvigorating his efforts to force oxygen down his throat. Suddenly, a man appeared next to our car, surprising me. He was wearing simple jeans and a hoodie. For some reason, he had a stethoscope around his neck.

"Is everything okay here?" he asked.

"No," I replied. "My son is struggling to get his breath. He's really constricted."

The man pulled off his stethoscope and listened to Jude wheeze. "You are getting air in," he said reassuringly. "It's not a lot, but it's enough. If you want, I can help get you to the ER, if that's where you want to go?"

Jude contemplated the man's words. The emotional turmoil on his face was plain.

"Son, I think if you can relax, you will feel better. Maybe a breathing treatment or an albuterol inhaler when you get home will help too." The stranger patted him lightly on the shoulder and gave me a knowing look. He wrapped the stethoscope around his neck and walked away from the hospital, into the darkness.

With an extraordinary force of will, Jude allowed his shoulders to relax and delicately slumped back in his seat. I heard a whistle of air sneak down his throat. Nearly imperceptible, his chest rose and fell a couple of times. "Let's go," he whispered.

"Go where?" I asked. "To the ER?"

"No," he quickly replied. "I have to do this. I have to see Simone."

I had no idea who that man was who appeared out of nowhere. I also have no idea where he went. But with a touch of assurance and an angel-like command, he had provided Jude with enough peace to let his lungs reopen. I dove into the driver's seat and raced away from the hospital. I called Jody en route, explained the situation, and asked if she could arrange a private entrance for us.

When we arrived at the gymnasium, everything was set. The school administration was incredibly responsive and helpful. We were able to drive past the gated area, where team entrances were privately accessed, and wheel Jude into the gymnasium through the locker room. He remained slumped forward in his wheelchair, nearly comatose, just hanging on to consciousness. He gasped for each breath with a strained, clicking staccato, while his head inadvertently bobbed up and down with the effort.

His sister met him on the gymnasium floor. When he saw her, he straightened up and his face enlivened. Sustained by nothing other than the deepest love, he coaxed the last vestiges of energy from his depleted reserves. Minutes earlier, I thought I was going to lose him. Suddenly, he began shaking hands, waving, and acknowledging a horde of friends who attended the game and were just waiting for Jude to show up.

Jody and I were able to join Simone on the court, with Jude lovingly watching from the boundary, clapping in her honor. The crowd joined him with an outrageous ovation. The noise honored the gravity of his journey and signaled to Jude, in no uncertain terms, that this was his community. They had fought, supported, and prayed from the outset. They had supplied a surplus of encouragement throughout his entire ordeal. These were the people he loved, and they were honoring his fight as much as they were honoring the seniors.

Before Simone went back to join her cheerleading squad, she walked over to Jude, bent down, and delicately kissed his cheek. He reached out with all the tender care of a protective big brother and stroked the side of her face. An enormous tear emerged and slid quietly down his cheek, tracing a lonely path until it came to rest in the hollow below his lower lip. Simone's eyes overflowed, and for the briefest moment, she let a quiver of emotion express itself on her chin. Neither of my children are criers. They rarely display public emotion. In that moment, their tears embodied the solemnity of the occasion. The two exchanged a look that only siblings who love each other dearly could share. That glance contained the richness of their history, the fortitude of their current bond, and the sorrow in knowing what must be. There were no words. Only profound love. Their crisp, unadulterated affection pierced the emotional glamour of senior night and drove directly into the hearts of everyone observing. Jude reached up, and they clasped hands. It was a physical expression of a bond that could never be broken. A big brother protecting his little sister by giving his entire heart to her. She would be responsible for carrying his love forward.

* * *

I took Jude home shortly after the game started. It was a testament to his fortitude that he had made it to tip-off, and it was incredibly touching to have his friends circle around and cheer him on before we left. The sheer force of their encouragement nearly levitated his wheelchair, like magic. Jude relished their support and soaked up their presence. While they surrounded him, however, he gave me a surreptitious glance that instantly explained his condition. He was absolutely spent.

After supplying him with meds and breathing treatments, he fell into a fitful sleep. I was so grateful he could drift off and create separation from the emotional and physical turmoil of the day. I loved him so much, but the suffering was unbearable. I silently fantasized, as he slept in a half-sitting position, that he would calmly stop breathing and be free of his torment. This thought unnerved me. To wish for someone you love unconditionally to be gone forever felt sacrilegious, almost evil. I rested next to him in bed, wracked with guilt, as if I was betraying him for thinking such thoughts. And yet it is the duty of every parent to enable their child to have the opportunity to choose the best path. For Jude, the best path was a cessation of this wretched existence.

Jude was rarely conventional, and history demonstrates he rarely behaved in a manner I thought best or appropriate. True to form, he awoke the next morning with a tiny spark, mildly refreshed, relaxed, and ready to take on the day. That afternoon, six of his closest friends were planning to come see him. Jude was noticeably excited about this, and he wanted to be prepared. Jody patiently took him through his morning routine. Simple steps that a healthy person could accomplish in minutes required painstaking effort and considerable commitment on Jude's part. He wanted to be clean and presentable, so she gave him a bath, just like she had when he was an infant. It took him over ten minutes to transfer from his wheelchair to the bathtub as his heart rate crept close to 190. Every physical act pressed his limit, even the stress of breathing. His cancer was inexorably ossifying his lungs, making him feel like he was inhaling through a straw. The strain was visible, almost grotesque. His body knew what was healthy and right, but those actions were deplorably denied. So, his body activated every resource at its disposal to keep the machine running, even if it meant hijacking muscles to operate well beyond their breaking point. His life engine was desperately sputtering and heaving. There was no gas left in the tank.

Despite his agony, he sat in the bathtub and let his mother clean him with water decanted in tender mercy. That physical act personified her constant, lifelong love for her child. The water gently sluiced through his hair and down his torso. She took soap and polished him like a rare jewel. He was as precious to her as he had ever been, and he could calmly rest in her loving care. There are some memories for which the decay of time will never find a footing. The image of Jody bathing Jude is indelibly imprinted in my memory. I have never seen such an expression of a mother's love as I did that morning.

We warned Jude's friends that he would have the energy to chat for maybe five, ten minutes at the longest. They caroused for three hours, playing wild games of Quiplash, telling stories, and rolling on the ground with gut-busting laughter. Jude sat in the middle of the crowd, holding court once again, elevating the energy with his wit and humor. The seven of them tore through the entire afternoon without a care in the world. Jody and I sat quietly next door and reveled in their celebration. Tears of joy and sorrow freely intermingled on our faces.

Late in the afternoon, when the party started winding down, I heard Jude shout my name. The volume and clarity shocked me. It was the Jude of old, the child with the thunderous, deep voice that would resonate like a division bell throughout our entire home. It was the voice that would keep us all awake when he played video games late in the night, and the voice that animated the stories he would tell. I could not see him, only hear him, and for a startling second, I thought all our prayers had been answered—my son fully restored, hearty and hale.

"Dad!" he boomed. "Hey, Dad!"

I leapt out of my chair and poked my head into the living room, shaky with shock and anticipation. He was as animated as he'd ever been, eagerly sitting upright. "What's up, bud?"

"Hey... what do we have going on tomorrow?" His voice echoed off the walls, supported by a look of such intensity and sincerity I was speechless.

"Well, I'm not sure," I replied noncommittally, eventually finding my own voice. I looked around the room at each of the young men, maintaining a placid expression. I knew, beyond a shadow of a doubt, what Jude would be doing tomorrow. But tomorrow could take care of itself. I wanted him to continue to do what he always did best, and what he had so clearly taught me to do: Find gratitude for each moment. "What did you have in mind?"

"Me and the fellas were thinking it would be fun to watch the Pro Bowl over here tomorrow. We could have chips and snacks and hang out." All his buddies looked at Jude, smiling and nodding. I could tell they were hesitant, however, holding something back. They had not journeyed with Jude the way I had, but only the most obtuse among them could be blind to his trajectory.

"That sure would be fun, wouldn't it?" I agreed, smiling and nodding with the other men. "I'll tell you what. Why don't we see what tomorrow brings and maybe we can make that happen."

Jude gave his assent and took some pictures with his fellas, while everyone agreed to connect in the morning. It was business as usual in our home. A bunch of energetic young men jostling, clambering for jackets, and teasing as they went.

FURTHER UP AND FURTHER IN

"It is quite useless knocking at the door of Heaven for earthly comfort: it's not the sort of comfort they supply there."

C. S. LEWIS

A few more friends and grandparents made quick entrances later in the evening. Jude entertained them all, summoning a degree of energy I thought impossible. The physical reserve endowed to the youthful was a marvel to observe. It was Jody's night to spend the evening with him, so she and all three kids stayed awake late into the evening. They shared stories, were silly, and absorbed the joy of familial fidelity. To describe the evening, or the entire day for that matter, as something precious, would be a gross misappropriation of an adjective. Each day we share with those we love is a blessing. That day was an ineffable delight.

I crashed in Jude's bed, capturing a few hours of much-needed rest. Since before Christmas, we had been burning empty tanks. Each day exposed new hurdles, relentless pressure, unsavory decisions, and novel aberrations requiring immense concentration and energy. We tackled each barrier with an intensity only love for a child could fuel. But everyone must sleep at some point, and I took a blessed reprieve that evening.

I awoke at five in the morning ready to relieve Jody. Ever since Jude's terminal diagnosis, I had stopped praying. Not because I was mad at God, did not believe in Him, or was dismissive. I did not know what to pray for, or even how to begin if I thought it would be worthwhile. I simply had nothing to say.

That morning, as I stilled my heart in the quiet solitude of Jude's bedroom, I bowed my head and prayed a simple request. I asked God to love my son.

I knew, as clear as a sunny day, what was about to unfold. As I forced my way up the stairs, my heart was so heavy I nearly toppled from the weight of it. Each step felt like I was tearing an irreparable hole into the fabric of my family. I wanted this final mountain to be unscalable—not because it was too tall or unnavigable—but because I still had a choice, some degree of agency, to choose not to climb it. I had no place in my heart to tackle this final leg.

I paused on the last step and peered across our living room through the great windows framing the inky blackness of a crisp, winter morning. Strewn across the floor were all the blankets and pillows used the previous night. It was a room of laughter. A place made for wonder, love, and contentment. I quested for an inner peace, a sense of *rightness*. I waited for stillness to descend, for God to wrap our home in His loving hand and declare *All Is Well*. I sat there with a bowed head, patient as I've ever been, waiting, waiting and ever yearning for the God of all comfort to cradle us under His wing.

I waited in vain.

Unsurprised and unsatisfied, I continued my journey. The crushing reality of the day squeezed my heart, forcing it to work at a desperate tempo. It throbbed so violently as I slowly walked down the narrow hallway to my bedroom that I had to wrap my arms around my chest just to keep it from exploding out of me. Dejected and tormented, I paused in the doorway, unable to push in, and gazed longingly at my son.

Jude was sitting upright, his bed propped at an angle that allowed him to breathe. There was a soft light emanating from behind his head, which set his cheeks and dark hair aglow, as if a halo was delicately resting above. His head was turned slightly, and he affectionately observed his mother slumbering peacefully next to him. He appeared to be watching over her, measuring her every breath, lovingly monitoring her as she rested.

Jody sensed my presence and woke with a start. It was apparent she had not been sleeping long, and she was desperately in need of more rest. I let her know I was ready to take over. I also let her know I thought it would be a good idea if we invited our closest family members to make a quick appearance later in the morning. At first, she looked at me like I was crazy. Why would we want to add to the chaos of the day? But when she saw my face, she realized what I already knew. She gave a brief nod of assent, eyes downcast, and exited solemnly.

I propped myself next to Jude and asked him about his evening. He chatted energetically at first, but admitted he was still painfully tired. "My head hurts, Dad," he said. He wasn't complaining. It was just matter of fact, like someone commenting on the weather or the color of a house. "It's odd, you know. These drugs make me foggy, but I still feel what's happening. I don't feel good."

"Should I tell you how you look?" I joked.

He smiled briefly. "My chin still looks sharp though, doesn't it?" He chuckled briefly and jutted his chin forward while he pursed his lips like the caricature of a supermodel. "I guess I've looked better, huh?"

The simple effort of leaning forward depleted him. I checked his pulse. 180. He was breathing, but his chest hardly moved, as if it was frozen in place. His hair was matted with sweat.

"You're as handsome as ever," I assured him. "Why don't you get some rest and maybe some ladies will come over later today."

"Really?" he asked. "Like who? I'm not ready to see anyone."

"I'm just kidding, son. Get a little rest. We will sort out the rest of the day when you wake up."

He lay back against the pillow and closed his eyes. I sat and watched him breathe, fervently praying for comfort and relief. For a while he seemed to drift, and then, with a startled jerk, he leaned forward, and his eyes shot open like a startled animal. He gesticulated with sharp, precise, geometric movements. I watched this display in curious fascination, wildly confused as to what he was doing.

"Jude," I whispered hoarsely. "Jude! What are you doing?"

He turned his head slowly, regarding me with beguiling sincerity. "I am destroying all those inferior to me," he chortled. Then he shook his head and snapped to attention, allowing reality to flood back into his consciousness. Between the pain medication and his lack of sleep, delusions were pushing to the surface.

"What?" I asked. "That doesn't seem like a nice thing to do."

"Yeah, I was only kidding," he replied. "I wouldn't do that to people."

"I know you wouldn't, son," I responded, gently patting his arm. "I know who you are."

He lay his head against the pillow and we sat in silence. The sun slowly rose, and glowing light bathed the room in a warm, golden hue. It was going to be a very rare, sunny day in the middle of winter, made rarer still by the circumstances unfolding in my bedroom. Jude rested there, staring into the light, somehow content despite his misery.

"It is so unfair," I suddenly blurted, surprising myself with my own vehemence. "Why did this have to happen to you?" I gripped his leg in frustration.

"I don't know, Dad," he answered in a whisper. "I don't know. But ..." He raised his head off the pillow and looked at me fiercely. "It doesn't help to get hung up on that question."

I sat with that comment, chastened. He was suffering, marching towards inevitability, but still teaching me about a proper state of mind.

"What have you learned?" I asked, the intensity and desperation in my voice impossible to mask. "What can you teach me?" I repositioned myself directly before him and held his hand. He gazed downward for a bit, rearranged his blankets, then looked at me sharply. He was thinking very, very deeply now. I waited patiently while the curiosity built. It wasn't characteristic of Jude to think too long or too hard about anything. Adversity, however, can chisel its way through the toughest veneers, working into the depths of one's soul, exposing our deepest character. I'd witnessed its transforming influence within my son. I was thirty years his senior but easily realized his crucible had granted him wisdom which far outstripped mine.

"You have to live with gratitude," he stated firmly. "And thankfulness."

"Thankfulness? How can you be thankful for this?" I did not want to argue, I only wanted to absorb, but I was incredulous.

"I have you, and Mom, and Simone, and Johann... I even have some great friends. Who could ask for anything more?" He panted for a bit as his muscles strained to pull in more air. "That is more than I deserve..."

I wept then, just like I weep now when I think of his answer. We both sat in silence for a long while, letting the room get brighter. Jude drifted again. It was Sunday, and the day grew more beautiful. Even though it was February, birds chirped outside. I mulled his answer over in my mind, letting his wisdom settle. I cherished his answer. I also knew it required serious contemplation. My heart was full to bursting with love for my child. It was also wracked with anguish from his wretched state. I was utterly torn between what was and what was to come. I wanted more time to live this wisdom with him. It was the cruelest of injustices that I could not extend our moment the way it deserved.

I finally mustered the courage to grip his hand tightly. "Son, I love you with all I have." Jude slowly opened his eyes and regarded me casually. My statement was not a revelation. This was not the first time he had heard this from me, and I was grateful for that. I've erroneously discarded much great parenting advice, but letting your child know they are loved is not one I've misplaced. "Do you know what is happening today?"

He cocked his head slightly, with a hint of confusion. He sat for a bit, mulling in silence, and then his eyes grew wide with understanding. A classic Jude smile, subtle and wry, crept across his face. "Yeah, Dad, I know."

There was no need to state what we both recognized. The knowledge hung in the air, like an executioner's scythe, threatening to rip apart the tranquility of the moment. We would not let it.

"What about if I have your cousins and uncles and aunts swing by?" I suggested. "Anyone else you want to see?"

"I need to see Bryce," he said fervently. "For sure Bryce."

"Okay," I agreed. "I think Emily will also want to come over."

"Yes," he agreed. "I've seen everyone else... I think. But I am tired, Dad. I don't think I can handle a crew of people."

"I hear you, son. We will make it quick. But you just say the word. If it gets to be too much, we will cut it off."

I sent the most solemn invitation any parent can possibly send. How do you encourage someone to come over for a final visit? There is no manual for this, nor should there be. It was horrible even thinking about, let alone articulating. The bitter gall of Jude's imminent reality sat in my belly, poisoning the beauty of that morning. The emotional dissonance created by Jude's serenity, in the midst of his imminent demise, was utterly confounding. He was content, at peace. Yet all the logistical effort was necessary. My duty was to enable him to die well. Part of that reality was the opportunity for those who loved him to say goodbye.

They came, quickly and quietly. Jude possessed the energy for fleeting interchanges. He graciously gave them their opportunity, looking at each person with keen interest—as if they were the most important thing happening to him that day. Soon it became too much, and we had to cut them off. This was disheartening, but he knew his limit, and he desperately wanted to hold something in reserve for his dear friend Bryce and for his siblings.

What was exchanged I cannot say. It was their moment to preserve and cherish. What I do know is that when Johann and Simone each approached their older brother, it was a picture of exquisite beauty, buoyed by a tenderness and love which set my heart on fire. Something sacred happened in that room, a covenant of fidelity, rife with an emotional theurgy that transcended comprehension. Those children recognized what they had in each other, and they somehow managed to simultaneously cherish its beauty and mourn its loss. Jude had to find the wisdom to encourage his siblings to blossom, fully aware it was his soil that provided the nourishment for their character. I still pray that what he provided has the power to buoy them indefinitely.

* * *

When everyone dispersed, the five of us began our precious day, the last day we would spend as a complete family. We never left the bedside. For seventeen months, Jude had carried us with his wit, charisma, selflessness, and gratitude. Now it was our turn to carry him. What we experienced with our son is much too holy to convey in a memory. It is writ upon our hearts. He was reminded how much he was loved, and how much he was appreciated for loving others. As he took his last breath, Johann and Simone lovingly held his hands, while the prayers from our bleeding hearts carried him beyond the threshold we who remain are barred from crossing.

PRAYER

"Prayer does not change God, but it changes him who prays."
SØREN KIERKEGAARD

After Jude's passing, the outpouring of love and support from family, friends, and the broader community could not be overstated. They carried my family. They also drew us back. Not that we were necessarily in danger of ejecting from our various social spheres or becoming ostracized from each other, but when you engage with such intensity, immersed in a fiery milieu, it creates a form of isolation. Others cannot fully comprehend your struggles or the maelstrom of emotion ensnaring your world. This produces distance, and if it wasn't for those willing to chase after us, those barriers would have propagated.

When you live life on the margins, you encounter more questions than answers. Life is easier when you remain embedded within the discrete confines of your protected world. Clear borders supply simple answers. But that is a delusion. The life we are granted is complicated, messy, and beyond explication. Jude's journey pulled many into his wake, and for some, his circumstances proved unsettling. His experience extended well beyond the borders of simple answers and demanded difficult questions. While attempting to make sense of that journey, struggling with their own confusion and frustration, many have approached me with questions. Those questions typically fall into three categories. Why didn't our prayers work? How could a loving God allow this to happen? How do you ever move beyond this?

These questions are not new. In many ways they define our very existence. Every culture in recorded history has wrestled with these conundrums. They have yet to be satisfactorily answered, and not for lack of effort. More has been written about prayer and the subject of suffering than the remainder of all other theological puzzles. Why have we struggled to find adequate answers?

Far be it from me to posit solutions to such vexing questions. Many who see much farther and deeper have wrestled more successfully than I ever will. However, I wonder if the struggle is less about the answer, and more about the question. Is it possible the questions these circumstances elicit are incorrect? Perhaps our answers lack satisfaction because they are being applied to wrong questions.

A dear friend, while struggling through her own unimaginable tragedy, once remarked that if prayer was a popularity contest, then Jude would still be with us. She is not wrong. The sheer volume of petitionary prayer lifted on his behalf lies beyond measure.

Loss forces us to confront our faith and our theology. We learn very quickly, and sometimes painfully, that the theology we practice and the theology we exhort is not the theology we experience. God doesn't just encourage us to pray, he commands it. But why bother if it is only empty incantations and hopeless utterances?

My faith tradition is dismissive of the exceptional. And yet most faith traditions, including my own, espouse that petitionary prayer, properly applied, should induce the miraculous. Is the current lack of miracles reflective of improper application, weak faith, or misplaced understanding? Would we recognize a miracle if one occurred? We are taught if we possess authentic faith, even that of a mustard seed, we can move mountains. Has anyone seen a mountain move?

I do not possess the gift of faith. My prayers for Jude were heartfelt, sincere, and desperate. They were directed towards the God I love, the God I know, the God I fear. Was it my hesitant belief or feeble faith that poisoned those prayers before they ever took flight? But even if that was the case, there were those who possess a deep, irrepressible faith who were praying on Jude's behalf. Surely God would listen to them. Does not the Bible instruct that if someone is sick, we should anoint them with oil and pray over them, and the Lord will heal them?

I have seen sick people anointed and fervently prayed for. They remained sick. Some died. Jude was prayed for. Incessant, voluminous prayers, faithful and sincere. Yet he suffered as no one should and died much too soon. Is the Bible a compilation of lies and empty promises? How does petitionary prayer work?

Until recently, the idea of testing prayer was unconscionable. The Bible is very clear about testing the Lord. However, the Enlightenment has so infiltrated our culture that it has laid deep roots in our theology and our disciplines. To that end, a few studies of the efficacy of prayer have been performed. From a purely scientific perspective, these studies are abysmal. The most famous study, the Study of the Therapeutic Effects of Intercessory Prayer (also known as the Templeton Foundation Prayer Study), aimed to assess the therapeutic effects of prayer on cardiac bypass patients. The study divided 1,800 cardiac patients into three groups. Two of the groups were told that they may or may not be prayed for, and the third group was informed they would be prayed for. The first group was not prayed for, the second groups were prayed for. There was no statistically significant difference between those prayed for and not.

What does this tell us about prayer? That depends on what you are trying to measure. There are so many flaws and biases in a study of this nature, its conclusions are meaningless. Even someone without any working knowledge of scientific inquiry can immediately recognize the pitfalls. Does anyone really believe that no prayers were uttered for persons in the group that were not supposed to receive prayer? What about from the individual undergoing treatment, or their spouse or children? What about relatives or church members oblivious to the study? A study without a control group is not a study at all.

Does anyone believe that intervention from God happens in a quantitative fashion? If the frequency, numbers, or duration of the prayers are important, does God grant the request only after a standard is met? If the type or style is important, does God grant favor based on His adjudication of form? Is the level of fervency or intensity recognized? What about practical content? Does God decide based on the reasonableness of the request? How faithful was the person doing the praying? Were they sincere and authentic in their belief?

I could fill pages with similar questions. Essentially the experiment lacked blinding, consistent data sets, had unreliable and ill-defined outcome measures, and was never replicated. With an instrument this poorly designed, can anything of value be drawn from it?

Yes. What this experiment did replicate was what we observe every day: the life we experience. Some people get sick and then get better. Some people grow ill and then die. Some people drive to the grocery store and return home with a car full of sundries. Others drive to the store and become paralyzed from a grisly highway accident. Many of these people are prayed for, both the ones who suffer and the ones who do not.

I took a short trip with my father-in-law recently where we discussed a recent prayer experience. He is a prayer warrior, has written numerous books on prayer, and participates in a plethora of prayer ministries. One of his prayer ministries has employees and volunteers who travel. The other members of their team routinely pray for safe travel. During a business trip two young ladies rented a car and drove from the airport to their conference. On the way they got into a frightening accident. Their car flipped multiple times, shot off the road, and crashed into a heavily wooded area many feet from the highway. Other than being emotionally and physically shaken, the ladies survived essentially intact. Of course they were grossly inconvenienced, missed most of the events they were trying to attend, and had to deal with rental car logistics and all the other rigmarole associated with the catastrophe. My father-in-law finished his tale by exclaiming, "It is amazing they survived. What an answer to prayer."

I find that conclusion preposterous. The petitions were for traveling safety, protection, and mercies. If the prayer had been answered in the spirit provided, then the ladies would not have gotten into a wreck at all. And if this was God's answer to prayer, if the ladies would have been killed if those prayers were not faithfully uttered, then what does that say about all the other people who have been sincerely prayed for but ended up injured or dead? Or what about those traveling who sailed along with no issues at all?

Is God a mercurial, erratic tyrant, randomly bestowing mercies or trouble for his whimsical pleasure? This is not the God I know or love. That is not a God anyone could love. Perhaps there is something else going on here.

When we try to quantify the physical effects of petitionary prayer in a scientific fashion, we immediately recognize it is not objectively possible. Beyond the questions already asked, consider just a handful of barriers we confront with simple observation: 1) Prayer effects on the receiver are not consistent or obvious. 2) There does not appear to be any correlation between style, type, quantity, or intensity of prayer and the effect on the receiver. 3) The nature of the request may or may not impact the efficacy of the prayer (prayers for healing versus prayers for faith or patience or resolution, etc.). 4) It is impossible to ascertain if an intercessory prayer was wholly ineffective simply because, once prayed for, there is no control group. What would the outcome have been if no prayer was uttered? 5) All previous studies on prayer, whether on the pray-er or receiver, have been extremely limited in scope and clarity.

This all leads back to the original issue. Investigating the efficacy of petitionary prayer is pursuing the wrong question. When we question whether prayer is working, we are making an erroneous assumption about our relationship to God and our relationship with his creation. There is a pervasive and altogether mistaken notion that Christianity is a vehicle for making our lives better. Christianity does not make your *life* better; it makes *you* better. We don't pray to procure gifts or plead with God to change the world for our benefit. We don't act a certain way, performing the correct rituals, so our requests will be granted. This is what the pagans did, which is no different from the modern-day prosperity gospel. Prayer isn't for something; it is a response *to* something—the gift we've already received. Jesus Christ.

Does one not get the impression, after reading the gospels, that Christ performed his miracles with extreme reluctance? The only miracle he was happy to oblige was the one no one asked him for—the forgiveness of their sins. He knew the rest of his miracles were necessary as signs, to extoll his divinity, but the real miracle, the only miracle necessary, was Christ incarnate, the fulfillment of God's promise.

When we ask why petitionary prayer did not work, what we are really asking is, "Why is the world not the way I want it to be?" And this is an entirely different question altogether. Suddenly we are making God in our image, instead of the other way around. We are attempting to measure the effect of prayer with an assumed or preconceived outcome. We have improperly flipped the script. We are falling prey to the same temptation Adam and Eve succumbed to. We want to be like God.

This is not to say there is something wrong with engaging in petitionary prayer. I cannot imagine a sane parent not praying for the health of their sick child. However, the intent, purpose, and context matters. The true value in petitionary prayer is its capacity to align ourselves with God's will. When we align ourselves with His will, what we discover is a radical acceptance of reality instead of our own desires or imagination. As James says, "When you ask, you do not receive, because you ask with wrong motives, that you may spend what you get on your pleasures."

Most of us believe we are praying God's will. When I prayed for Jude, I certainly thought so. What sort of loving Father would will my son suffer and die? For petitionary prayer to attain its true value, to bear the fruit for which it is intended, it must be employed after the dissolution of the ego. When Christ is in me, just as He is in the Father, then petitionary prayer serves to form us from the inside out. We transfer God into the world. Ultimately my praying for Jude was about Jude and about me. It wasn't about God. Now, this doesn't get God off the hook. Just because I wasn't employing petitionary prayer correctly doesn't mean Jude's suffering was acceptable. But that observation must be applied to a completely different question.

Jude had a feeding tube which was inserted through his nose and snaked into his stomach. The tube was taped across his face and dangled behind his ear when it wasn't in use. When in use, which was frequent, it was attached to a food bag that hung from an IV pole and pushed through a pump. He hated that tube. It pulled the side of his nose, irritated his cheek, and tickled the back of his ear. When puking it would expel from his stomach and out his mouth, drooping like a three-foot slimy noodle from his lips. This forced us to delicately feed it through his mouth and up his nose to release it, like filling a Kleenex with a giant night crawler. It was irritating and gross, but that tube helped keep him alive. Soluble food would slowly drip into his stomach, nourishing him when the ravages of chemo prevented him from eating. The tube was frustrating, but very necessary.

When we were on a schedule, which we vigorously adhered to, his bag of food would be exhausted sometime between two and three every morning. An alarm would sound, and we would change the bag. Jude was able to do this himself, but it was a bit of a hassle, and with his amputation, getting out of bed and hanging implements on an IV pole was tricky. So, I woke up every night and changed the bag.

Sleep was necessary for Jude, and he hated the interruption of the feeding alarm. I made sure to wake myself a few minutes before I thought the bag would be finished, intercept the alarm, and surreptitiously change the bag without waking Jude. This meant I laid awake waiting to make the change. Sometimes I would only have to wait a few minutes, sometimes it would take nearly an hour. As I waited, every single night, I would get down on my knees in front of Jude's door and pray with unbounded passion. I prostrated myself before the Almighty on that cold hardwood, pleading for Jude's life. This went on for months. I have never been more single-mindedly dedicated to a task. My knees even developed two livid purple spots, painful to the touch, which served as grim reminders of my dedication and desire.

As the months wore on, so did my prayers. One early morning, while I rested my cheek on Jude's door—simultaneously sweating and weeping in supplication—I heard a voice. It was clear as a cold bell. "Enough," it commanded. The word was not repeated. There was no elaborate vision, flash of lightning, or repetition. But the word *enough* echoed through my heart and soul.

That single word was suffused with meaning. I am not a Charismatic. I am not keen on the idea of God physically speaking to people. I believe the Holy Spirit operates with more subtlety than that. Despite my resistance to this idea, that word was undeniable. Packed within was a very clear message: God heard me. He acknowledged my request, He acknowledged the plight of my son, and He acknowledged He loved us both. I did not need to pray for Jude's physical healing any longer. God did not reveal what would happen. He did not provide assurance. He just acknowledged it was enough.

Our petitions for corporeal intervention in this world have been answered once and for all. The incarnate Christ is that answer. The miracles of the Old Testament pointed to that answer—providing hope—and the miracles of the New Testament declared the answer with undeniable clarity. Christ is the fulfillment of physical miracles. All the minor stuff—restoring sight, healing the lame, curing the sick, turning water into wine—is unnecessary now. The evidence is rather clear. God has already physically intervened in the natural world. That work is done.

This does not mean petitionary prayer is valueless. To the contrary, petitionary prayer is incredibly important and necessary, just not in the way most of us imagine. The benefits, even without material or physical change, are significant. Without getting into the weeds too deeply, let me take a moment to outline what this looks like.

There are four areas for which petition plays a role. First, petitionary prayer is therapeutic. It has obvious physiologic effects on the pray-er, developing empathy, emotional support, and bonding with the afflicted. It is also cathartic and allows one to see their inner self more fully. Second, it is moral. It exposes our dependence on God, revealing our lack of control. This then produces humility, which aids in resisting temptation and enabling objective awareness. Third, it is relational. Petitionary prayer fosters empathy and serves as a tool to help us love our neighbor. If performed in the presence of the pray-ee, it can also communicate that burgeoning love, establishing an immutable connection. Finally, it is spiritual, as it develops receptivity to the will of God and catalyzes solemnity and reverence.

In addition to those benefits, I also believe the effects of petitionary prayer, the tangible "intervention" we seek, lies in its capacity to invest others, and ourselves, with the fruits of the Spirit. Ultimately prayer is relational. The only way we can draw closer to God, to appreciate His magnificence and love more fully, is to take on His fruit, which He bestows when we ask. The true miracle of prayer, and its decisive power, lies in its capacity to change the heart and spirit of the pray-ee and pray-er.

The Ascension was God incarnate, the physical Christ, leaving this world. In His wake He gifted us His Spirit. Petitionary prayer is our interaction with the Spirit and the Spirit's work in us. It is not a physical interaction, where literal seas are parted, mountains flattened, or cancer eradicated. Rather, it is the cultivation and endowment of spiritual fruit. Petitionary prayer grants us access to the spiritual garden.

To illustrate this assertion, suppose you were in a horrible accident and you mangled your arm. The doctors doubted it was salvageable. Collectively your friends and family prayed fervently that your arm would be saved, while also praying for your patience, faith, fortitude, and self-control during your time of trial. I aver the prayers God entertains are the latter, not the former. Prayers for physical healing, safety, and forbearance of calamity, while not necessarily a waste of time (for some of the reasons outlined above), are not received with the intention they are directed. Those prayers can also be dangerous. For they turn our focus to God as the giver when He is the gift. We hold out our arms, waiting for Him to fill them. But instead of waiting for Him to provide treasure, we must realize He is the treasure—and more precious than anything we think we've lost.

BITTER CRUELTY

"I want to know Christ—yes, to know the power of his resurrection and participation in his sufferings, becoming like him in his death."

PHILIPPIANS 3:10

In 1992, I had the opportunity to visit the Taizé monastic community in Burgundy, France. This ecumenical commune boasted a collection of dedicated Christian men from a myriad of faith backgrounds, determined to live in kindness, simplicity, and peace. The Church of Reconciliation, formed on their grounds, was born out of the storm of World War II. Young Germans volunteered their time for the construction, working shoulder to shoulder with French and Swiss monks in an act of Christian solidarity. As the community grew, so did its heterogeneity. Taizé is ecumenism at its finest. For me, the entire experience was profoundly moving and a purposeful demonstration of living in a community of believers committed to Christ's mandate to love God and neighbor. I sat at the feet of Brother Roger, the founder, while he patiently explained what a posture of ecumenical love looked like. The men of Taizé were firm adopters of that posture. Their faith in practice proved inspiring.

After Taizé, in the dead of winter, I traveled to Germany and visited the infamous concentration camp at Dachau. This was the longest running camp of the German regime and served as a model for all subsequent camps. Like

Taizé, it was also ecumenical, in that it housed a host of Jews, Catholic clergy, and Protestant dissidents. Because of my timing and the weather, my travel companion and I were the only visitors. We walked through the memorial in eerie silence. It took little imagination to conjure, through our mind's eye, the fetid conditions of the incarcerated. We solemnly paged through the handwritten ledger notarizing those condemned to die, and even entered the appalling crematorium specially engineered to service the mass of bodies unceremoniously heaped for processing—bodies that were sacrilegiously accumulated through intentional executions and the abhorrent, deprived conditions. An oppressive pall of evil hung over that camp. As we trod through its all-too-wide confines, we were sickened by our recognition of the pervasive sin and suffering in this world. The contrast to Taizé could not be starker.

Thirteen years later, Brother Roger was mercilessly stabbed to death by an unhinged woman, killed in the middle of a compound devoted to unconditional love.

How is it possible to make sense of a world so dissonant? Beauty is all around, and yet it is easily marred by foul wretchedness. Much like a victim dying from cancer, our world teases us with glimpses of what should be, while being poisoned by what is. This juxtaposition of health and disease creates a capricious existence simultaneously beset with delightful flourishing, calamity, joyful relationships, evil, faith communities, and injustice. Why would a God, who we claim is fully good, loving, and omnipotent, allow such atrocities?

Epicurus, a Greek philosopher living three hundred years before Christ, is attributed with formalizing this penetrating question. While his authorship is in doubt, the dilemma he presents troubles us to this day: "Would God be willing to prevent evil but unable? Therefore, he is not omnipotent. Would he be capable, but without desire? So, he is malevolent. Would he be both capable and willing? So why is there evil?" No one has satisfactorily answered this question.

When Jude was diagnosed, we were so absorbed by the daily trials that it was months before I could reflect upon the injustice of his circumstance.

When I finally did, frustration overwhelmed me like a storm surge. My prayers to God were met with silence. There was no mercy. No healing. No respite from the gnawing, parasitical demon of cancer. It painstakingly eviscerated Jude while God callously watched, unmoving. I remember calling my brother after Jude's amputation, despairing beyond reason, and admitted the entire affair was dangerously testing my faith. He quickly responded, "It isn't really faith if it can't be tested."

Just like our question regarding petitionary prayer, when we ask the question, "How could a loving God allow this to happen?" we are asking from the wrong viewpoint. When the question is reframed, we realize what we are really asking is, "What is wrong with God?" And when we distrust the Almighty, we can only be left with two options: a disdainful atheism or a modern-day paganism. These are not comforting options.

When tormented by calamity or evil, instead of questioning God's integrity, we should really be questioning our own. Instead of blaming God for our less-than-ideal circumstances, or decrying the injustice of life's vicissitudes, we should be asking, "How do I appropriately respond to adversity?"

When Jude was at a low point during his chemotherapy regimen, he intently regarded me with eyes moist and bloodshot from the intense strain of heaving. As he wiped the bile from his lips, he slowly shook his head and lovingly asserted, "I am so glad this happened to me and not any of my friends. I would never want my friends to have this." I have never been more humbled or prouder. His attitude reflected the very heart of Christ. Unbeknownst to either of us, Jude was closing in on the beatific vision that is so elusive for our sinful natures.

We will forever be denied that vision if we become stuck on the *why* of evil. The brilliant Reformer Martin Luther lost both an infant and a teenager. The premature deaths of his children assailed his sensibilities. He personally battled numerous illnesses, limiting his fervor and effectiveness. Like many living in the sixteenth century, suffering was frequent and a salient feature of everyday life. Luther was a priest, and a man dedicated to both understanding and pastoral care. Yet when dealing with the problem of evil, he adamantly advised any and all to cease explication. For if you do, he warned, you will stand at the edge of an abyss capable of swallowing both your reason and your faith.

Luther's advice is rarely taken. We work overtime to understand the dilemma of evil. There is a fancy word in the theological lexicon, *theodicy*, which plagues many brilliant minds. Although a unique word, its meaning is simple: Theodicy is the defense of God's goodness and omnipotence in light of the existence of evil. In other words, it is justifying God. There are many types of theodicies, and one can easily spend years poring over the nuanced versions. The problem every theologian eventually runs into, however, is that the source material available for justifying God is His revelation, the Bible. And what one realizes, after devouring pertinent scripture, is that the Bible is not a theodicy. It is quite the opposite.

Long before Epicurus and the early church fathers, potentially before Moses—the author of the first five books of the Bible—God anticipated our consternation concerning the friction between His attributes and the presence of evil. Knowing how our curious and demanding minds worked, he gave us the story of Job. Now, we all know Job's story. How he was beloved by God, blessed by God, and loved God. But he was given over to Satan to be tested. Eventually Job lost everything, except his life.

Through it all, Job continued to love God. When Job was ill and mourning the loss of all he cherished, three friends came to provide solace. For seven days they simply sat with him in silence. Much can be gleaned in silence, and there is a lesson for us there. For when they began to speak, everything unraveled. Contrary to their best intentions, they expounded a foolish theology, criticizing Job and encouraging repentance to curry God's favor. In the face of this ridicule Job defends his love for God. He recognizes the goodness of God and extolls God's righteousness. As inspiring and virtuous as Job was, however, even he falters. Job defends his own righteousness. And this is the true source of his consternation. He cannot understand why God would torment him, considering his authentic, sincere faith and righteous actions. Here is where Job runs up against the question so many of us ask: Why would a God I love, and who loves me, allow this to happen?

Enter Elihu. He is the fourth friend. A younger man, who has waited until the others have exhausted their specious advice. He chastises Job's friends but doesn't stop there. He also chastises Job. He criticizes Job for making a claim to righteousness, as if he deserved God's blessings. For Job has defended his own virtue at the expense of God's grace and questioned God's justice amid his perceived abandonment.

This is the first key point to the story of Job, and one we often miss. Our suffering is not retributive. God is not singling you out for his Holy Wrath. Your suffering is part of the larger picture of suffering, which is a deeper theological issue, and something we will return to. But the important first point is that regardless of the cause of your suffering, despite the apparent injustice, the *why* of suffering is not critical. It is the *how* of suffering you must attend to. How do you respond to abject torment?

Jody challenged Jude before each hospital check-in to demonstrate God's glory in the way he responded to his ailment. It was his duty to make all those tasked with taking care of him feel positive about the work they were doing, regardless of how Jude was feeling. Jude accepted this challenge and adopted an attitude of privilege. He exuded this attitude with diligent salubrity. And as he worked at it, a peculiar phenomenon manifested. His attitude grew with his efforts. Jude became more. As he expanded, so did his foundation of gratitude and thankfulness. His persona inevitably attracted his caretakers, who then worked doubly hard for Jude's sake. This in turn buoyed his spirit, cultivating fortitude and endurance. What Jude never articulated, but what he thoroughly understood and defended against daily, was the knowledge that when you turn your suffering into bitter resentment, the hell you experience is unlimited.

The second key point is Job's insistence that good is always greater than evil. Evil and suffering often get misrepresented. There is an unhealthy notion that evil is an entity unto itself—as if it has its own quantifiable personality and qualities. Job was wise enough to deny evil the credit it tries to exact. Evil, and its subsequent suffering, is simply a deprivation of good. It cannot exist autonomously. This doesn't mean we can or should ignore it, but when we are tempted to accede evil as victor, we are making a category error. Despite impressions, despite personal intuitions and even lived experience, evil can never overtake good. It is, and will always be, parasitic.

Enter God. This is the anticipated denouement. We eagerly await an elegant explanation of the problem of evil. God will dash Epicurus before he can ever ask the question. But God surprises us here. This is where Luther's solution demonstrates its genius and where we are reminded of our finitude. This is where the faithful and righteous Job is brought to his knees.

God, unsurprisingly, acts as an equal opportunity arbiter of his own attributes. First, God chastises Job's three friends for their improper theology and clearly indicates that it is better to have no theology than bad theology. While this is a very small part of God's dialogue, its implications are far-reaching and severe. Expanding theology does not always infer expanding wisdom or spiritual vitality. It may, in fact, choke them out.

Then God gets down to the serious business of explaining Job's position in the cosmos. First, God takes Job on a cosmic journey and heartily defends His intimate knowledge of creation, disabusing Job's claim of neglect. Then God narrows His focus to the habitation Job is intimately familiar with, providing details about the very animals Job is accustomed to. Job becomes keenly aware that his working knowledge of everyday life is limited and feeble. As God continues to provide details of creation, it becomes both obvious and overwhelming to Job that God in fact possesses supreme wisdom, authority, and sovereignty. God is paying attention to every detail, and the inner workings of the entire universe are precisely tuned to function as He permits. Job unabashedly recognizes he is neither suffering due to divine neglect nor due to a lack of God's justice. God's apprehension is infinite. Injustice is impossible in the face of omniscience.

Job's response reveals the final key point to Job's story. Job realizes true humility and acknowledges his utter incomprehension of God's ways. God's transcendence supersedes our understanding. What He reveals is that His love for us is coupled to His power, grace, and care for all creation. It is impossible for us to apprehend the whole of suffering by only considering the tiny slice of Job's suffering. We are too small, too finite, to grasp the entire picture. God has only gifted us the capacity to engage suffering on a personal level. What we discover, through narrowed focus, is that there is meaning in it.

Job's story is revealing. It is not satisfying. It is not even particularly pastoral. When we ask the question, "How could a loving God allow this to happen?" we are squarely reminded we are too small for the question. It is a question we are asking out of depth and out of context. And when we twist the question to ask, "What's wrong with God?" he very precisely and convincingly provides an answer: Nothing.

Job teaches us that our time would be better spent examining ourselves. "How do I fit into a world with suffering?"

God created us out of an act of pure love. He also created us in His image. This was the beginning. What we need to remember is that it wasn't the end. There is an odd notion afoot in Western Christianity that we need to "return to the Garden." While this idea is comforting, God did not create us as a static enterprise. We have a role to play. A job to do. There is no "going back." God never intended us to stay put. The story is very clear that creation was created *good*, and we were created *very good*. We were not created *ideal* or *perfect*.

Part of the telos of humanity is movement in an upward spiral towards God. This spiral began at creation. The garden of Eden was the Great Permission—permission to begin our journey towards God. Although we are created at an epistemic distance from the Creator, through our growing love of God, others, and our tending to creation, our trajectory spirals ever upwards as we continually learn more, love more, become more. The garden permits this spiral. It promotes and enacts this spiral. While we cultivate the garden, we clearly see God interacting with his nature as the *summum bonum*—the highest good. While our focus remains steadily fixed on Him, our pathway remains obvious and carefree.

In that garden we only had one primary rule: Never take your eyes off God. This is the true meaning of the tree of knowledge. It wasn't some tempting fruit or succulent delicacy that captured our vision. It was the serpent fooling us into thinking we could be like God. We elected to avert our gaze from the Creator and look to ourselves. Instead of resting peacefully in the comfort of God's objective values, we became convinced of our own capacity to determine principles. Instead of remaining incorporated into the beauty of creation, firmly ensconced within the divine spiral of love, we chose to set ourselves apart. We rejected God's objective, pure love, and inappropriately elevated our subjective worth above His.

The original path laid before us, our vocation, became obscured by our own pride. Thankfully God, in His complete and unconditional love, provided us the opportunity to reclaim the spiral by sending us a guide—His very own Son. God did not abandon us. But instead of moving steadily upward on God's path, as was the original intent, we now must arduously bushwhack along a path of our own devising.

C. S. Lewis once said that humility is not thinking less of yourself but thinking of yourself less. In the garden we took our eyes from God and started thinking of ourselves. We were created with complete humility, which we divested. When we lack humility, then what we love becomes misaligned. I always find it interesting how many books and sermons expostulate sin. We've all heard of the seven deadly sins and their numerous offshoots. We are constantly on guard to root out sin in ourselves and expose sin in others. Much of theology reflects this, as it has become propositional in nature. We attempt to arbitrate sin. This, ironically, is also a sin. When the dust settles, there really is only one sin: Idolatry. And idolatry is nothing other than misplacing our love.

Disordered love is evil, which leads to suffering. Suffering reminds us we are not in control—the antithesis of pride. This leads to humility. And humility points us back to God. Oddly then, there is something about evil, adversity, and calamity that directs us to God, not away from Him. After our self-induced fall, the very nature of creation changed. Creation's engine, its telos, is now driven by adversity.

Even odder still, God's faithfulness demonstrates this. He would love nothing more than to pull us from the path of our own choosing. But he made a covenant with us, to continue to love us despite our broken and sinful nature. He has the much harder job. We're only required to keep our eyes fixed firmly on the embodiment of love. This should not be difficult. And yet we continually step off the spiral, and He must let us, or He would impugn His integrity. For God created us as objects from love, for love. He did not create puppets. Evil was our choice. If God took away evil, he would also take away our ability to love.

Humanity is now on a path of sanctification. God has blessed us with that path. We did not have to fall off the spiral, but it is possible, having fallen, we will finally understand what it means to embrace humility. Much like the child who touches the hot stove, they only need to experience it once to never touch it again.

There is a reason why there are so many biblical references to rejoice in suffering. We are even called to consider it pure joy! How is that possible? The entire idea seems abhorrent to me. When Jude was in the midst of his suffering, there was nothing joyful about it. He was in misery. I was embittered, frustrated, helpless, and hopeless. I felt like God had rejected us. He was torturing my son. He was silent. He was cruel. However, that torture burned away, in merciless fury, any remaining vestige of pride. I was not in control. Jude was not in control. Jude's journey proved the antithesis of pride. Suffering is the reversal of the original sin.

There is a very bitter irony in Jude's journey. The person my son became—a selfish boy turned man who learned to love his neighbor and embrace humility—would not have evolved so sublimely without his crucible of suffering. It transformed him. The evil of his cancer forced him to confront his own inadequacy. He chose to embrace adversity, not in a macabre masochistic fashion, or as a foe to be conquered, but as an undesirable companion serving as a guide. In this, we find joy.

Now, there is a very clear danger in this recognition. It is a danger we often fall prey to, damaging both ourselves and others. This is the danger of mistaking evil for good. Jude was transformed by the evil happening to him, but what he suffered through was not good. Nothing does more harm to God's character, or to our capacity to love Him, than trying to justify evil. Evil is never a virtue. It does not come from God.

In the book *A Severe Mercy*, Sheldon Vanauken brilliantly describes the sublime love he and his wife shared and how ultimately their love became prioritized above all else—including love for God. He goes on to say that his wife's illness and subsequent death became a "severe mercy" in the sense that it shocked them both into the realization that God was more important than their love for each other. He defends his wife's suffering as God's instrument for his own good.

I find this deeply troubling. God is maximally powerful and knowledgeable. Could the Almighty not have concocted a more benign mechanism to shock them to their senses? Could not God have creatively manipulated a reasonable dynamic for Jude's transformation, while keeping him safe in the process? Absolutely. God is wholly good. He does not use evil. Evil is not a sword to wield. It is only the deprivation of good—which is impossible for God. There are many Christians who claim the deprivations we suffer in our tormented lives are all part of God's perfect plan. I disagree. God's plan is not perfect. How do I know this? Because I'm in it. And so are you. The moment we chose ourselves, the original plan was perverted. Now God, in his infinite wisdom, grace, and love, manages the plan we've chosen. Somehow, he handles this perverted plan in accordance with His ineluctable will. It is complicated. It is messy. We cannot fully understand it. Despite our best efforts, God will not be thwarted, but we will suffer in the meantime.

God clearly did not want Jude to suffer and die. God did not want the Columbine murders. God does not want the fracturing of His church, corrupt governments, or the wholesale degradation of his creation. Anyone who attempts to justify these atrocities as chosen instruments of a perfect plan is speaking with the voice of the adversary. To remain faithful to us, however, God must maintain a posture of divine impotence, as we proceed down our chosen path of sanctification.

When we first asked about evil, we were asking in the wrong context. We were directing the question to God. We now understand it is self-inflicted. This knowledge does not solve what we so readily experience, however, and which begs the follow-up question, "Why is my own suffering so awful?" This is where Job's story is instrumental. We don't know. It is beyond our ken. It is too much for our insignificant minds to handle.

What we do know is that God, in His grace, mercy, and love, provided a way out. We are like Narcissus, caught in our own reflections, captivated by our desire for something other than God. The hot burner remains irresistibly attractive. God sent his Son, who graciously places His hand on the burner next to ours. He suffers with us, fully revealing our inadequacy, as He teaches us how to properly respond to suffering. Through Him, we see our first true love. And in His resurrection, He provides hope as His new life demonstrates what we will have once we allow Him to pull our hand away.

The book of Job teaches us we can have two responses to suffering. We can either be consumed by our own misery, curse God, and die, or we can tear our clothes, expose our nakedness, and recognize our inadequacy. If we choose the latter, we may never understand the why of suffering, but we will understand our need for God. And that is worth any price.

This is easy to say in hindsight. It is easy to talk myself into this understanding after the fact. I did not see this when Jude was suffering, and Jude did not understand as he shouldered a suffocating burden of misery. It is alluring, and almost natural, to push God away out of frustration, anger, or disgust when we suffer. Humanity loves to destroy that which it doesn't understand. As Jude succumbed to his disease, it became very tempting for me to destroy God.

In his book *Can God Be Trusted?*, the theologian John Stackhouse provides a simple syllogism to cling to when we are ravaged by evil and find ourselves staring into Luther's abyss:

> Premise 1: Jesus Is Good
>
> Premise 2: Jesus Is God
>
> Conclusion: God Is Good

Job recognized this and pinned his faith to it, even though he didn't understand it. Jude lived it, even if he didn't recognize it. As Paul says, "Hate what is evil, cling to what is good." It isn't faith if it can't be tested.

All of Christianity participates in the Eucharist, also known as Communion. It is the most revered of the sacraments. And sacraments, by their very nature, are something of a mystery. As we participate, it is not our job to analyze or fully understand what is occurring, just like the problem of evil. What we do recognize is that the Eucharist means "thanksgiving," and Communion means to "have union with." For us, then, to participate in the Eucharist is to be thankfully invited into the depths of a sacred mystery. We become what we eat.

As we partake of the body and blood of Christ, we symbolically digest Christ into ourselves and are spiritually transformed into His body. This transformation is driven through remembering—and when we re-member, we become something new. What we specifically remember is the suffering of our Savior. The bread is broken, like Christ's abused body. The wine is poured, like the lurid shedding of Christ's blood. The grain in the bread is refined through pressure, the wine from crushed grapes. As we ingest those elements, we give thanks that we too can become one with the body of Christ. When we suffer, we experience the wages of sin. We pay the price for turning away. It is the cumulative price accrued by our collective rejection. This suffering is nondiscriminatory. What appears random, cruel, and unjust is exactly that. But that is the only way we can be shown what it was to be Christ. The paradox of Communion is thanksgiving through Christ's suffering. Those broken pieces, the symbolic parts of Christ's nature that were forged through His sacrifice, now become whole. Suffering makes us one with God.

A HOLE WITHOUT MEASURE

"To love another person is to see the face of God."
VICTOR HUGO

In the early fall of 1991, Jerry Sittser drove his family home from an educational evening out. His wife was homeschooling their four children, and field trips were part of the curriculum. Jerry's mother, Grandma Grace, was also participating, as she had come to visit for a long weekend. Jerry's four children were young and energetic. The seven of them conversed about the evening's activity in what could only be described as an organized cacophony. Diana Jane, four years old, was the spunkiest of the lot and vociferously inserted her opinion amongst her siblings—whose ages ranged from eight to two. It was a busy and rewarding time for Jerry and his wife, Linda. They were deep in the throes of parenting.

Their car was struck by a drunk driver, mercilessly killing Linda, Diana Jane, and Grandma Grace. In one heart-rending instant, Jerry lost his daughter, wife, and mother. The world he knew, and the future he imagined, were obliterated.

Thirty-two years later, a week before he perished, Jude spoke with Jerry. Jerry happened to be a pastor and a theology professor at Whitworth. He was also Jude's great-uncle. Jude's motives for speaking to Jerry were twofold. First, he wanted a Christian professor's perspective on euthanasia. As his burden of misery magnified, Jude thought a great deal about the ethical and moral implications of speeding along his inevitable process. Jude was not afraid to die, he just loved living. Cutting that joy short seemed sacrilegious. He knew our perspective. He desired an independent, ethically minded source for confirmation. We strongly encouraged this endeavor.

His second objective, and one Jody and I were not aware of, was recruitment. Jude was deeply concerned about the fate of his family, including his parents. He wanted to ensure someone with a profound working knowledge of familial loss would watch over us.

After Jude passed away, Jerry honored Jude's request and graciously checked in with Jody and I, delicately guiding us through our unenviable emotional turmoil. One evening the three of us were chatting on the phone, and Jerry recollected some of his own personal travails after the accident. Jerry now has three thriving adult children. He is happily remarried, embedded in his community, and flourishing as a grandparent. The accident is long past. And yet, as he spoke about the loss of his four-year-old dynamo, he was overcome with grief and broke down sobbing.

"How do you move beyond the loss of a child?"

There are libraries bursting with books dealing with grief and loss. Different authors have alternate perspectives and various remedies. Just like the two questions we've already tackled, this inquiry is also misplaced. The question possesses an implicit assumption. By its very nature, it infers a solution. However, losing a child is not the same as losing a job, a reputation, or even a parent. Children are part of us. They comprise the very fabric of our being, and when one is taken away, it tears a hole in the tapestry of our lives.

There is a pithy statement: "Time heals all wounds." A hole is different from a wound. Most wounds, by their very nature, lend themselves to healing. A hole is quite the opposite. Each child comprises a uniquely sized substance and shape. The hole they leave can only be perfectly filled by them.

Perhaps time may act as an emollient to dull the poignancy and dampen the intensity—but it will not heal. At the core there is no wound, there is only loss, and time cannot replace something that is missing. When Jude departed, a colorful, intricate, and critical component of our family's artistry was torn from the fabric. Every parent who has ever lost a child recognizes this. Hence Jerry's sorrow, three decades removed, over the death of his daughter.

Jude taught me how to fully love. When he died, I was both unsure and afraid of loving that way ever again. Bernard of Clairvaux said, "True love is precisely this: that it does not seek its own interests." When Jude was sick, I gave up any and every thought of myself. His travail enabled me to see the beauty and freedom one can attain with complete self-surrender. This magnified my marriage and my relationship with my other children. After Jude passed, the thought of going through the agony of another lost love unnerved me. Suddenly I lived in fear of that happening. What if I lost another child? What about my wife? I loved them desperately—with total abandon. Their loss would unravel my very existence. Life after Jude became palpably undesirable.

Thankfully I came to realize how remarkably selfish that attitude was, and how it represented the very antithesis of what Jude taught me to be. Retreating from loss, making yourself less, is not a solution. It is damaging to yourself and those closest to you. So, with God's grace and through prayers and friendship, Jody and I eventually learned that life must and can be navigated with joy and sorrow simultaneously. They are not mutually exclusive. Much like twin tracks meandering through a field, we strive to straddle both paths, attempting to honor and carry forward Jude's personality while embracing God's glory and our present companionship. Fortunately, we have a clear picture of how to do this. Before us stands both the cross and the empty tomb. Loss and redemption, sorry and joy, death and resurrection remain affixed in our hearts. We live in the shadow of the cross while squarely facing the empty tomb, always thirsting for the joy it brings.

This is not always easy. Grief, like cancer, can be parasitic. Unlike cancer, however, it can be tended, nurtured, and managed. What you must not do with grief is either dismiss it or embrace it. If you dismiss it, it will continue to grow unchecked and unhindered until it washes over you in an all-consuming rush. If you embrace it, it will dominate your life, devour your priorities, rupture your relationships, and poison your soul.

Grief is best thought of as an artificial reservoir held back by an emotional dam. Grief daily pours into that reservoir, slowly filling, pressing against the dam. Managing the reservoir in a judicious fashion is the safest way to handle the inflow. The wise person lets grief drain out the spillway in calculated increments, ensuring the reservoir never becomes over-filled, potentially rupturing the dam, all the while limiting the outflow to a degree that the spillway does not become overloaded either. It is a delicate process and takes practice and experience to manage correctly. As one becomes more accustomed to grief, it becomes apparent how full the reservoir has become and what steps are required to ease the pressure. There is nothing enjoyable about this discipline. Left unchecked, however, grief will be catastrophic.

Grief attacks are a different animal altogether. Tending the reservoir can limit the attacks, but no one is fully immune. Time is the best defense against an acute assault, but even time is not impenetrable. There have been moments, shocking in their intensity, where the horror of Jude's suffering abruptly gripped me like a rampaging fever. I imagine there are similarities to an epileptic seizure. There is little warning, and the effects are ravaging. In the throes of such an attack, I've found myself wrestling my car to the side of the road, sprinting out of a meeting, my clinic, or even the church sanctuary as grief consumed me. I am always left emotionally raw and fragile.

In 1969 Elisabeth Kübler-Ross introduced a model labeled the five stages of grief. In this model, she described a tendency for grievers to journey through Denial, Anger, Bargaining, Depression, and Acceptance. This model has been criticized over the years, and rightly so, for every grief journey is unique. She is not wrong, however, in that these stages will be encountered at some level, at some time, during most grief journeys. What I've discovered, and what others corroborate, is the idea of a staged, linear journey is something of a misnomer. There are no obvious hurdles one clears as the griever slowly progresses towards a definable endpoint. I think a more apt approach would be to imagine one's grief journey as a wheel, or sphere. As one cycles through their grief, they encounter Kübler-Ross's stages. These stages sometimes arrive in pairs or triplets. Occasionally, they may all interrupt one's progress simultaneously. As time passes, and as the sphere of grief rotates, one re-encounters these stages over and over, when they may be dressed in different guises.

My aim here is not to provide a travelogue of grief. Everyone's eventual encounter is so unique and situation-specific that the topic can only be approached with broad strokes. The critical element is to acknowledge that grief must be taken seriously. Each potential stage should be properly recognized and tended. For grief can be insidious, furtively wending its way into your psyche, camouflaging its aura while silently twisting the fabric of your personality. Suddenly your vibrant, colorful life becomes dull and vapid, and you find yourself becoming short and ill-tempered from minor trivialities. Some of these personality adjustments are temporary, necessary, and forgivable. But it is important you don't let grief become chronic and allow its influence to alter your sensibilities. Welcoming chronic grief, either intentionally or inadvertently, will desiccate your heart and crystallize into bitter resentment. And we already learned that bitter resentment eventually poisons your ability to love God and others.

Grief, like adversity, will expose our deepest flaws. It shone a spotlight on my immature faith. St. John of the Cross highlights the time in a Christian's walk when their faith will be tested. He calls this the "Dark Night of the Soul." Before the Dark Night our souls are caressed and nurtured by the Spirit. Prayer comes easy, participation in worship brings only joy. Religious experience and participation take on a delightful urgency because of the pleasure they bring. The initiated believe their spiritual depth is nearly limitless and their foundation of faith unshakeable. But, John says, a time will come when this simpleness will be removed and a self-reckoning introduced. Enter the Dark Night.

Jude's death enveloped me like the blackest night. God was hidden in that inky darkness. Praying was a heavy weight. There were no words. I had no idea what to say. I would only sit in silent darkness, weeping tears of frustration, anger, and despair. My previous life had been immersed in music and song. I loved to worship through music. Singing became impossible. The first Sunday I attended church after Jude's funeral, I opened my mouth to sing and nothing emerged. I could only sit in the pew while tears streamed down my face. I thought this would pass quickly. I was foolish. For two years I tried to sing but could only muster croaking sobs. Why would I even consider praising God? He had taken my child. Loving Him seemed beyond repair.

It was in this deep pit, at the heart of the Dark Night, that I realized the book of Job, for all its brilliance, provides one grave disservice. At the end of the story, Job is rewarded. God blesses him for not losing faith and remaining stalwart in the face of adversity. Now here I was, desperately clinging to God, and where was my reward? The story of Job would be much more powerful and provoking if it ended with verse nine. It teases us with prosperity, as if that is somehow earned *through* righteousness, not despite our unrighteousness.

Job, however, is about suffering. It says less about grief. Although they are cousins, suffering points to humility. Grief, on the other hand, manifests from loss, and we only mourn that which we love. The antidote for grief is love.

Jude's death wounded my heart so deeply, it paralyzed my desire to love. The only tangible emotion, readily accessible and always lurking, was despair. Joy felt unreachable. Life was a pale shade of gray. I locked myself in this dungeon of despair and let my Dark Night compress me into one dimension. While I lay there flat, unmoving, allowing despair to suffocate, I curiously wondered why we bother with life at all. If joy can be severed in an instant, is our existence truly a gift? Would it not be better to have never been born?

That thought pulled me back to Jude. He read the book of Ecclesiastes the last month of his life, and he had asked that very same question. As he swam through the murky depths of despair, bereft of hope and suffering unbearably, he rejected the temptation to fall prey to this emotion. It would have been so easy for him to give in. Instead, he focused on thankfulness, gratitude, and loving his neighbor. He eagerly greeted every day he was alive, even the very day he perished, with gracious expectation.

In 1678, John Bunyan published *Pilgrim's Progress*. In this allegory, he describes Christian, an everyman character, and his progressive journey on the path to the celestial city. At one point on his journey, Christian is captured by the giant of Despair and imprisoned within his Doubting Castle. There Christian is beaten, starved, and mercilessly tortured by Despair. The Giant encourages Christian, with all the reason at the Giant's disposal, to commit suicide. Life is but despair. There is only one escape.

As he contemplates this tempting solution, Christian discovers something in his pocket that he had all along. The key of Promise. This key unlocks the dungeon and enables escape from Despair's clutches. As John Bunyan wrote about Christian's trial of despair, Bunyan too was in prison. Separated from his wife and children, suffering through impoverished conditions and grieving the loss of his family, Bunyan was keenly aware of despair's temptation. In his story Bunyan's character, Christian, is imprisoned on Wednesday and discovers the key on Sunday, Resurrection Day. We are reminded then—I was reminded then—that while suffering points to the cross, grief points to the empty tomb. The key of promise is forged from the rolled-away stone of the tomb. It opens the door of hope, which defeats despair, and reveals the fruit of the resurrection: True joy which defeats even death.

Armed with the key of promise, I stepped out of the dungeon. Now, I would love to report that stepping out exposed me to all the beauty, truth, and joy available to the Christian experience, but this would be a frivolous fiction. Valleys, by their very nature, are shadowed. The first step out of a valley is uphill. As is the second and third. Depending on the depth of the valley, the rim may be perceptible only as a distant longing. Your path forward may be obscure, or even impenetrable. Now that I had been blinded by the Dark Night, my only certainty was the knowledge there was no going back to simple faith and mollycoddled theology. That way was forever closed. My trust in God was deeply bruised. What was left to draw me forward, to recapture joy and ignite a doused faith?

In Dostoevsky's novel *The Brothers Karamazov*, Father Zosima is a fictional monk, characterized by his wisdom and teachings on love, forgiveness, and humility. The foundation for most of his saintly advice is unconditional love. In the novel, Zosima is approached by a lady whose faith is slipping. When she was young, she had a simple faith, but she is afraid it was born more out of a fear of death than anything authentic. Because, like the rest of us, she cannot see beyond the veil of death, she desires proof—some concrete, irrefutable evidence demanding conviction. Zosima immediately responds that there is no question of proof, but that it is possible to be convinced. He says, "Try to love your neighbors actively and tirelessly. The more you succeed in loving, the more you'll be convinced of the existence of God and the immortality of the soul. And if you reach complete selflessness in the love of your neighbor, then undoubtedly you will believe, and no doubt will even be able to enter your soul."

Love brings clarity to the hidden pathway which wends its way up and out of the valley. Not the idea of love, or a fanciful, idealistic imaginary for the fidelity of humanity. True, unconditional love. And this is no easy task. The greatest thing Jude ever taught me was to love someone for who they are, not for who you want them to be. I had enough difficulty doing this with my own son. How much harder to accomplish with someone to whom you have no familial ties? Dostoevsky was keenly aware of this as he further states, "Love in action is a harsh and dreadful thing compared to love in dreams." It is, however, the only remedy for grief, and the best tool for shoring up a shaky foundation of faith.

How does one move past the loss of a child? As Jerry Sittser so poignantly demonstrated in his emotional reaction, you do not. It is a question out of context, and one that could only be asked by someone who has never lost a child. The tapestry cannot be rewoven. The hole cannot be filled. Instead, one must learn to live with loss. This can only be accomplished by recognizing the suffering and grief this loss thrusts upon you will only either drive you inward—into a pool of self-absorbed pity that will stamp out faith and extinguish love—or towards the pain of the cross and the joy of the empty tomb. It is your choice.

EPILOGUE

THE END OF THE JOURNEY

"And I heard a loud voice from the throne saying, 'Look! God's dwelling place is now among the people, and he will dwell with them. They will be his people, and God himself will be with them and be their God. He will wipe every tear from their eyes. There will be no more death or mourning or crying or pain, for the old order of things has passed away.'"

REVELATION 21:3–4

Time can never be frozen. One of the more troubling aspects of continuing life after the loss of Jude is recognizing that progress is not the same as abandonment. As Jude's siblings mature, enrich their lives, and expand their world, I walk forward with them, reveling in their growth, while guilt-ridden that each step I take in their company is one step further from their brother. I am haunted by the notion that something is always missing. Their joy softens my grief, but it also underscores the permanence of Jude's absence. With time comes the painful clarity that the world I once knew, and the future I imagined, is irrevocably lost. As much as I may wish or dream, there is no road to that future. Jude is forever irretrievable.

Ironically, it is Jude's attitude and admonitions which allow me to move forward with joyful anticipation. For I know nothing would upset him more, or hasten my chastisement, if he knew I was chained to his grave. He would be the first person waving me on, encouraging me to anticipate each day with graciousness and thankfulness. He would tell me to thank God for the grace and beauty of Jody, the gift of Johann and Simone, and the selfless support of my current community. And in his own Jude fashion, he would remind me not to think about what I lost but remember what I had, forever appreciating the twenty years we shared together. Even now, I marvel how Jude was never the son I ever hoped for or imagined—he was always so much more.

With Jude pushing me forward, I stagger along, like all of us, living in a world with both a cross and an empty tomb. Our present hue is not permanent, but only the still gray of the dawn before the world is made new. Ever anticipating that sunrise, I relish the blessings bestowed as a child of God: my incredible wife, my beautiful children, and a family of faith which supersedes any border. Even still, there are days Jude's injustice moves me to shake my fist at God and scream with tears of anger. Some days I fall to the ground and weep tears of anguish because of his horrible suffering. I mourn a future that will never be, and for my family that is forever distorted because of his absence. Yet I also find joy in the memory of his personality, the flourishing of his friends, and an appreciation for the faith, wisdom, and perspective he bludgeoned into me, despite my obstinance. I hunger for the promised supernatural restoration, keeping my eyes focused ever outward and upward, knowing the ultimate terminus of Jude's journey and my journey are congruent.

Mostly though, I miss my son.

ACKNOWLEDGMENTS

There are many who walked alongside our family during Jude's trial who deserve both thanks and praise. The breadth of people who came to our aid is too expansive to name individually, and for that I apologize, as each individual, however small the gesture, contributed to the maintenance of our sanity and energy. Church members, neighbors, friends of friends, and even strangers inserted themselves into our whirlwind and served as an unyielding tether. Simply saying "Thanks" seems a disservice to the term.

Our "Facebook family" was especially beneficial. Social media is rife with ills, but in this instance it proved invaluable. You buoyed Jude with your comments, anecdotes, and prayers.

The oncology team at Seattle Children's Hospital deserves special commendation. Everyone functioned at a fevered pace, every day stepping into another child's war. The fortitude required to serve in that capacity is immense.

The staff and pastors at Cornwall Church in Bellingham, Washington, held our hands while we grieved, enabling us to provide proper treatment for Jude's memorial.

My staff kept my practice afloat and gracefully managed my frustrations, anxiety, and discordant schedule.

Our immediate family proved invaluable. The phone calls, check-ins, food, transportation, encouragement, prayers, and the continuous help with the myriad other logistical details which surround a trial of this nature kept us all afloat and able to focus primarily on Jude's care.

Jon and Leanne not only organized meals but also provided a quiet space for me to simply "be." It is a true friend who lets you march into their home, burst into tears, and then leave without expressing gratitude or supplying an explanation.

Much gratitude to Eric, Kyle, and Jon who, however unwittingly, helped pick up the pieces while I traveled through the "Dark Night."

Thanks to Donna, Amy, Jack, Diane, Stacia, and Carolyn for providing valuable feedback regarding the initial draft of the *The Revelation of Jude*.

Insight from Rebecca, my editor, and Steve, my designer, gave me the confidence and assurance to move forward with this project.

Jerry, who has walked his incalculable road of grief, provided insight, encouragement, and spiritual sustenance both for Jude and the writing process.

Johann and Simone asked for nothing, graciously weathered Jude's storm, and offered their brother more love than they could spare.

Jody's strength and love are ineffable. She brought Jude into this world, loved him throughout, and bore his burden with an incalculable fortitude. She is God's gift to me.

www.ingramcontent.com/pod-product-compliance
Lightning Source LLC
Chambersburg PA
CBHW030450100526
44580CB00002B/65